Galleries & Museums

15 National Gallery of Rome, Palazzo Barberini
16 National Gallery of Rome, Palazzo Corsini
17 Villa Farnesina
18 Capitoline Museums and Gallery
19 Museum of the Palazzo Venezia
20 Doria Pamphilj Gallery
21 Colonna Gallery
22 Gallery of the Academy of St Luke

23 Spada Gallery
24 Barracco Museum
25 Museum of Rome
26 Roman National Museum (Museo delle Terme)
27 Borghese Museum and Gallery
28 National Etruscan Museum of the Villa Giulia
29 National Gallery of Modern Art
30 National Military and Art Museum, Castel Sant'Angelo
31 Vatican Galleries and Museums

Map of Rome galleries and museums

- 29
- 28

Villa Borghese

VIALE D'ANNUNZIO
VIA DEL BABUINO
VIA PINCIANA
CORSE D'ITALIA
SALARIA
VIA PIAVE
- 9
- 13
- 8
PIAZZA DI SPAGNA
VIA CONDOTI
- 7
- 6
- 12
V. GREGORIANA
VIA FRANC. CRISPI
- 3
- 2
V. D. MACELLI
- 5
VIA SISTINA
- 4
VIA VITTORIO VENETO
VENTE SEPTEMBRE
-ELLI
VIA DEL
V.D. MERCEDE
VIA BARBERINI
VIA D. TERME
Museo Nazionale
VIA DEL TRITONE
- 15
QUATTRO FONTANE
- 26
- 22
Palazzo Quirinale
VIA DEL QUIRINALE
VIA NAZIONALE
V. AGOSTINI DEPRETIS
CAVOUR
Sta.
CORSO
V. XXIV MAGGIO
VIA MILANO
Palazzo Doria
- 21
- 20
V. IV NOVEMBRE
S. Maria Maggiore
V. PLEBISCITO
- 19
VIA PANISPERNA
V. CARLO ALBERTO
VIA DEI FORI IMPERIALI
VIA CAVOUR
VIA GIOVANNI LANZA
VIA MERULAN
- 18

Art centres of the world—Rome

General Editor: G. S. Whittet

Art centres of the world Rome

Ronald Bottrall

Michael Joseph

Designed and produced for Michael Joseph Ltd,
26 Bloomsbury Street, London WC1
by George Rainbird Ltd,
Marble Arch House, 44 Edgware Road, London W2
Phototypeset by V. Siviter Smith & Co. Ltd, Birmingham 12
Printed and bound by Grafoimpex, Zagreb, Yugoslavia
House Editor: Mary Anne Norbury
Typographer: John Wallis
Endpapers: John Flower

First published 1968

Contents

Acknowledgements   *page*   6
List of colour plates   7
List of illustrations   8
Introduction   11
The National Gallery of Rome – Palazzo Barberini   13
The National Gallery of Rome – Palazzo Corsini   22
The Villa Farnesina   29
The Capitoline Museums and Gallery   31
The Museum of the Palazzo Venezia   47
The Doria Pamphilj Gallery   54
The Colonna Gallery   62
The Gallery of the Academy of St Luke   66
The Spada Gallery   70
The Barracco Museum   75
The Museum of Rome   79
The Roman National Museum – Museo delle Terme   82
The Borghese Museum and Gallery   93
The National Etruscan Museum of the Villa Giulia   109
The National Gallery of Modern Art   118
The National Military and Art Museum – Castel
    Sant'Angelo   126
The Vatican Museums and Galleries   130
  I The Vatican Picture Gallery   130
 II The Museums of Antiquities   141
III The Vatican Library and Annexes   155
 IV Gallery of Tapesties, Stanze and Loggia
     of Raphael   165
Out of doors and incidentals   171
Art for sale   185
Galleries, museums and sale rooms   190
Author's Acknowledgements   192

Acknowledgements

The publishers and producers wish to express their gratitude to the museums, galleries and photographers who have courteously assisted the author in obtaining the material for the illustrations reproduced in this book. They would especially like to thank the following:

Scala Istituto Fotografico Editoriale, Florence, who supplied all the colour transparencies; Fratelli Alinari Soc. p. AZ, who supplied all the black and white photographs with the exception of the following where our thanks are due to the kind co-operation of: The British Museum, 108; Mario Carrieri, Milan, 8, 14, 25, 93, 95, 98, 100, 102, 103, 107, 108, 109; J. Allan Cash, F.I.I.P., F.R.P.S., 94; John R. Freeman, 99, 107; The Mansell Collection, London, 34; Julian Wontner, London, 1, 15, 32, 35, 36, 39, 50, 61, 72, 96, 104, 111.

List of colour plates

facing page

I Hans Holbein the Younger, *Henry VIII*, 1540   16

II Raphael, *The Triumph of Galatea, c.* 1513   33

III Diego Velazquez, *Innocent X*, 1650   64

IV Caravaggio, *Madonna of the Palafrenieri*, 1605—6   81

V Dosso Dossi, *The Enchantress Circe, c.* 1530   96

VI *Sarcophagus of the Spouses, c.* 530   96

VII Melozzo da Forlì, *Sixtus IV Nominating Platina Prefect of the Vatican Library*, 1477.   113

VIII *Fibula from the Regolini-Galassi Tomb, c.* 650   144

IX Michelangelo, *The Creation of Man, c.* 1510   161

X Fra Angelico, *St Peter Ordaining St Stephen as Deacon and St Stephen Distributes Alms*, 1447—49   161

List of illustrations

1   The Barberini Palace   *page* 13
2   Simone Martini and assistants, *Madonna and Child, c.*1319   14
3   Fra Filippo Lippi, *The Annunciation, c.*1443   16
4   Pietro da Cortona, *Ceiling of the Great Hall,* 1633–39   *facing* 17
5   Bartolomeo Veneto, *Portrait of a Gentleman, c.*1520   17
6   Angelo Bronzino, *Stefano Colonna,* 1546   20
7   Quentin Massys, *Erasmus of Rotterdam, c.* 1517   20
8   The Corsini Palace   23
9   Bartolomé Esteban Murillo, *Madonna and Child*   24
10 G. B. Gaulli (Il Bacciccia), *Clement IX, c.* 1667   24
11 Canaletto, *Rialto Bridge, Venice,* 1744   25
12 G. B. Piazzetta, *Judith and Holofernes*   26
13 Caravaggio, *St John the Baptist, c.*1603   27
14 The Villa Farnesina   29
15 Michelangelo, The Capitoline Museum (Palazzo Nuovo)   31
16 *She-wolf,* early 5th century B.C.   *facing* 32
17 *Dying Gaul, c.*200 B.C.   *facing* 32
18 *Mosaic of Doves;* Roman copy, *c.*130 A.D.   33
19 *Capitoline Venus;* Roman copy, 2nd century B.C.   35
20 Alessandro Algardi, *Innocent X,* 1649–50   38
21 *Spinario,* 1st century B.C.   38
22 *Seated Etruscan,* 7th century B.C.   41
23 Caravaggio, *St John the Baptist, c.*1600   45
24 Guercino, *The Burial and Reception into Heaven of St Petronilla,*
    *c.*1621   45
25 The Palazzo Venezia   47
26 *Cross* from Rosciolo, 1334   50
27 The Doria Palace   54
28 Caravaggio, *Rest of the Flight into Egypt, c.*1596   56
29 Pieter Bruegel the Elder, *The Battle in the Gulf of Naples,*
    *c.*1560   58
30 Annibale Carracci, *Rest on the Flight into Egypt,* 1600–4   60
31 Hans Memling, *The Deposition, c.*1485   61
32 The Great Hall   *facing* 65
33 Paolo Veronese, *Portrait of a Gentleman*   *facing* 65
34 Madame Elizabeth Vigée-Lebrun, *Self-portrait*   68
35 The Spada Gallery   71
36 Francesco Borromini, The 'perspective'   71
37 Guido Reni, *Cardinal Bernardino Spada* (detail)   72
38 Michelangelo Cerquozzi, *Masianello's Revolt*   74

39	The Barracco Museum	75
40	*Five women prisoners in a palm grove;* Assyrian, 7th century B.C.	76
41	*Stele* of a man on horseback; Greek, early 5th century B.C.	77
42	The staircase of the Braschi Palace	*facing* 80
43	*The Tiber Apollo;* Graeco-Roman copy, ?2nd century B.C.	84
44	*Discobolos of Myron,* Lancellotti copy, ?1st century B.C.	87
45	*Dying Niobid, c.* 440 B.C.	87
46	Apollonius son of Nestor, *Boxer, c.* 50 B.C.	88
47	*Young Girl of Anzio, c.* 250 B.C.	88
48	Decoration of the Villa of Livia	90
49	*The Ludovisi Throne, c.* 470–60 B.C.	92
50	The Borghese Museum and Gallery	93
51	Johannes Wilhelm Baur, *View of the Borghese Villa,* 1636	94
52	Gian Lorenzo Bernini, *Apollo and Daphne,* 1622–25	95
53	Correggio, *Danäe, c.* 1530	95
54	Domenichino, *Diana Hunting,* 1618	*facing* 97
55	Jacopo Bassano, *The Last Supper*	*facing* 97
56	Gian Lorenzo Bernini, *David,* 1623–24	98
57	Raphael, *Deposition,* 1517	101
58	Girolamo Savoldo, *Tobias and the Angel, c.* 1540	102
59	Antonello da Messina, *Portrait of a Man, c.* 1474	108
60	Paolo Veronese, *St Anthony Preaching to the Fishes* (detail), *c.* 1580	108
61	The National Etruscan Museum of the Villa Giulia	109
62	*Centaur* from Vulci, *c.* 600 B.C.	111
63	*Head of Hermes, c.* 500 B.C.	111
64	*Apollo of Veii, c.* 500 B.C.	*facing* 112
65	*Head of a Youth,* called 'Malavolta', *c.* 430 B.C.	114
66	*The Chigi Vase;* Protocorinthian, *c.* 640 B.C.	114
67	*The Ficorini Cista, c.* 300 B.C.	117
68	The National Gallery of Modern Art	118
69	Andrea Appiani, *Vincenzo Monti,* 1805–10	119
70	Giovanni Segantini, *At the Fence,* 1885–86	123
71	Giuseppe De Nittis, *Races at the Bois de Boulogne,* 1881	125
72	Castel Sant'Angelo	126
73	Lorenzo Lotto, *St Jerome, c.* 1508	129
74.	Giovanni di Paolo, *Annunciation,* 1445	132
75	Fra Angelico, *Virgin between St Dominic and St Catherine of Alexandria*	132
76	Raphael, *The Madonna of Foligno,* 1512	135
77	Leonardo da Vinci, *St Jerome, c.* 1482	137
78	Sir Thomas Lawrence, *George IV*	140
79	Carlo Maratta, *Clement IX,* 1669	140
80	*Apollo Sauroctonos;* Roman copy, ?1st century B.C.	143
81	*Cnidian Venus;* Roman copy, ?1st century B.C.	143
82	*Laocoön, c.* 150 B.C.	*facing* 145
83	*Apollo Belvedere;* Roman copy, ?1st century B.C.	*facing* 145
84	*Augustus of the Prima Porta, c.* 23 B.C.	*facing* 145
85	*Mars of Todi,* first half of the 4th century B.C.	*facing* 145
86	*Amphora of Exekias, c.* 540–530 B.C.	154

10   List of illustrations

87	Pinturicchio, *Disputation of St Catherine, c.*1495	158
88	Botticelli, *The Burning Bush, c.*1482	*facing* 160
89	Perugino, *The Delivery of the Keys, c.*1482	*facing* 160
90	Michelangelo, *The Prophet Jonah, c.*1511	162
91	Michelangelo, *A Slave* (ignudo), *c.*1511	163
92	Michelangelo, *The Last Judgment* (detail), *c.*1540	164
93	The Arch of Titus	171
94	*The Arch of Constantine with the Colosseum*	172
95	*Trajan's Column,* A.D. 113 and *SS Nome di Maria*	173
96	*Statue of Marcus Aurelius with the Palazzo Senatorio*	174
97	*S. Maria in Cosmedin and Bizzaccheri's Fountain*	174
98	The Farnese Palace	175
99	*Contemporary engraving of the Moses Fountain,* 1589	176
100	*Lion* (detail of the Moses Fountain), 19th century copy	176
101	Gian Lorenzo Bernini *Ecstasy of St Teresa,* Cornaro Chapel, S. Maria della Vittoria	177
102	*Dolphins on the Triton Fountain,* Palazzo Barberini	177
103	*The Dioscuri, Obelish and Fountain,* Piazza del Quirinale	177
104	*The Trevi Fountain*	178
105	*The Pantheon with Obelisk and Fountain*	179
106	*Elephant and Obelisk,* Piazza della Minerva	180
107	*The Piazza Navona*	181
108	Engraving of the *Spanish Steps* showing the *Fountain of the Barcaccia* in the foreground	182
109	Detail from the *Fountain of the Moor*	183
110	*The Obelisk of Flaminius,* Piazza del Popolo	183
111	*The Piazza San Pietro*	184
112	Arnaldo Pomodoro, *Sphere No. 6,* 1963–65	186
113	Frank Kupka, *Rhythms in Black and White,* 1921	186
114	Giacomo Balla, *Decor for Stravinsky's 'Feux d'Artifice',* 1917	186
115	Tano Festa, *Da Michelangelo No. 2,* 1966	187
116	Max Ernst, *Aerolian Harp,* 1963	187
117	Pini Pascali, *Decapitated Rhinoceros and Giraffe,* 1966	188
118	Claudio Bruni with Luigi Russolo's, *I Capelli di Tina,* 1911	188
119	Renzo Vespignani, *Steps to the Swimming-pool,* 1967	189
120	Carlo Lorenzetti, *Structure in Steel and Yellow Enamel,* 1966	189

Introduction

Rome is not the most beautiful city in the world — Venice has that honour — but it is an unexampled monument of history, art, civilization and religion. To quote Derek Verschoyle, 'In the range and scope, the variety, the quantity, and the intrinsic quality of its resources, it remains not merely unequalled but unapproached among the greatest artistic treasures of the world.' The barbarians inflicted great wounds on the city, but in more recent times, owing to indifference and deliberate pillage, Rome has suffered more damage from its citizens than from its enemies, with the possible exception of the Sack of Rome by the German mercenaries of the Emperor Charles V in 1527. The worst offenders were the popes, in particular Sixtus V and Urban VIII. The depredations of the latter, the Barberini pope, and his family were so devastatingly widespread as to provoke the famous pasquinade *'quod non fecerunt barbari, fecerunt Barberini.'* By a curious irony, however, some of the greatest despoilers of ancient Rome were the creators of the Rome that we know. The popes preserved as well as destroyed, as can be seen from the great collections of art that they assembled.

Much remains and a great deal of it can be seen on foot. Walking is the best way to get acquainted with Rome and however well one knows, or thinks one knows, the city new discoveries will constantly appear, so packed with history and art are the narrow streets. Of the ancient Roman monuments only one building, the Pantheon, remains 105 tolerably intact. The extent of the damage and the length of time that it lasted can best be imagined if we recall that the Roman Forum, plundered and half buried, was used as a market and known as the *Campo Vaccino,* or cow pasture, well into the 18th century, as the engravings of Piranesi show. The Vatican, Lateran and National Museums have preserved precious fragments from the past, but it is difficult for us to envisage the grandeur of the imperial city as it was at its zenith at the end of the 1st century A.D. Similarly, little remains of early Christian Rome, but the catacombs, the mosaics in the churches and the sarcophagi help us to recreate this world.

Medieval Rome is visible in the additions to the Castel Sant'Angelo 72

and the Milvian Bridge, the Torre delle Milizie and other landmarks, but it is during the period 1500–1650 that Rome grew to be as we see it now. First the classic period of Bramante, culminating in the Cancelleria, followed by great architectural conceptions of Michelangelo, the father and son Antonio di Sangallo, Vignola, Peruzzi, Maderno and Domenico Fontana. Then came the dynamic flowering of the baroque style exemplified in the works of Bernini, Borromini, Pietro da Cortona and Rainaldi. In the late 17th and early 18th centuries the masterpieces grow fewer and farther between, but we are grateful for Carlo Fontana's S. Marcello, Ferdinando Fuga's Palazzo della Con-
104 108 sulta, Nicola Salvi's Trevi Fountain, Francesco de Sanctis's Spanish
27 Steps, Valvassori's façade of the Doria Pamphilj Palace, Cosimo
110 Morelli's Palazzo Braschi and the ensemble of the Piazza del Popolo. The less said about Roman building in the 19th century, and the 20th century up to the outbreak of World War II, the better.

It must not be forgotten that the new discoveries of the World and Man, the natural sciences, the revival of interest in antiquity, the beauty of landscape, the nobility of the human body, commonly called the Renaissance, but more correctly named the Rinascimento, came from Italy. Without patrons, the ideas and the art of the men who rebuilt European culture could not have developed and patrons were found in Rome in the persons of popes, cardinals and noblemen, whose munificence can be estimated by the treasures of the Vatican Museums, the Capitoline Museums, the Borghese Gallery and, on a smaller scale, of the Doria, Colonna and Spada Galleries. Whatever artistic crimes against the past the popes may have been guilty of, the art of the western world would have been very different if the pontiffs had not called Perugino, Raphael, Michelangelo, Gaulli, Lanfranco, the Carracci, Bernini, Borromini, Algardi and many others to Rome.

Art in Rome lies everywhere, in the Roman ruins, in the churches, in the fountains, in the private palaces, in the public buildings and in nooks and crannies. For this reason any book dealing only with the museums and galleries, rich in masterpieces as some of them are, can only give a faint idea of the extraordinary effect produced by Rome as a whole, an effect far surpassing that of any other city in the world. The blend of colours, the harmony of line, the russet ruins of the Palatine against the dark ilex background, the brilliant baroqueness of the
107 Piazza Navona, the steps rising to the bare façade of the Aracoeli,
111 Bernini's colonnade embracing the faithful on the way to St Peter's, the meandering presence of the Tiber, all this makes up the most exciting scene that man, by accident or design, has ever achieved.

The National Gallery of Rome
Palazzo Barberini

The Barberini Palace was constructed on the site of the Sforza Palace, 1 acquired by Urban VIII in 1625. Carlo Maderno was the first architect chosen by the pope and he is responsible for the two sober wings of three stories each. Bernini took over the work on the death of Maderno in 1629 and built the brilliant façade overlooking the Via delle Quattro Fontane, which has immense windows and a loggia over the portico. Francesco Borromini and Pietro da Cortona also collaborated in the building of the palace which was finished in 1632. The rectangular staircase on the left was designed by Bernini, the beautiful oval spiral staircase on the right by Borromini.

The National Gallery of Rome had its origin in the purchase by the state of the Corsini Palace in 1883, when the owners, Princes Tommaso and Andrea Corsini, gave their collections of paintings and

1. The Barberini Palace

13

2. Simone Martini (*c.*1284–1344) and assistants, *Madonna and Child, c.*1319
tempera on wood $28\frac{3}{4} \times 16\frac{1}{2}$ in. (73 × 41·5 cm.)

sculpture to the government. This collection was started about 1737 by Cardinal Neri Corsini, nephew of Clement XII and eventually comprised 600 pictures. To this was added by Duke Giovanni Torlonia in 1892 the pictures now in the Torlonia Rooms. Shortly after, 187 paintings came from the Monte di Pietà Gallery, and these were followed by paintings from the Odescalchi, Colonna-Sciarra and Chigi collections. The latest important gift is the collection bequeathed in 1961 by the Duke of Cervinara. This consists mainly of French paintings of the 18th and 19th centuries. In 1949 the Barberini Palace was sold to the state and it was decided to use the main state rooms to house the Rome National Gallery. Unfortunately only a part of the palace was made available for the Picture Gallery and it was therefore decided to house those pictures before 1600 in the Barberini Palace and to keep pictures after 1600 in the Corsini Palace. There are altogether over 1700 pictures and it is hoped to house them all eventually in the Barberini Palace.

Room I. In *Madonna and Child* by Simone Martini and assistants, 2 the transparent colours model the figure of the Virgin, which is delicately painted. *Madonna and Child with Angels* by Giovanni da Milano dates from the middle of the 14th century. It is charged with emotion and brilliantly coloured, with hard, wiry drawing. Probably painted in Florence, it retains strong elements of the Lombard style. Another *Madonna and Child,* a delightful work in the International Gothic style by Michele Giambono of Venice, is signed and datable about 1432. A fine crucifix probably by a painter from Lucca, Bonaventura Berlinghieri, and another by an unknown Tuscan artist are good examples of 13th century work in the Byzantine style. *Scenes from the Life of Christ* by Giovanni Baronzio, the most important painter of the Rimini school of the 14th century, is remarkable for its iconographic originality. Another *Scenes from the Life of Christ* is a magnificent panel, probably by Giovanni da Rimini, datable around the middle of the 14th century.

Room II. The triptych *Ascension, Pentecost and Last Judgment* by Fra Angelico is probably a late work datable about 1447. It is well organized, painted in clear, bright colours and has a dream-like quality. *Madonna and Angel worshipping the Infant Jesus,* attributed to the Master of the Triumph of Chastity who painted in the style of Domenico Ghirlandaio, is a delightful work with a river scene in the background. *Madonna and Child* dated 1437 by Fra Filippo Lippi is far inferior to his *Annunciation* painted about 1443. The latter shows 3 great mastery of perspective and immense decorative skill. The Virgin

3. Fra Filippo Lippi
(*c.*1406–1469)
The Annunciation,
*c.*1443 oil on panel
61 × 56¾ in.
(155 × 144 cm.)

I. (opposite)
Hans Holbein the
Younger (1477/8–1543)
Henry VIII, 1540
oil on panel
34⅝ × 29⅜ in.
(88·5 × 74·5 cm.)

stands in an attitude of grace and meekness, bowing towards a curly-haired angel who kneels before her bearing a lily. At the side are two donors. Piero di Cosimo's brilliantly-coloured *Magdalene* has little of the oddity of this eccentric genius, except that the saint is probably a portrait of a Florentine lady reading a book. The painting, an early work, shows the influence of Signorelli in the firm lines and the influence of Leonardo in the soft lights of the flesh against a dark background.

Room III. *Madonna with St Paul and St Francis* and *St Sebastian and two Donors* are by Antoniazzo Romano, a little-known and neglected painter. The first came from the Convent of St Paul in Poggio Nativo near Rieti. It was painted around 1488 and resembles the *Madonna della Rota* in the Vatican Gallery. The second is influenced by Piero della Francesca and has a charming background with Mount Soracte depicted against a luminous sky. *St Jerome* belongs to the School of Perugino. The saint, in a white gown, kneels with the two Holy Children behind him, in a superb landscape of rocks and trees.

ANNO · ÆTATIS ·   · SVÆ · XLIX ·

Bartolomeo Veneto's *Portrait of a Gentleman* is a highly accomplished 5
work painted about 1520 with firm Northern outlines and a fine view
of the foothills of the Venetian Alps in the background. The *Madonna
with Saints* by Nicolò di Liberatore, called L'Alunno, a follower of
Carlo Crivelli, shows saints Francis, John the Baptist, Jerome and
Clara in Gothic niches on each side of the Virgin. Perugino's *St
Nicholas of Tolentino* is part of the great polyptych painted for the
Church of the Annunciation in Florence which was started by Filippo
Lippi and finished after his death by Perugino.

Room IV. *Portrait of a Young Man* may be by Lorenzo Lotto or by
one of his pupils. Francesco Francia's *St George and the Dragon* is an
early but vigorous work of the Bolognese painter. In an elegant and
delicately painted landscape the saint advances on a cowering dragon
who has a broken lance in his back. The princess kneels praying in
from of a medieval castle. Lotto's *Holy Conversation*, signed and
dated 1524, is a splendid picture notable for the fresh and sensuous
figure of St Catherine on the right. The intense light falls on the finger-
nails of the saint, on the right hand of the Madonna and on St Anthony
Abbot's book. Marco Palmezzano's *St Jerome*, dated 1503, is remarkable for the lively landscape. *The Lute Player* by the Milanese Andrea
Solario is a fine composition, *c.* 1515, in harmonious colours.

Room V. This room contains the only 17th and 18th century Italian
pictures in the Gallery. *The Massacre of the Niobids* and *Diana*

4. (opposite) Pietro da Cortona
(1596–1669) *Ceiling of the Great Hall,*
1633–39 fresco

5. Bartolomeo Veneto
(before 1502–1555) *Portrait of a Gentleman,*
c. 1520 oil on panel
$28\frac{7}{8} \times 20\frac{7}{8}$ in. (73·5×53 cm.)

Hunting are archaizing works by Andrea Camassei, a disappointing pupil of Domenichino, who had a good deal to do with the decoration of the palace. *The Missionary's Family* by Marco Benefial, who was half French, is an intense study of a tropical scene.

Room VI. *The Creation of the Angels* on the ceiling is by Andrea Camassei. Domenico Beccafumi's *Madonna and Child with the Infant St John* painted about 1517 has the easy elegance and brilliantly luminous colours which are characteristic of this Sienese master. The three pictures by Sodoma, born in the north but Sienese by adoption, cover a long period of this artist's career. *The Rape of the Sabines* about 1510 and *The Mystic Marriage of St Catherine* about 1530 both show the influence of Leonardo and Raphael, but the second is a subtle and moving picture. *The Three Fates* about 1539 is decorative, but mannered and luridly lighted.

Room VII. On the ceiling is Andrea Sacchi's fresco, in cold tones of grey and blue, livened by reds and yellows, of *The Divine Wisdom*, which caused the painter enormous trouble. Divine Wisdom is enthroned over the world surrounded by eleven females who symbolize her qualities. In spite of his great efforts to rival Pietro da Cortona, Sacchi failed to achieve a harmonious composition. A delightful *Madonna of the Scarf* is by the Master of the Kress Landscapes who belonged to Fra Bartolomeo's group. *Madonna and Child* (on easel) by Andrea del Sarto is an early work displaying his refined sense of beauty. The *Madonna and Child* on the right-hand wall, dated 1509, generally attributed to Andrea, is almost certainly by Franciabigio who painted the *Portrait of a Man*. The *Holy Family* by Fra Bartolomeo and that by Andrea del Sarto, both late works, make an interesting contrast, Fra Bartolomeo more weighty and monumental, Andrea softer and more delicate. Bronzino's magnificent *Portrait of Stefano Colonna*, the captain of Charles V, in armour, signed and dated 1546, is paralleled at a somewhat lower level by Girolamo Sicciolante da Sermoneta's *Portrait of Francesco II Colonna*, 1561. An opening in this room leads to the Chapel decorated with frescoes of New Testament scenes by Pietro da Cortona and G. F. Romanelli.

Room VIII. On an easel in the centre of the room is Raphael's *La Fornarina* reputedly representing his mistress Margherita Luti, the baker's daughter. In spite of Raphael's name on the yellow and blue striped band round her arm, there is strong ground for believing that this picture was painted, at least in part, by his principal assistant Giulio Romano, about 1518. The *Pietà* by the Master of the Manchester Madonna is a curious transcription of Michelangelo's *Pietà* in

St Peter's. The room also contains a good *Portrait of a Gentleman* by Federico Zuccari, a pleasant *Holy Family* by Marcello Venusti, based on a Michelangelo drawing, two competent Cardinals *Ricci* and *Savelli* by Scipione Pulzone and a sentimental *Ecce Homo* by the Spanish Mannerist Luis Morales.

Room IX. On the ceiling is a neo-classical fresco *The Chariot of the Sun* by Carlo Maratta's pupil Giuseppe Chiari. *Madonna with St Anne, the Infant Jesus and the Infant St John* by the Bergamesque painter Giovanni Cariani has a delightful landscape background. The baroque *St Jerome* is by Domenico Tintoretto, son of Jacopo. The two brilliantly-painted small canvases, *The Adoration of the Shepherds* and *The Baptism of Christ* attributed to El Greco are probably sketches for a large work, the altarpiece of the Colegio de Doña Maria de Aragon in Madrid, though they may be workshop replicas. The restoration of 1946 has revealed the finely-painted detail and silvery tones previously hidden by varnish. Tintoretto's splendid *Christ and the Woman taken in Adultery*, an early work *c.* 1547, exemplifies his great gift of opening up architectural space. As often, the picture is divided into areas of light and shade, with the chief figure deep in the centre and the other figures placed in groups, and Tintoretto still retains the old Venetian harmony of colours. The *Portrait of Philip II* attributed to Titian is in poor shape and is probably a copy of a lost original.

Room X. The frescoes depicting *Vulcan invoked by a King* and the *Sacrifice of Juno* are by Pietro da Cortona. *Venus and Adonis*, attributed to Titian, was once in the possession of Queen Christina of Sweden. It is probably a workshop copy of the Prado picture, which was painted in 1553. Jacopo Bassano's *Adoration of the Shepherds, c.* 1565, a favourite subject of his, is a somewhat mannered composition. *Venus and Adonis* by the Genoese Luca Cambiaso, is well-drawn, decorative and original in design.

Room XI. This room has several examples of the Ferrarese painters Benvenuto Tisi, known as Il Garofalo, and Ippolito Scarsella, known as Il Scarsellino. Garofalo's *The Vestal Claudia and the Statue of Cybele* and *King Picus being transformed into a Woodpecker* derive respectively from Ovid's *Fasti* and *Metamorphoses*. The miracle of the effigy of the Magna Mater proves the chastity of the Vestal Claudia and Circe casts the spell on King Picus. Denis Calvaert's *The Mystic Marriage of St Catherine* is not a notable picture, but it is a reminder of the great influence this Antwerp painter had as a teacher on Reni, Albani and Domenichino. Girolamo da Carpi's *Portrait of a Gentleman*

6. (left) Angelo Bronzino (1503–1572) *Stefano Colonna,* 1546
oil on canvas 45¼×38¾ in. (115×97 cm.)
7. (right) Quentin Massys (1464/5–1530) *Erasmus of Rotterdam, c.*1517
wood transferred to canvas 23¼×18⅛ in. (59×46·5 cm.)

is a good example of the work of this painter, who was active in Bologna, Rome and Ferrara. Bartolomeo Passarotti's *Fish Market* and *Butcher's Shop* are genre pictures by this able portraitist from Bologna. Scarsellino's limited but lyrical art is best seen in *Noli me tangere* and the *Raising of Lazarus,* though neither equals Garofalo's statuesque *St Cecilia* with its delicate romantic background.

7 Room XII. The *Portrait of Erasmus of Rotterdam* by Quentin Massys, probably painted in 1517 as part of a diptych for Sir Thomas More, is a beautiful example of this painter's portraits of scholars sitting at a desk with books and papers. *Portrait of an Old Woman* of the 16th century Dutch school is a penetrating psychological study, while Joos van Cleve's *Portrait of Bernardino Clesio, c.* 1530, prince-bishop of Trent, is objective and realistic. The two pictures of the 15th century Westphalian School *Adoration of the Magi* and *Circumcision of Jesus,* Simon Marmion's *Crucifixion,* the Master of St Sebastian's *Pilgrims at a Sanctuary* and Hans Maler's *Portrait of Wolfgang Tanvelder* are worth noting.

Room XIII has a magnificent *Portrait of Henry VIII* attributed to Hans Holbein the Younger. The King appears, at the age of 49, in the clothes he wore for his marriage to Anne of Cleves in 1540. The fine *Deposition,* a triptych ascribed to Maerten van Heemskerck, may be by Dirk Jacobz Vellert. Worth noting are *Diana and Actaeon* by Joseph Heintz and *Judith* by Jan Massys, Quentin's son and pupil.

Rooms XIV and XV contain the Cervinara Bequest. At the entrance is a *Madonna and Child* by Bartolomeo Montagna painted under the influence of Giovanni Bellini. There follow paintings by: Louis Léopold Boilly, *Grandfather's Birthday;* J. F. Schall, the Alsatian painter, *The Canary* and *The Indiscreet Dog;* François Boucher, *Morning* and *Evening* at the mill; and six good views of romantic ruins and fantasies from Italy and France by Hubert Robert.

Room XV has some excellent pictures, particularly: Bernard Bellotto's *A View of Old Dresden* and *Schlosshof,* the Imperial Castle in Lower Austria; *Girl in a Striped Veil* by J. B. Greuze; Nicolas Lancret's *The Rendezvous* and *Family Group;* Jean Honoré Fragonard's *Annette and Lubin;* Antoine Le Nain's *The Young Singers;* Francesco Guardi's magnificent *The Canal of the Giudecca;* and Boucher's charming *Little Gardener,* signed and dated 1767.

Room XVI contains new acquisitions of which the busts of *S. Filippo Neri* by Alessandro Algardi and *Antonio Barberini* by G. L. Bernini are very fine.

Room XVII is the Great Hall of the Palace with the huge illusionist fresco by Pietro da Cortona, painted 1633–1639, on the ceiling. It is called *The Allegory of Divine Providence* but it might just as well have been named 'The Triumph of the Barberini Family'. The architectural framework is not meant to expand the actual shape of the vaulting. Instead there is an apparently open sky where figures are floating or coming into the room. The complicated decorative scheme is completely successful and has never been equalled. The Allegory shows Divine Providence achieving her aims through the agency of Urban VIII, whose antecedents are indicated by three enormous Barberini bees in the middle of the wreath held by Faith, Hope and Charity. On the walls are works by Carlo Maratta and Pietro's defeated rival Andrea Sacchi. Urban VIII surveys the triumphal scene through the eyes of his *Bust* by Bernini and assistants.

The Director is Professor Italo Faldi.

The gallery is open on weekdays except Monday: May 2 to September 30 from 9 a.m. to 4 p.m.; October 1 to April 30 from 9.30 a.m. to 4 p.m.; Sundays and Holidays from 9 a.m. to 1 p.m.

The National Gallery of Rome
Palazzo Corsini

An account of the collection and its history is given at the beginning of the section on the Palazzo Barberini, to which pictures earlier than 1600 were moved in 1952. The Corsini Palace, in the Via della Lungara, was built for Cardinal Domenico Riario, nephew of Sixtus IV, in the 15th century. In the next century Queen Christina founded an Academy in the palace, took up residence and died there in 1689. The palace passed into the hands of the Corsini family and was completely rebuilt by Ferdinando Fuga 1732–1736. In 1797 Giuseppe Bonaparte, as ambassador to the French Directoire, occupied the palace and in 1800 Madame Letizia, mother of Napoleon, came to live there. In 1883 it was bought by the Italian State and became the seat of the Accademia dei Lincei.

Passing through the large Atrium, where are sarcophagi and marble busts, we ascend the fine double staircase to the first floor. In the vestibule are statues, mostly by neo-classic sculptors. *Psyche borne by the Winds*, 1821, is by John Gibson, the English sculptor who came to Rome in 1817 and died there in 1866. He worked with Canova and Thorwaldsen and in his time was regarded as little inferior to them. *Vulcan* and *Vesta*, 1844, by Pietro Tenerani and *Minerva* and *Ceres* by Antonio Solà from Barcelona are noteworthy. The pictures are still arranged as a family collection, which means that some of them are too high to be seen easily.

Room I contains views of Rome and landscapes. Two *Landscapes* (1051, 523) are by the little-known Master of the Betulla (birch-tree). There are a number of Roman architectural fantasies of which the best are by G. P. Pannini (2348, 2349) and Hubert Robert (1558). *Porticus of Octavia* (36) is by Antonio Gaspari. There are two scenes of buildings on fire (2210, 2211) by the 18th century Neapolitan painter Alessio de Marchis. He was a specialist in painting fires and if he could not find one he would set fire to houses to give himself a suitable subject. There are four sharply-observed oils and ten watercolours by Gaspard van Wittel, called Vanvitelli, of which the best are *Castel Sant'Angelo* (1415), the *Quirinal Palace* (1410) and various

8. The Corsini Palace

views along the Tiber. High up are two pictures showing the influence of Claude by Claude Joseph Vernet, *Shipwreck on a rocky coast* (466) and *Harbour scene* (472). Agostino Tassi's *Landscape with Diana and Pan* (2399) clearly shows the influence of Adam Elsheimer. *Landscape with Cephalus and Procris* (1084) is a good work of Paul Brill. *Bust of Clement XII* by Pietro Bracci.

Room II contains the Foreign Schools. There are two dexterous portraits attributed to the Utrecht painter Paulus Moreelse of which *Portrait of a Gentleman* (845) is particularly good. Jan van Ravensteyn's *Portrait of an Old Man* (911) is a powerful exercise in severe realism. There are a *Snow Scene* (189) by Lucas van Uden and Hunting Scenes of which the best are No. 972 by Philips Wouwerman and three *Boar Hunts* (821, 839, 836) by Frans Snyders. *Still-life* (944) by Andrea Benedetti is in the Flemish style. There are two charming miniature views, *Reims Cathedral* (926) by Gillis Neefs and *Interior of Antwerp Cathedral* (204) by Pieter Neefs the Younger and Frans Francken III.

Room III continues the Foreign Schools. *Man in a steeple hat* (885) is a lively portrait by Willem Moreelse. Two early works of Rubens are *Madonna and Child* (900) painted about 1614 and *St Sebastian* (388) being de-arrowed by angels *c.* 1610. *Sentry* (973) by Barent

9. (left) Bartolomé Esteban Murillo (1617–1682) *Madonna and Child*
oil on canvas 64⅝ × 42½ in. (164 × 108 cm.)
10. (right) G. B. Gaulli (Il Bacciccia) (1639–1709) *Clement IX, c.*1667
oil on canvas 29⅛ × 24¾ in. (73·9 × 62·8 cm.)

Fabritius shows strong influence of Rembrandt, whose pupil he probably was. Sir Anthony van Dyck's *Madonna and Child* is an uninspired work of his Roman period. Two *Portraits* (884, 890) by Jan Verspronck show the influence of Italian portraiture. Willem Kalf's *Interior of a Kitchen* (968) is a good example of the early work of this great master of still-life painting. *Portrait of a Woman* (872) by Thomas de Keyser is a penetrating study. Joos de Momper's excellent *Landscape* (1329) is outshadowed by the charming *Snow Scene* (1528) by Jan ('Velvet') Bruegel. Murillo's *Madonna and Child* (464) is finely modelled and completely free from sentimentality. The gold, old rose and varied blues blend into a harmonious whole. There are three good portraits by Justus Sustermans of *Vittoria della Rovere* (428), *Cosimo III* (414) and *Young Girl* (367). The chiaroscuro of Gerbrandt van den Eeckhout's *Supper at Emmaus* (1072) shows his debt to Rembrandt. Pierre Mignard's *Madonna and Child* with boy dressed as a Carthusian (1526) is a tired academic piece.

Room IV. Genoese school of 17th century. Domenico Fiasella's

11. Canaletto (1697–1768) *Rialto Bridge, Venice,* 1744
oil on canvas 27⅝×34¼ in. (70×92 cm.)

Hagar and the Angel (1696) has Caravaggesque lighting. *Charity of St Laurence* (1517) is a glowing work with strong chiaroscuro by Bernardo Strozzi. Andrea Ansaldo's *Flight into Egypt* (1704) is competent and unexciting. G. B. Gaulli's *Portrait of Bernini* (1451) is good, coming as it does from a developer of Bernini's ideas, but it cannot match the superb *Portrait of Clement IX,* painted about 1667, a master- 10 piece of technique and psychological penetration. Gaulli's sketches for the *Gesù* (1470) and *S. Agnese* (1667, 1668) are good, but give little idea of the grandeur of the finished work. The two portraits of noblemen (894, 904) by Giovanni Bernardo Carbone are examples of aristocratic Baroque painting, so much to the taste of the Genoese nobility. Magnasco's *Witches* (1505, 1506) and *Hermits* (1534) are typically melodramatic works of this master of phantasmagoria.

Room V. Venetian school of the 18th century. The four views of Venice, recently cleaned, by Canaletto are not among his most important works but they are excellently painted: *Grand Canal* (1037), *Rialto Bridge* (1033), *Piazzetta and Library* (1005) and *St Mark's* 11

12. G. B. Piazzetta (1683–1754) *Judith and Holofernes*
oil on canvas 31½ × 37 in. (80 × 94 cm.)

Square (1061). The two views (24, 26) by Luca Carlevaris, Canaletto's precursor as a painter of Venetian views, make an interesting contrast. G. P. Tiepolo's *Old Faun and Young Satyr* (1515) is an excellent piece of painting by the great master, but it is less interesting than 12 *Judith and Holofernes* (601) by Giovanni Battista Piazzetta with its bold shadows, fine draughtmanship and dramatic effects.

Room VI. Emilian and Tuscan schools of the 17th century. The three dramatic pictures by Giacinto Brandi *Noah drunk* (933), *Lot and his Daughters* (2365) and *David* (835) have striking colours. Of the three pictures by Carlo Dolci, *Madonna of the Veil* (92) illustrates best his slick technique and deep-felt piety. Guercino's *Magdalene Scourging Herself* (1757) has fine effects of light. Franco Furini's *Andromeda* (186) has Titian-red hair and fine flesh tones set off by a blue mantle and a yellow girdle. *Monsignor Ottaviano Prati* (1498) is a good portrait by Sassoferrata. Giovanni Lanfranco's *St Agatha Healed by St Peter* (211) gives only a slight idea of the abilities of this great fresco painter.

Room VII was the bedroom of Queen Christina and is the only room preserved from the 15th century building. It is divided by two

13. Caravaggio (1573–1610) *St John the Baptist,* c.1603
oil on canvas 39×52¾ in. (99×134 cm.)

columns and the ceiling is frescoed with grotesques by the Zuccari.
Queen Christina died in this room on April 18, 1689 and she is com-
memorated by her famous words, 'I was born free, lived free and shall
die emancipated'. *Narcissus* (1569) painted by Caravaggio about
1600 is a fine composition in a bad state of preservation. Caravaggio's
St John the Baptist (433), painted about 1603, shows the saint as a   13
youth in a romantic pose, with red draperies which form the base of a
triangle leading up to his contemplative face. *Madonna and Child*
(107) may be an early work of Caravaggio, but the palette of cold
deep blue, purple and yellow suggests Orazio Gentileschi as the
author. Carlo Saraceni's *Madonna and Child with St Anne* (Q.1) is
notable for its gay and enchanting colours. There are *bambocciate*
(genre pictures of Roman lower-class life) by Pieter van Laer of
Haarlem, *The Water-carrier* (965) being one of his best works.
    Room VIII. Followers of Caravaggio. *Herodias* (45) by Simon
Vouet is firmly modelled. Le Valentin, the most faithful of all the followers of Caravaggio, is represented by three pictures of which the
best is *Christ Casting the Moneylenders out of the Temple* (1261).
Mattia Preti's *Resurrection of Lazarus* (1499) is a well-organized

composition. *Portrait of a Painter* (1155) is attributed to Gerrit van Honthorst, called Gherardo della Notte because of his habit of painting by candle-light.

Room IX. Carlo Maratta's *Maddalena Rospigliosi* (2344) is a fine portrait while his austere *Gentleman* (336), a late work, shows his interest in the French, Dutch and Flemish portrait painters. Pompeo Batoni's *Clement XIII* (1925) is delicately handled. His exquisite *Nativity* (272) is in a magnificent silver frame of 1748. On the central stands: *Adoration of the Magi* (156) and *Adoration of the Shepherds* (163) are two decorative pictures by Giovanni Francesco Romanelli. Of the four sugary rococo works by Francesco Trevisani *Mater Dolorosa* (512) and *Madonna Reading with Child* (176) are the most attractive. *Jacob's Dream* (986) by Domenico Fetti is set in a wild landscape and a lurid sky. *Portrait of a Lady* (1548) by Anton Raphael Mengs is extremely disappointing.

Room X. Neapolitan school of the 17th and 18th centuries. Luca Giordano's *Self-portrait* (1881) is interesting and his *Jesus and the Doctors in the Temple* (394) overcrowded. G. B. Caracciolo's *St Onuphrius* (1535) shows the influence of Caravaggio tenderly reinterpreted. *Expulsion of Heliodorus from the Temple* (1536) is a dramatic and well-composed work by Francesco Solimena. *St Pellegrinus* (1483) by Pietro Novelli is a characteristic work of this Sicilian painter from Monreale. Salvator Rosa is represented by four *Landscapes* (106, 110, 503, 1466) and a *Battle Scene* (500) but the *Portrait of his Wife* (1571) is his best painting here. There are also pictures by Gaspare Traversi, Sebastiano Conca, Bernardo Cavallino and Jusepe Ribera.

Room XI. In the passage are four curious 'Anamorphoses' (artificial perspectives) of the French 17th century. On the ceiling is Fratel Andrea Pozzo's exciting *Mission of the Society of Jesus* (1426) a sketch for his virtuoso ceiling in St Ignatius. The three pictures by G. M. Crespi, *Death of Joseph* (1237), *Young Woman* (1938) and *St Hyacinth with the Virgin in Glory* (1538) are sensitive and sincere. There are also pictures by Gaetano Gondolfi, Carlo Maratta, G. F. Romanelli, Andrea Sacchi and Donato Creti.

Room XII has a number of Neapolitan *Still-lifes*, a pleasing *Fish and Crustaceans* (526) by Marco de Caro and two panels of fruit and flowers (50, 66) by Abraham Bruegel.

The director is Professor Italo Faldi.

The gallery is open on weekdays except Tuesday from 9 a.m. to 2 p.m.: Sundays and Holidays from 9 a.m. to 1 p.m.

The Villa Farnesina

Across the road from the Palazzo Corsini is the Villa Farnesina, a mar- 14
vellous example of a Renaissance villa, built by Baldassare Peruzzi,
1508–1511, for the banker Agostino Chigi, who entertained there in
fantastic luxury. It passed in 1580 to the Farnese family and in 1731
to the Neapolitan Bourbons. In 1927 it was acquired by the State and
now houses the administration of the Accademia dei Lincei.

We enter from the garden (passing through a small hall) the Loggia
of Psyche, whose arches are now glassed in. The overall design for
the gallery is certainly by Raphael, inspired by the episode of Cupid
and Psyche in the *Golden Ass* of Lucius Apuleius, though he took little
part in the execution, which he left to his assistants Giulio Romano,
G. F. Penni and Raffaelino del Colle. The beautiful festoons of fruit
and flowers are by Giovanni da Udine. The whole conception is
illusionist, with curtains and birds flying in the sky. The two great
'tapestries', executed by Penni and Raffaelino del Colle, probably

14. The Villa Farnesina

from cartoons by Giulio Romano, represent *The Council of the Gods* and *The Wedding Banquet of Cupid and Psyche*. In the spandrels are groups of nude figures, of which the best are *The Three Graces, Venus, Ceres and Juno, Jupiter and Cupid* and *Venus and Psyche*. Tradition holds that Raphael had a hand in *The Three Graces*, particularly the one whose back is turned, but it is more probable that all of them are by Giulio Romano.

In the adjoining room is an exquisite frieze with mythological figures by Baldassare Peruzzi, of which the most noteworthy are *Diana and Actaeon, Hunt of the Calydonian Boar and the Duel of Meleager* and *Myth of Orpheus*. Against the dark blue background the figures move in an agile and decorative manner.

The Loggia of Galatea is famous for Raphael's magnificent fresco *The Triumph of Galatea, c.* 1513, based on the episode of Polyphemus and Galatea in a poem by the Florentine Angelo Poliziano. Here is movement in a classical composition and every movement is related to the superb, Venus-like figure of Galatea who, her dark red cloak fluttering in the wind, has turned to listen to the love song of Polyphemus. Galatea is in a chariot drawn by two dolphins, surrounded by tritons and nymphs, while winged Cupids above aim their arrows at her heart. This lighthearted work is also a supreme example of composition where the permanence of a golden minute is captured. On the left is Polyphemus, a huge, relaxed figure by Sebastiano del Piombo, in a grotesque blue tunic added later. The room, whose decoration was organized by Peruzzi in strict accordance with the architectural background, contains lunettes of Ovidian *Metamorphoses* by Sebastiano del Piombo. On the ceiling by Peruzzi himself, are the constellations, the planets and the signs of the zodiac, which are placed as at December 1, 1446, the birthday of Agostino Chigi.

On the first floor are two rooms. The first is the Room of the Perspectives, brilliantly frescoed with illusionist architecture to give the impression of an open loggia. On the walls are admirably subtle frescoes of Ovidian subjects in the form of a frieze. The whole is the work of Peruzzi. In the second room, formerly a bedroom, is Sodoma's impressive *The Marriage of Alexander and Roxana, c.* 1512, based on a drawing by Raphael. The luxurious colouring and handsome detail are somewhat marred by awkward distortions and lack of harmonious composition.

The Villa is open on weekdays from 9 a.m. to 1 p.m.

It is closed on Sundays and Holidays.

The Capitoline
Museums and Gallery

The works of art housed in the Palazzo Nuovo, the Palazzo dei Conservatori and the Palazzo Caffarelli have as their nucleus the oldest
collection in the western world, which dates from 1471, when Sixtus
IV 'restored' to the Roman people a number of valuable bronzes and
placed them in the Palazzo dei Conservatori. This nucleus was increased over the years by discoveries and acquisitions of which the
most important is the collection of Cardinal Alessandro Albani,
bought in 1733. The collection is divided into three main sections, the
first of which is rather confusingly called the Capitoline Museum.

Capitoline Museum
Housed in the Palazzo Nuovo, completed by Girolamo Rainaldi at the 15
end of the reign of Innocent X, is an important collection of antique
sculpture, begun by Clement XII and added to by other popes. It was
opened to the public in 1734.

15. Michelangelo (1475–1564)
The Capitoline Museum
(Palazzo Nuovo)

Ground Floor. In the Inner Courtyard is a Fountain by Giacomo della Porta and above it a huge statue of a river-god called Marforio, formerly the companion of Pasquino in the dialogues of the 'talking' statues. In the niches are two 2nd century statues of *Pan* from the Theatre of Pompey. In the Atrium are colossal statues of *Minerva* (2), *Diana* (19) and *Mars* (16). On the right of the Courtyard is a small Egyptian collection, containing sculptures from the Isaeum Campense and two dog-headed apes from the tomb of Nectanebes II, 358–341 B.C. Returning to the Atrium we enter on the left the three Rooms of the Oriental Cults. Room I has a relief of a Mithraic sacrifice (9) and other representations of Mithras. An *Altar* (18) dedicated to the Magna Mater represents the legend of the Vestal Claudia who, in 204 B.C., drew to Rome with her girdle the ship carrying the image of the goddess. Room II has three statues of Serapis and an Alexandrian votive relief of the 2nd century (15). Room III has statues of the cult of Zeus Dolichenus. Returning to the Atrium we enter on the right Room I. In the middle is a *Base* (1) with a relief of the Labours of Hercules. Room II has a vigorous *Bust of an Old Man* (1) from the time of Trajan and the famous *Amendola Sarcophagus* (4) portraying a battle between Romans and Gauls, in a style resembling that of Pergamum, 2nd century A.D. In Room III is the colossal sarcophagus of the 3rd century A.D. formerly known as that of Alexander Severus. The dead couple are on the lid and on the sides are reliefs of the story of Achilles.

Returning to the Atrium opposite the statue of Mars we ascend the stairs to the first floor. The Gallery has on the walls 537 inscriptions. *Leda and the Swan* (7) is a much-reconstructed copy of an original by Timotheus of the 4th century B.C. A very drunken *Old Woman* (10) (modern head) may be a copy of an original by Myron the Younger who worked at Smyrna in the second half of the 2nd century B.C. *Winged Psyche* (22) is from a 4th century B.C. original. The *Athena of Velletri* (31) is a good copy of a bronze original of the end of the 5th century B.C. *Head of Probus* (33) is the best of the rare portraits of this emperor. *Krater* (34), a decorative vase of the 1st century A.D. rests on a *Wellhead* from Hadrian's Villa with an archaizing relief representing a procession of twelve gods (Dei Consentes). *Herm of Jupiter Ammon* (49) may be a copy of an original of the 4th century B.C., or a Hellenistic work. *Wounded Niobid* (52) is a copy of a 4th century original

16. (opposite above) *She-wolf,* early 5th century B.C. bronze height 32⅝ in. (83 cm.)
17. (opposite below) *Dying Gaul, c.* 200 B.C. marble

18. *Mosaic of Doves,*
Roman copy, *c.*130 A.D.

II. (opposite) Raphael
(1483–1520)
The Triumph of Galatea,
*c.*1513 fresco 116×100 in.
(295×225 cm.)
The Villa Farnesina

on this popular theme. The huge *Head of Aphrodite* (53) may be a Hellenistic original. *Sarcophagus* (57) of the 3rd century A.D. has reliefs of the Rape of Proserpine. *Roman Lady* (61) with hair stylized in rows of thick curls, from the Flavian era, is in the guise of Venus. *Statue of a Gladiator* (65) is a poor 17th century restoration by Monnot, incorporating a good copy of the torso of the Discobolos of Myron. *Cupid the Archer* (67) is a good copy of the famous 4th century bronze by Lysippus. *Statue of Hercules* (68) shows him struggling with an animal, probably the Arcadian Stag, but in the 17th century restoration by Alessandro Algardi a Hydra was added.

We turn back to the first doorway on the right into the Hall of the Doves named after the celebrated mosaic. *Sarcophagus* (8) of a child has a scene of the myth of Prometheus, 3rd century A.D. The *Mosaic of the Doves* (9) is of very fine workmanship (60 tesserae to a square centimetre) and comes from the centre of a room in Hadrian's Villa. It is probably a copy of a work, much admired by Pliny, by Sosus of Pergamum. In the glass cases are the *Tabula Iliaca* (63), a relief representing in minute detail the events of the Trojan war by Theodorus of the 1st century A.D., and pieces of shields of Achilles (75, 76) by the same sculptor. In the centre of the room is a *Child* pressing to her breast a dove which is being attacked by a dog, for which the restorer has substituted a snake. It is a Roman copy of a Greek work of the 3rd to 2nd century B.C.

Continuing along the Gallery we turn right into the Cabinet of

19 Venus which contains the *Capitoline Venus*, the most famous statue
in the museum. It is a splendid Roman copy, 2nd century B.C., in
Parian marble of a Hellenistic original deriving from the Cnidian Venus
of Praxiteles of which about fifty replicas are known to us. The
Capitoline Venus is more self-conscious than the Cnidian, but she is
better balanced, more solid and more compact. Acquired for the
museum by Benedict XIV in 1750, it was one of the many statues
removed to Paris by Napoleon. It was returned in 1816.

At the end of the Gallery to the left is the Hall of the Emperors con-
taining 65 busts of Roman emperors of which the more important are:
Augustus (6) with a crown of myrtle, represented at an advanced age;
a *Woman of the Flavian period* (15), supposedly Julia daughter of
Titus, with the characteristic hair-style of the period; *Plotina* (21) wife
of Trajan, her best portrait; *Faustina the Younger* (32) wife of Marcus
Aurelius; *Head of Heliogabalus* (55). On the walls are two reliefs
Perseus and Andromeda (F), 2nd century A.D. and *Endymion asleep*
(H), 1st century A.D. In the centre is a *Seated Statue of Helena* (59)
mother of Constantine, deriving from the Aphrodite of Phidias.

The Hall of the Philosophers contains 79 busts of philosophers,
poets and others of which the best are: *Herm of Socrates* (3); *Herm of
Asclepias* (15); *Theon of Smyrna* (17), a mathematician and commentator on Plato; *Sophocles* (22–23); *Euripides* (30–31); *Homer*
(39–41); *Demosthenes* (43); *Epicurus* (53); *Cicero* (56), an Augustan
copy of the original *c.* 43 B.C., *Lysias* (73), the orator; *Theophrastus*
(74). On the walls are a series of friezes (A).

The Main Hall has a rich ceiling with the arms of Innocent X. In the
centre: statues of *Zeus* (1) and *Aesculapius* (5) in white and black
Egyptian marble, copies from the period of Hadrian of Greek originals
of the 4th century B.C. *Young Centaur* (2) laughing and *Old Centaur*
(4) weeping, are signed works of Aristeas and Papias of Aphrodisium,
who worked in Hadrian's Villa, from which come these statues, copies
of late Hellenistic bronzes. Colossal statue of the *Infant Hercules* (3)
in green basalt, 2nd century A.D., with a base on which are lively reliefs
depicting scenes from the myth of Zeus. Around the room (left to
right): *Young satyr* (6) a Hellenistic work. Colossal statue of *Apollo*
(7) with cither, copy of a 4th century original. *Hera* (11) a copy of an
original of 420 B.C. attributed to Agoracritus and wrongly restored as
Ceres, has the head of Faustina, wife of Marcus Aurelius. Statue of
Apollo (20) is a replica of the so-called Apollo of Omphalos in Athens,
a 5th century work attributed to Calamis. *Statue of a Youth* (21) perhaps a young Roman in the guise of Hermes Logios, is from the time

19. *Capitoline Venus,*
Roman copy,
?2nd century B.C. marble

of Hadrian, a copy of a type of 4th century B.C. statue attributed to Scopas. *Statue of an Old Lady* (22) with a look of terror on her face, was probably part of a genre group in Hellenistic style. *Apollo* (30) is in the archaic style and of the Kassel type, copy of an original *c.* 460–450 B.C. *Pothos* (31) wrongly restored as Apollo with a cither, is from an original by Scopas. *Wounded Amazon* (33) is a copy signed by Sosicles of an original bronze of the middle of the 5th century B.C. by Cresilas. She must originally have leaned on a lance. Her head is particularly fine with a sweet, melancholy expression on her face.

Room of the Faun has 140 Roman inscriptions of which the most important is the *Lex de imperio Vespasiani.* Statue of a *Drunken Faun* (1) in red marble holding up a bunch of grapes, is from the time of Hadrian and may be a copy of a late Hellenistic work by the sculptors from Aphrodisium who worked at his Villa. *Sarcophagus* (5) depicts the Hunt of the Calydonian Boar. *Child* (8) with a mask of Silenus is a charming work of the early years of the Empire. *Sarcophagus* (11) of the 2nd century A.D. has figures of Endymion and Selene, the cover, which does not belong to it, has low reliefs associated with the death of a wife – the three Fates, the soul of the deceased, Pluto and Proserpine. *Boy with a goose* (17) is a replica of a bronze by Boëthos of Chalcedon, which existed in Rome in the time of Pliny. *Sarcophagus* (19) has exquisite scenes of the infancy and education of Dionysus, 2nd century A.D.

Room of the Gladiator contains statues, mainly from Hadrian's

Villa, sent to Paris in 1797, after the Treaty of Tolentino, and brought back in 1816. *Wounded Amazon* (1) is from an original by Phidias which existed at Ephesus. The head is in the style of Cresilas and the figure probably leaned on a lance. Colossal *Head of Alexander the Great* (2) is a copy of a 4th century B.C. original. *Statue* (3) of Antinoüs, or some other person, in the semblance of Hermes, is a graceful copy from the time of Hadrian of an original from the 4th century B.C. *Apollo with cither* (4) is a type of the Lycian Apollo of Praxiteles. *Head of a Young Man* (6) has been, with no evidence, identified as the younger Brutus. *Satyr Resting* (7) is one of the best of about 70 copies of an original of Praxiteles. It gave its name, as 'The Marble Faun', to Nathaniel Hawthorne's novel. The satyr, leaning against the trunk of a tree, is slightly drunk, which Hawthorne seems to have missed. *Head of Dionysus* (8) is a Hellenistic copy of an original by Praxiteles. *Statue* (9) is an expressive work possibly representing the Cynic philosopher Bion of Borysthenes. *Eros and Psyche* (12) is an attractive Hellenistic group from the beginning of the 2nd century B.C. In the middle of the room stands the *Dying Gaul,* formerly believed to be a gladiator, hence the misnaming of the room and Byron's erroneous description of him 'butcher'd to make a Roman holiday'. The statue was found in the Gardens of Sallust in the 16th century at the same time as *Gaul Killing his Wife* in the Ludovisi Collection of the Museo delle Terme and is also a Roman copy, in Asiatic marble, of part of the great bronze group of statues dedicated by Attalus I of Pergamum to commemorate his victory over the Gauls in 239 B.C. It can be dated about the beginning of the 2nd century B.C. The body is admirably modelled and the proud, resigned face of the dying man gives the figure great nobility.

Palazzo dei Conservatori
This palace was begun by Nicholas V about 1450 and was remodelled from designs by Michelangelo in 1563–1586 by Girolamo Rainaldi, Tommaso dei Cavalieri and Giacomo della Porta. It contains the Rooms of the Conservatori, the Museum of the Palace and the Picture Gallery (Pinacoteca).

From the Piazza we enter the central door and pass into the Courtyard. On the right is a colossal head of *Constantine the Great* brought from his Basilica in 1486. On the left are reliefs representing the provinces subject to Rome, which once decorated the Temple of Hadrian in the Piazza di Pietra. The Entrance Hall has a number of books, engravings and prints, including a set by Hubert Robert, illustrating the history of the Capitol. Through the door on the right we ascend the stairs to the First Landing where are reliefs from triumphal arches of which the most notable is that of Marcus Aurelius sacrificing before the Temple of Jupiter Capitolinus. On the Second Landing, ornamented by stuccoes, 1575, of Luzio Luzzi, is a relief of Hadrian pronouncing the funeral eulogy on his wife Sabina and a 13th century statue of Charles of Anjou, King of Sicily, attributed to Arnolfo di Cambio.

At the top of the stairs are the Rooms of the Conservatori. Room I, of the Horatii and Curiatii, has good frescoes by Giuseppe Cesari, known as the Cavalier d'Arpino, in imitation of tapestries, portraying episodes of the origins of Rome and the early kings. Against the shorter sides of the room are statues of *Urban VIII*, 1640, by Bernini and assistants and *Innocent X*, 1649–1650, by Algardi. The Bernini 20 statue in marble is mostly studio work but it has grandeur and catches the light effectively at many angles. By contrast, Algardi's bronze, a great masterpiece of portraiture and one of his finest works, lacks the dynamic vision of Bernini's statue. Room II, of the Captains, has two beautiful doors in carved wood of 1643 and a splendid painted ceiling from the Palazzo Mattei Paganica, formerly at the foot of the Capitoline Hill. Room III, of the Triumphs of Mars, has a carved wooden ceiling of 1569 and pictures by G. F. Romanelli, Pietro da Cortona and Francesco Albani. In the middle is the famous *Spinario*, a bronze 21 statue of a boy taking a thorn out of his foot, an elegant creation of late Hellenistic eclecticism. The bronze *Bust*, once supposed to be of L. Junius Brutus, is Italic-Etruscan work of the 2nd century B.C. Only the head is antique. There is Hellenistic influence but its basic Etruscan nature is seen in the set features and the lack of concern for detailed analysis. *Statue of a Camillus*, or acolyte, is Roman of the 1st century A.D. The bronze *Krater* was a gift of King Mithridates of Pontus to the Eupator gymnastic association of young men at the end of the third war against the Romans, 63 B.C. Room IV, of the Wolf, has in the middle the celebrated bronze *She-wolf* of the early 5th century B.C. It is 16 known that it was in the Lateran Palace in the 10th century, but its earlier history is unknown. The linear, geometrically-ornamented head marks it as Etruscan and the rendering of the anatomy links it with the art of Veii. It is remarkably unrealistic, but a powerful and austere masterpiece. The twins were added in 1509 by Antonio Polaiuolo. It is believed by some to be the wolf that stood on the Capitol and was struck by lightning in 65 B.C. The hind legs certainly bear traces of damage which might be attributed to this cause. On the wall

20. (left) Alessandro Algardi (1595–1654) *Innocent X*, 1649–50
bronze
21. (right) *Spinario*, 1st century B.C.
bronze

facing the windows are fragments of the *Fasti Consulares et Triump-hales*, from the Arch of Augustus in the Forum, framed in an archi-tectural design by Michelangelo. They contain lists of consuls, tribunes and censors and records of the triumphs of the great captains of Rome. Room V, of the Geese, has two Roman bronze ducks and a bronze vase in the form of a Head of Isis. The *Head of Medusa, c.* 1630, was presented to the Museum in 1731 by the Marchese Francesco Bichi as the work of 'a most celebrated artist' and was soon attributed to Bernini. In spite of some unusual features, the brilliance and technical wizardry stamp it as by the great master. In the middle of the room is a *Dog* in rare green marble known as *'verde ranocchia'*. Rooms VI-IX contain Hellenistic works, tapestries, frescoes and pictures of minor importance. Room IX has a fine ceiling, *c.* 1516–1519. Room X, the Old Chapel, has on the walls *Madonna and Child with Angels*, a charming fresco by Antonio da Viterbo, end of 15th century, and *Saints* by G. F. Romanelli. In the Corridor are landscapes and views of Rome by Gaspard van Wittel (Vanvitelli), a Flemish tapestry of the 16th century depicting *Trajan at the Colosseum*, *Charity* by Lodovico Carracci, *St Jerome* by Annibale Carracci and an

Adoration of the Magi attributed to Jacopo Bassano.

To the right is the Museum of the Palace of the Conservatori. Rooms XII–XIV are the Sale dei Fasti Moderni, through which we pass and turn right into Room XV, the Gallery of the Orti Lamiani containing sculptures from this site on the Esquiline. *Old Fisherman* (3) and *Old Woman* (5) with a lamb are crude examples of late Hellenistic realism. *Seated Girl* (4) is a refined example of earlier Hellenistic art. *Head of a Centaur* (7) belongs to the second school of Pergamum. *Bust of Commodus* (12) as Hercules has a touch of the grotesque which gives liveliness and point to this somewhat absurd figure. In the centre of the room is the splendid *Esquiline Venus*, a young woman probably connected with the cult of Isis, a copy of a Greek bronze of the 5th century B.C. She is of peasant type, short and stocky and is binding her hair. She is also compact and well-proportioned according to a mathematical scale. Room XVI, the room of the Magistrates, has two statues of *Magistrates* (2, 5) giving the sign for the initiation of the Circensian games by throwing into the arena a *mappa*, a kind of banderole, 4th century A.D. *Artemis* (4), copy of a 4th century B.C. original, is restored to represent Christian Rome. Rooms XVII–XVIII, the rooms of the Archaic Monuments, have a headless female statue of a *Young Woman* (2) from a bronze original ascribed to Calamis; a fine funerary stele of a *Girl with a Dove* (12) in Ionic style of the 6th century, perhaps from Southern Italy; *Head of a Lion* (11) possibly a Greek original of the middle of the 5th century B.C. In the middle of Room XVIII is a *Statue* (13) which may represent either a Hero mounting a Chariot or Theseus lifting a Rock, from a bronze original of the middle of the 5th century B.C.

The Gallery has a miscellaneous collection of which the most interesting object is a colossal marble foot (16) wearing a sandal adorned with marine motives. It may have belonged to a statue of Isis. From the Gallery we enter left Rooms XIX and XX, of the Christian Monuments, which have sarcophagi with Christian motives including four of the Good Shepherd (1A, 2, 21, 23). There is also a statuette of the *Good Shepherd* (14) from the second half of the 3rd century A.D. Room XXI, the Room of the Chimneypiece, contains a *Sarcophagus* (1), in splendid condition, depicting Meleager hunting the Calydonian Boar. On the lid are the dead couple, the woman holding in her hand a musical instrument, first half of 3rd century A.D. In the glass cases are Greek vases, mirrors, etc. and antefixes, many Etruscan, of the 6th and 5th centuries B.C. from Capua. On a stand is the *Oinochoe Tittoni*, a wine jar incised and painted with scenes of the Trojan Games, 7th century B.C. Rooms XXII and XXIII contain part of the Castellani Collection donated by Augusto Castellani in 1866. The larger and more important part is in the Etruscan Museum, Villa Giulia. In the first room are glass cases containing Etruscan, Italic and Faliscan vases. In the centre, Case 9, are objects from the Castellani Tomb, discovered in 1861 at Palestrina and dated early in the 6th century B.C., including a large bronze amphora, a cylindrical cista in gold leaf decorated with oriental designs and a silver goblet. Case 10 contains a reconstruction of a Tensa, end of 4th century B.C., a triumphal chariot used to carry images of the gods at the opening of the Circensian Games. It is overlaid with bronze and decorated with reliefs representing scenes in the life of Archilles. In the second room are glass cases containing Corinthian and Attic vases with red and black figures, including an amphora (64) signed by Nicosthenes, c. 530–520 B.C. In the centre, Case 11 contains the splendid *Krater* (135) signed by Aristonothus, an Ionian or Etruscan work of the middle of the 7th century B.C. On one side Ulysses and his companions blind Polyphemus, above whose head is the artist's signature, and on the other side two boats, one with sails the other with oars, are on the point of giving battle. This is the oldest known Greek vase bearing a signature. Case 12 contains a fine terracotta polychrome statuette of a seated Etruscan in a reticulated tunic and mantle held over the right shoulder by a brooch. The hair is arranged in the style of the 7th century B.C. from which this portrait of the dead man dates.

Room XXIV contains important bronzes. *Head and Hand of the Emperor Constans II* (2, 3) are a part of a colossal masterpiece of late Roman portraiture. In glass Case 4 is a *Dancing Lar* with a rhyton (drinking horn) in his hand, 1st century A.D. Rear half of a colossal *Bull* (5) is of fine workmanship. Two *Globes* (6, 8), one from the obelisk in the Piazza di San Pietro, and the other formerly held by the hand of Constans. *Horse* (10) is a lively copy of a work by Lysippus. In the middle are a *Funeral Bed* (11) badly restored as a Bisellium (seat of honour) of the 1st century A.D. with equisite damascene decoration on the bedhead and back, and a *Litter* (12), found on the Esquiline by Castellani and reconstructed with bronzes. Room XXV contains sculptures found in the Gardens of Maecenas on the Esquiline. *Fighting Hercules* (2) is a copy of an original by Lysippus. *Flaying of Marsyas* (6) in Phrygian marble is a fine copy of a Hellenistic work from Pergamum or Rhodes, 2nd-1st century B.C. *Dancing Maenad* (9) in relief, is probably from an original by Callimachus of the 5th century B.C. *Headless Aphrodite* (10) is a copy of

22. *Seated Etruscan,* 7th century B.C.
terracotta height 57⅛ in. (144 cm.)

a 5th century work attributed to Callimachus. *Head of an Amazon* (11)
is a replica of the famous 5th century statue of Cresilas. In the centre
is a large rhyton (18), part of a fountain by Pontius of Athens, with
elegant figures in the neo-Attic style of the 1st century A.D.

Braccio Nuovo. At the end of the Gallery we turn left through the
Passage of the Roman Wall and enter the New Wing. Room I contains a *Base* (2) dedicated to Hercules by the dictator Minucius, col-
league of Q. Fabius Maximus in 217 B.C. *Fragment of a Fresco* (35)
possibly portrays M. Fannius talking with Q. Fabius Rullianus, Consul
in 322, and is reputedly the oldest example of Roman painting known.
Room II contains more examples of Republican art, including a fragment of a frieze (11) of a ritual dance. Room III has a statue of an
Unknown Man (7) with the busts of his ancestors and heads of
Agrippa (9), *Claudius* (10), *Domitian* (11), *Trajan* (14) and *Lucilla*
(25) daughter of Marcus Aurelius. Room IV has on the floor a mosaic
with Mercury, Plenty and the Personifications of the Seasons. *Apollo*
(3) shooting an arrow, probably a Greek original of the 5th century
A.D. is possibly by Pythagoras of Rhodes. It was brought as war booty
to Rome, altered and placed in the temple of Apollo Sosianus.
Aristogeiton (8) is the best replica of one of the statues from a bronze
group of the tyrannicides (including Harmodias) by Critias and

Nesiotes, 476 B.C. which stood in the Agora at Athens. Room V has four fragments (1, 4, 7, 8) of a greystone frieze richly decorated with trophies, victories and candelabra, 1st century A.D. In the middle is an archaic *Base of a Candelabrum* (7) with the divinities of Delos. Room VI has sarcophagi of the Republican era and a neo-Attic *Relief* (13) of the contest between Apollo and Marsyas. Room VII has on the floor a polychrome mosaic of the Rape of Proserpine and Personifications of the Seasons, 3rd century A.D. Fragments 4, 7, 8, 10 are parts of a colossal female statue from the Area Sacra of the Largo Argentina, possibly from the Temple of Fortune.

Palazzo Caffarelli

This palace at the south-west end of the Palace of the Conservatori was built for Giovanni Pietro Caffarelli in 1580 by Gregorio Canonica. It was formerly the German Embassy and was opened as the Museo Nuovo in 1925. We return to the Gallery at the end of which we descend a staircase and enter the Passage of the Roman Wall. In front is a tufa wall in blocks from the podium of the Temple of Jupiter Capitolinus, the most celebrated sanctuary of the Roman world. It is reputed to have been founded towards the end of the era of the Kings. It was reconstructed in the days of the Republic by Sulla and twice during the Flavian era. The hollow cube of marble (9) formerly contained the cinerary urn of Agrippina the Elder, which during the Middle Ages was used to measure grain. *Base* (11) of a statue of Cornelia, daughter of Scipio Africanus and mother of the Gracchi, is from the Porticus of Octavia and bears a famous inscription. *Base* (12) has an inscription from the beaked column erected in the Forum in honour of the Consul C. Dullius after his naval victory over the Carthaginians off Mylae, 260 B.C. Rooms I and II contain cinerary urns and fragments of sarcophagi. Room III has archaic and neo-Attic sculpture. In the archway is a relief of an *Athlete Purifying Himself* (26) before making a sacrifice, an archaizing work of the 2nd century A.D. Room IV contains Hellenistic art. *Fragments* (3, 5) are from a frieze depicting the War of the Giants. *Torso of Hercules* (11) is a copy of a 4th century B.C. original, possibly by Scopas. Nos 17–21 and 23 are from erotic groups of satyrs, maenads, nymphs and hermaphrodites. In the middle is a statue of the muse *Polyhymnia* (24) in a pensive pose, an exquisite original (or copy) of the 2nd century A.D. From this room a door opens into the Garden which contains fragments of funerary monuments from the Via Flaminia, fragments of fluted columns from the Temple of Jupiter, a vigorous group of a *Lion Attacking a Horse*, much restored in the 16th century, and a sepulchral relief of the charioteer Cotta Calpurnius. In Room V are a *Votive Relief* (6) with Asclepius (Aesculapius) and a female figure who may be Hygeia, original Greek work of the second half of the 4th century B.C. Headless *Aphrodite* (9) derives from the same original by Praxiteles as the 'Aphrodite of Arles' in the Louvre. It is the only copy which preserves the right arm. *Athena* (16) is a fine replica of the 4th century statue by Cephisodotus which was in the temple of Zeus Soterios at Piraeus. In the middle is a headless *Praying Woman* (17) in green basalt, from a bronze original of the end of the 5th century B.C. Rooms VI and VII contain altars, funerary urns, sarcophagi and portrait busts, of which the most interesting are *Corbulo* (6) the famous general of the reigns of Tiberius, Claudius and Nero, who was father-in-law of *Domitian,* himself brilliantly portrayed here (18). Room VIII, formerly the Chapel of the German Embassy, contains replicas of Greek sculpture of the 5th century B.C. *Kore* (2) possibly a goddess, is a copy of a Peloponnesian bronze *c.* 460 B.C. *Discobolos Resting* (3) is probably a copy of a work by Naucides, son of Polycleitus, from the beginning of the 4th century. *Athena* (18), a colossal statue, is a fine replica of an original by Cresilas, *c.* 430 B.C. In the middle are fragments from the Cella of the Temple of Jupiter. Room IX has a *Torso of Apollo* (10) from an original datable earlier than 450 B.C. and a *Statue of a Wounded Niobid* (15) from an original of the end of the 4th century or beginning of the 3rd century. Room X has fragments of a sarcophagus of Asiatic type (11, 12) and a portrait-bust of *Caracalla* (28).

We now return to the entrance to the Rooms of the Conservatori, ascend the staircase, and reach the Landing of the second floor, where are the *Apotheosis of Sabine,* from the so-called Arco di Portogallo, and two pieces of marble intarsia work from the temple of Junius Bassus, representing a *Bull Attacked by a Tiger.* From this landing we enter the Pinacoteca Capitolina.

Picture Gallery

The Picture Gallery was founded in 1749 by Benedict XIV on the basis of the collections of Prince Gilberto Pio of Savoy and Cardinal Giulio Sacchetti. It has subsequently lost some of its treasures to the Vatican and to the Academy of St Luke, but gained from bequests, notably that of Count Francesco Cini, 1881.

Room I. *Portrait of a Girl, c.* 1510, by an unknown Ferrarese painter (4) is a work of charm and delicacy. The *Holy Family* (5) by Dosso Dossi, an early work probably from his Roman period, shows great energy in composition and the splendid colouring gives a joyous atmosphere to this fine psychological study. The beautiful *Madonna and Child with Saints*, 1513, by an Emilian master was commissioned by Alberico Malaspina of Carrara. Four lyrical pictures by Garofalo (6, 11, 21, 22) have delightfully poetic landscapes. His *Annunciation* (14) is more formal. *Presentation in the Temple* by Francesco Francia has been much repainted. *Adoration of the Magi* (23) by Scarsellino is a lively work by this Ferrarese painter.

Room II. The two panels *Strength* (1) and *Temperance* (3) by Veronese, *c*. 1556, formed part of the decoration of a ceiling and have splendid colour effects. *Rape of Europa* is a good workshop copy of the original in the Doge's Palace at Venice. *Portrait of a Lady*, with the attributes of St Margaret, by Girolamo Savoldo is beautifully modelled in a plastic style. Giovanni Bellini's signed *Portrait of a Young Man*, *c*. 1500, painted against a sky and cloud background, shows great force of character. *Woman Taken in Adultery, c*. 1512, is an unfinished work by Palma Vecchio. Titian's *Baptism of Christ, c*. 1512, is an early work in the style of Giorgione with a splendid portrait of the donor, possibly a Spanish merchant. *Man with a Crossbow*, 1551–1552, by the great portraitist Lorenzo Lotto is a fine study in seriousness. Domenico Tintoretto's *Magdalene* is a luminous, if rather affected work.

Room III. The two double-portraits by Van Dyck of the engravers *Pieter de Jode, Father and Son*, 1627–1629, and of the painters *Lucas and Cornelius de Wael* (10) both in fine impasto, are penetrating character studies. *Portrait of Man with a Dog* by the Bolognese Bartolomeo Passarotti is lively and well painted. *Romulus and Remus Fed by the Wolf*, 1617–1618, by Rubens, painted with the assistance of J. Wildens and F. Snyders, is a warm and exuberant work, with a fine contrast between the skin of the wolf and the luminous flesh of the children. *Portrait of a Man* by Velasquez, in sombre tones, is remarkable for the intent gaze of the sitter, who may be Bernini. There are pictures of some interest by Jean Leclerc, *Christ before the Doctors;* Carlo Maratta, *Holy Family;* Simon Vouet, *Allegory of Vanity;* Luca Cambiaso, *Madonna and Child;* and Denis Calvaert, *Marriage of St Catherine.*

Room IV. *Death and Assumption of the Virgin*, 1514, by Cola dell' Amatrice was painted for the Dominican church in Ascoli Piceno. *S. Biagio* by Neri di Bicci is a sensitive work in delicate colours. *Madonna and Saints*, 1495–1496, by Macrino d'Alba of Vercelli is finely painted, as are the primitive *Baptism of Christ* and *St Francis Receiving the*

23. (left) Caravaggio (1573–1610) *St John the Baptist, c.*1600
oil on canvas 52×38⅝ in. (132×98 cm.)
24. (right) Guercino (1591–1666) *The Burial and Reception into Heaven of St Petronilla, c.*1621 oil on canvas 283×166½ in. (720×423 cm.)

Stigmata by Bicci di Lorenzo. *Ascension* by Barnaba da Modena is an austere work remarkable for its skilful combination of colours. *St Mary Magdalene* (17) and *St Bartholomew* (19) are calm compositions by a follower of Pietro Lorenzetti. *Holy Trinity* by Nicolò di Pietro Gerini has at the foot of the crucified Christ two members of the family of Francesco Baroncelli, Tribune of Rome after Cola di Rienzo.

Room V contains the Cini collection of ceramics of which the most important are the Saxon porcelain, clocks and tobacco boxes in glass cases. The neo-classic *Madonna and Child* by Pompeo Batoni has the delicate elegance and frigid charm of his maturity. There are also a genre piece of Roman 'low life' by Michelangelo Cerquozzi and landscapes by Gaspard van Wittel (Vanvitelli), (?) H. Seghers, Jan Asselyn and Isaack van Ostade. At the end of the room is Caravaggio's *St John the Baptist, c.* 1600, probably the Pio original, which is lighter 23 in colour, more refined, and more sensitive than the version in the Doria Gallery.

Room VI was constructed for Benedict XIV by Ferdinando Fuga in 1747–1748 to hold the Sacchetti collection. Above there is a *Bust of Benedict XIV* by P. A. Verschaffelt, 1749. This room contains the most important easel pictures of the great architect and decorator Pietro da Cortona. All were painted for Marcello Sacchetti. *Triumph of Bacchus,* c. 1620, *Sacrifice of Polyxena,* c. 1622, and *Rape of the Sabines,* c. 1629, have groups of figures set in contrast. In the *Polyxena* they look like a static frieze whereas in the *Rape of the Sabines* the figures appear in depth. In all of them an antique fable is used as a platform for drama and they established a mode which was copied up to the 18th century. Worth noting are *Diana and Endymion* (1) by P. F. Mola, *Joseph Sold into Bondage* (6) by Pietro Testa and *Academic Exercise* (13) by G. B. Gaulli, called Il Bacciccia, painted for his son Giulio. In a niche is a colossal statue of *Hercules* in gilt bronze found in the time of Sixtus IV during the demolition of the Ara Maxima.

24   Room VII is dominated by the huge *Burial and Reception into Heaven of St Petronilla* by Guercino, commissioned by Gregory XV in 1621 for an altar in St Peter's. This magniloquent masterpiece is less vigorous than Guercino's earliest work but it is better balanced. The composition is divided into two parts, the lower part, portraying the burial, is filled with huge realistically-modelled figures. Domenichino's *Sybil* is a copy of the Borghese Gallery picture. *St Sebastian* by Annibale Carracci is a fine piece of decoration. The lively *Gipsy Fortune-Teller* is a variant of Caravaggio's Louvre picture. Worth noting are Giovanni Lanfranco's *Erminia among the Shepherds,* Guercino's *St John the Baptist* and *St Matthew and the Angel* and four paintings (4, 5, 7, 8) by Guido Reni in the pale palette of his later years.

Room VIII. *Madonna and Child* (3) by Pietro da Cortona. Three *Landscapes* (4, 16, 18) formerly attributed to Domenichino are probably by Agostino Tassi. *Self-portrait* (13) by Francesco del Cairo is an interesting example of this neurotic painter.

Room IX (corridor) contains a *Madonna and Child* (7) by Francesco Albani and an interesting *Parable* (15) by Domenico Fetti, 1622.

The Inspector is Professor Carlo Pietrangeli.

The museum is open every weekday except Monday from 9 a.m. to 2 p.m.; Tuesdays and Thursdays also from 5 p.m. to 8 p.m.; Sundays and Holidays from 9 a.m. to 1 p.m.; in summer every Saturday from 9 p.m. to 11.30 p.m.

The Museum of
the Palazzo Venezia

The Palazzo Venezia is the first great work of civil architecture in
Rome. It is generally agreed that it was planned by the 'complete man'
of the Renaissance, Leon Battista Alberti (though some attribute the
designs to Bernardo Rossellino) and that it was built about 1455–
1467. The palace was constructed, partly with stone from the Colosseum, for the Venetian Cardinal Pietro Barbo, who later became Paul
II, and finished by his nephew Marco Barbo, Patriarch of Aquileia. It
remained a papal residence until 1564 when it was handed over to the
Venetian Republic for its embassy and for the titular cardinal of St
Mark's. After the Treaty of Campoformio, 1797, it passed to Austria
and until 1915 it was the seat of the Austrian ambassador to the
Vatican. In 1917 the Italian state took possession of the palace and it
was restored by F. Hermanin. During the Fascist period it was occupied by Mussolini, who often addressed the Roman crowds from

25. The Palazzo Venezia

the balcony overlooking the Piazza di Venezia.

The palace is a severe brown building, battlemented with arched windows and doorways, which successfully harmonizes the robustness and strength of the Middle Ages with the elegance of the early Renaissance. The door of the main entrance from the Piazza, ornamented with the arms of Cardinal Barbo, is attributed to Giovanni Dalmata. A second and larger door, also attributed to Giovanni Dalmata, with half columns in the Composite order and Barbo shields on the upper plinths, opens on to the Via del Plebiscito. This door leads into an atrium and then into a courtyard with a pleasing portico surmounted by a loggia, an elegant but unfinished work by Giuliano da Maiano. Adjoining the palace and facing the Piazzetta di San Marco is the Palazzetto di Venezia, 1455–1468, which originally closed the Piazza Venezia to the south and was removed to its present site in 1911 because it obstructed the view of the Victor Emmanuel Monument. The courtyard was the *viridarium* or garden of the palace. In the centre is a little fountain with a pine-cone, the symbol of the old 'Pigna' quarter.

The Museum occupies several of the papal apartments in the palace and a number of rooms in the Palazzetto. It was originally intended to be a collection of medieval and renaissance art but bequests, particularly the Wurts collection, the Alfredo Barsanti collection of bronzes and the small porcelain collection of Prince Fabrizio di Motta Bagnara, have greatly altered its character. The museum is broken into two parts by a number of rooms given over to temporary exhibitions. The former contents of these rooms are in store or in circulation. The remaining rooms on the Piazza Venezia side are closed at the time of writing for re-arrangement.

The Museum now begins at Room XI. The excellent oval *Adoration of the Child* is by Andrea della Robbia. *Scenes from the Life of St Julian,* after cleaning seen to be Lorenzo Lotto, are curiously primitive in execution. *Ascent to Calvary* and *Madonna and Child* by Paolo Farinati of Verona are beautifully coloured. In the glass case is Hispano-Moresque majolica of the 16th century and on the wall above the door a Brussels tapestry *c.* 1510. Room XII has, painted on leather, *Incidents from the Life of Taddeo Zuccari* by his brother Federico. *The Redeemer,* part of a fresco by Benozzo Gozzoli, is admirably drawn. In the glass case are wooden models of pilasters decorated with grotesques, Emilian work of the 16th century. Room XIII. *Madonna and Child with St John* by Domenico Puligo is a good linear study in reds and greens with a pleasing landscape seen through the window on the left. This is Puligo's first independent work, but it still shows the influence of Ridolfo Ghirlandaio. Lorenzo Sallatini's *Adoration of the Magi* has a striking star in the sky above a northerly mountain landscape. The remarkable *Vision of St Bernard* by Bacchiacca has a very small Virgin and Child seen floating gracefully on a cloud. There are excellent 16th century Brussels tapestries with hunting scenes and a painted chest from Ferrara, 15th century. Room XIV. *Prodigal Son* by the Monogrammatist of Brunswick is remarkable. *Assumption of a Soul into Heaven* by an anonymous painter of the Venetian school of the 16th century has a strong resemblance to the early work of El Greco. There are majolica of the 15th and 16th centuries and Brussels tapestries by G. Pannemaker. The adjoining Cappelletta has a rich collection of Italian majolica of the Renaissance. Room XV has a ceiling, put together from fragments of fresco and stucco from the Palazzo Bindo Altoviti, by Giorgio Vasari, representing *Ceres and the Seasons.* The glass cases contain small bronzes and plaques from northern and southern Italy, Sicily, Austria, Germany and the Netherlands, among them a fine Flemish lion from the beginning of the 16th century. On the walls are a Chinese Umbrella dinner service and a magnificent porcelain service made for the French East India Company, both of them 18th century. Room XVI contains the Alfredo Barsanti collection of larger bronzes. Case 1 has notable figures of people, animals, reptiles and crustaceans by Andrea Briosco. The other cases have works by Roccataglia, Susini and various northern Italian sculptors. Of particular interest in Case 5 is Giambologna's *Rape of Deianeira.* On the central table are two pieces by G. F. Susini, *Horse Being Killed by a Lion* and *Bull·Being Killed by a Lion.* Room XVII. G. M. Crespi's *Moses Saved from the Waters* is a fine example of the last great Bolognese painter, notable for its direct approach, good colouring and masterly play of light. His *David and Abigail* shows David in military garb with a well-painted group on the left. Donato Creti's *Acis and Galatea* is a pastoral scene whose landscape owes much to Claude and whose figures show the influence of Poussin. In the centre are an 18th century Neapolitan sedan chair and a clavichord. Room XVIII has two charming anonymous 18th century pictures of a *Lady* and a *Young Prince,* a fine wooden figure of the *Archangel Michael, c.* 1485, standing on a devil and weighing souls, by the Tyrolean master Michael Pacher and a *Bust of Duchessa Giacinta Sanvitale Conti* by the Carrara sculptor Giuliano Finelli. Room XIX is a long corridor with arms and armour.

  Room XX. From the School of Giovanni Bellini are *Moses rescued*

26. *Cross* from Rosciolo, 1334
silvered metal height 34⅝ in. (88 cm.)

from the waters and *Encounter at the Golden Gate*. Girolamo da
Cremona's triptych of the *Nativity and Annunciation* is a delicious and
delicate work in miniature detail. The wooden sculptures of the 16th
century are from Bavaria and Swabia. In the glass case are Flemish
and German wood-carvings and Italian majolica, including a large
Roman vase from the workshop of Diomede Durante. Room XXI.
Madonna and Child, a wooden relief of the school of Niccolò dell'
Arca; a fascinating 13th century crucifix on loan from the church of S.
Tommaso dei Cenci; and *Mystic Marriage of St Catherine* by a
Florentine master of the second half of the 14th century. On each side
of the far door are fine statues of a *King* and *Queen*, Ulm 15th century.
Room XXII. Spanish *Madonna Enthroned*, with Child and angels
above, of the 15th century Valencian school; *Hosea* by the Master of
the Bambino Vispo; a lovely *Nativity* by the pseudo-Pierfrancesco
Fiorentino; and the *Prophet Daniel* and *Redeemer Blessing* by the so-
called Master of 1419. A good *Madonna and Child* is attributed to
Stefano di Zevio. In glass cases are 15th century engraved ivory and
bone objects, Umbrian fabrics, medieval bronzes and 13th and 15th
century crosses from the Abruzzi. Room XXIII. *A Doctor of the Church*
by Francesco de'Franceschi; a charming *Madonna and Child* by
Ottaviano Nelli from Gubbio; a triptych in a Gothic frame of *Madonna
and Child with Saints* by Simone de Bologna; and a *Choir of Angels*
by Paolo Veneziano, in a round golden nimbus against a black background. On a small Venetian chest of the 16th century reclines a
Spanish lady in wood and stucco of the 15th century. Room XXIV.
Our Lady of Mercy with Saints is by the Master of Staffalo. Triptych
of *Madonna Enthroned* by Nanni di Jacopo has angels and two saints

on each side. *Stories of St Catherine of Siena* by Bicci di Lorenzo is divided into two parts by a richly-gilt pillar. The glass case contains church vestments, gilded coffers, bronzes and locks. The Gothic sideboard of the 15th century is from Verona. Room XXV contains minor paintings of the 14th and 15th centuries. The charming triptych on wood of *Madonna and Child* with four saints is from the school of Gentile Bellini. *Christ Carrying the Cross* by Francesco Zaganelli da Cotignola is a dramatic and well-painted work. *Agony in the Garden,* a curious archaizing painting, is attributed to the Emilian Master of the Sagra di Carpi. *The Redeemer,* attributed to the Venetian Benedetto Diana, is smoothly painted and highly finished. Panel of *The Assumption of the Virgin* by Michael Wolgemut, Dürer's master, is a fine example of this painter's work. There are wooden sculptures by Niccolò da Venezia and Nicolà di Nuto. In the glass cases are a silver-gilt chased beaker with ship motifs, Gröningen 1669, a Processional Cross of the 15th century in gilded silver from Alba Fugens by (?) Nicolà di Guardigrele, a silver-gilt chased beaker, also with ship motifs, Dordrecht, end of 17th century, and a Processional Cross in silvered metal dated 1334 from Rosciolo. Room XXVI. *Angel of the Annunciation,* German 15th or 16th century, is painted on one of the folding doors of an organ. *Venus* and Cupid with bow and arrow, signed HS, is German work of the first half of the 16th century.

Room XXVII has fine Meissen porcelain from the Motta Bagnara collection. Room XXVIII has a portrait of *Benedict XIV* by Pierre Subleyras and one of *Clement XIII* by Pompeo Batoni. Each is represented seated in a large gilt chair making the sign of the benediction, but the Frenchman by his superior precision of design and expression produces a better picture than Batoni, whose usual delicacy of touch is absent. A good *St Jerome* by Garofalo has a fine romantic landscape background. There are two Brussels tapestries of the 16th century. The silver from the Wurts collection is mostly 17th and 18th century, from Germany, Russia, England, Switzerland and Scandinavia. Room XXIX has two magnificent ovals, one at each end of the wall, the first, embroidered with gold thread and silk, Fontainebleau work of the middle of the 16th century, represents the *Rape of the Sabines;* the second, Flemish *c.* 1560, represents a *Hunting Scene.* Both are from the Doria Pamphilj Palace. The three tapestries are 17th century depicting Roman scenes. (1) and (3) are *Scenes of Triumph,* (2) *Homage Paid by the Victor to an Image.* Room XXX has, left and right, two fine 16th century Persian carpets of the 'Polonaise' type. In glass cases is Chinese porcelain of the 18th century. Room XXXI. The striking *Pietà* by Orazio Borgianni has a remarkable resemblance, in its foreshortening, to Mantegna's *Dead Christ* in the Brera Gallery, Milan. The Swiss painter Hans Asper's portraits of a *Man* and *Woman* are good. *Flight into Egypt* is a charming work by the 17th century Bolognese painter Giovanni Giuseppe del Sole. *Lamentation of St Peter* by Guercino is an impressive but stylized late work, showing the influence of Guido Reni. Room XXXII has a *St George and the Dragon* attributed to the Milanese Camillo Procaccini. *Battlefield* is a vigorous painting by Adam Frans van der Meulen of Brussels who was a specialist in contemporary warfare. The two 18th century porcelain reliefs are by Doccia from designs of Massimiliano Soldani. The Flemish 16th century tapestry depicts Apollodorus presenting to Trajan a model of his column. In the glass case are 16th century Florentine embroidery, a 17th century Burmese table-cloth, 17th century German ivories, including a fine hunting-horn, and an 18th century silver water-jug by Vincenzo Belli of Rome. Room XXXIII has a highly formalized *St Francis* in a niche by Sassoferrata. A delightful, almost miniature, *Hunting Scene* is by the German 17th century painter from Frankfurt-am-Main, Johannes Lingelbach. In the glass case is silver from Russia, Germany and Portugal. Room XXXIV, on the left, contains pastels by John Russell, Louis Vigée, Rosalba Carriera, Pietro Antonio Rotari and M. Quentin de la Tour. There are three notable Beauvais tapestries of 1760 from cartoons by François Boucher. In glass cases, 18th century fans and costume jewellery. Room XXXV has three more Boucher tapestries, J. L. Kreul's *Woman and Child*, a French 16th century portrait of *Maria Feodorovna*, Princess of Würtemburg, executed for Paul I of Russia and a small *Coast of Normandy* attributed to R. P. Bonington. In the glass cases are a collection of rings, 15th to 18th centuries, and 18th century fans. Room XXXVI has admirable portraits of a *Man* and *Woman* attributed to Jacob Gerritsz Cuyp. *Portrait of a Girl with Puppy* is by the English painter Cornelius Johnson van Ceulen. The child is in a fine ruff, be-jewelled bodice and crinoline skirt. On the table is a good *Double Portrait* on copper attributed to Nicolas Regnier of Maubeuge. Room XXXVII has two *Bacchic Scenes* by Giulio Carponi and two painted doorstops by G. B. Cassisa. The two oval marble reliefs of the *An-nunciation* (Virgin and Angel) in fine period frames are attributed to François Duquesnoy of Brussels, known as Il Fiammingo. The oval marble in the centre of the wall, *Head of a Bacchante*, is of the school of Bernini. The five splendid Barberini tapestries are by Giacomo della Riviera from cartoons by G. F. Romanelli. On the right, under the windows, are three cases of musical instruments, 16th to 18th centuries. Room XXXVIII has a good *Country Scene* by Johannes Lingelbach, who worked in Amsterdam before and after coming to Italy, *Mystic Marriage of St Catherine* by Ciro Ferri, and a reposeful *Madonna* by Simone Cantarini from Pesaro. *Marriage Feast at Cana* by Francesco Solimena, in his time a great international painter, is dramatic, well-constructed and beautifully coloured, with ingeniously arranged figures. *Marine Landscape* is a good work by Jan Porcellis of Ghent. In a case are maquettes by Bernini, Algardi, Duquesnoy, Bouchardon, Bracci and others. Room XXXIX has two small 18th century tapestries by José del Castillo of Madrid from cartoons by Murillo. They represent *Two Boys Eating Grapes and Water-melon* and *Two Boys and a Dog Playing*. The fine *Portrait of Cav. Cesare Cavalcabò* is attributed to Ambrogio Figino. Three tapestries: (1) Flemish 18th century, country scene with castles among trees and a stork (2) Aubusson 18th century, pastoral scene with fountain on the left and bridge in the centre (3) Aubusson 18th century, pastoral scene with mill on the left, shepherd and shepherdess, sheep and cows. On the right of the door is a Saxony vase in relief representing an orchard with birds. The fine 18th century writing-desk is from Modena. Room XL. *Flowers and Fruit* attributed to Mario di Fiori, *Portrait of a Genoese Gentleman and Child,* an aristocratic baroque work of G. B. Carbone, and a brilliantly-painted *Mater Dolorosa* by Bernardo Strozzi, the Genoese Capuchin. Carlo Maratta's *Cleopatra* is a large canvas in the grand manner with every trick of the trade, well-harmonized colours, a finely-modelled figure in bejewelled and wonderfully-patterned clothes – a portrait perfectly suited to contemporary taste. Daniele Crespi's *Portrait of a Man* combines severe realism with chiaroscuro and a psychological study of the introspective subject. On the walls are three pieces of embroidery in colours and silver and gold thread. The three cases of porcelain contain fine examples of Capodimonte relief work. Room XLI. A 16th century Flemish tapestry of the *Redeemer* is in a black frame of the period. Series of ten angel candle-bearers, two on each painted wooden panel, are Umbrian school *c.* 1480. A 16th century Spanish Barqueño has gilded decoration. *Bust of a Prelate* is of the first half of the 17th century. The 18th century Venetian mirror has an incised female figure, a rich glass frame and four lamps.

The Director is Professor Maria Vittoria Pace Brugnoli.

The museum is open on weekdays except Monday from 9 a.m. to 2 p.m.; Sundays and Holidays from 9.30 a.m. to 1 p.m.

The Doria Pamphilj Gallery

27 The immense .Doria palace, dating in part from 1435, and owned
successively by Cardinal Fazio Santorio, the Della Rovere, Aldobrandini and Pamphilj families, passed to the Doria family of Genoa,
who added Pamphilj to their name. It is a combination of three buildings. The façade, c. 1734, looking on to the Corso, by Giovanni
Valvassori, has a noble entrance-gate surmounted by an animated
balcony and richly-ornamented windows and is regarded as the
finest example of rococo architecture in Rome. The south façade,
1643, giving on to the Via del Plebiscito is by Paolo Ameli and that
facing the north, c. 1660, in the Piazza del Collegio Romano is by
Antonio del Grande. The 16th century courtyard, in the style of
Bramante, has a portico with Doric columns and an upper loggia of
Ionic columns. The entrance to the Picture Gallery is by a small door
at 1A Piazza del Collegio Romano.

27. The Doria Pamphilj Palace

54

The pictures and sculpture form the most important of the Roman patrician collections and date from the period of Donna Olimpia Maidalchini, the sister of the Pamphilj pope, Innocent X, with later additions. The paintings, mostly from the 17th century, are a product of keen collecting instincts, good taste and a wish to display wealth in a worthy way. The setting is magnificent. The pictures remain, for the most part, as they were originally arranged, which means that some are hung too high and others are difficult to see because of the angle at which the light enters the gallery, which consists of four long *bracci* (wings) and a series of rooms. The best light is about mid-day.

Braccio I has a ceiling by Annibale Angelini in the Pompeian style. Titian's *Spain Succouring Religion* (10) is probably a workshop copy, in muted colours, of the picture in the Prado, Madrid, while the *Herodias* or *Salome* (29) is a charming early work. *Portrait of a Man* (15) by Tintoretto is a dark monotonous composition which contrasts unfavourably with the pastel shades of Correggio's *Triumph of Virtue* (20), an unfinished sketch in tempera for the picture in the Louvre, with *sinopia* in the top left corner. The double portrait (23) *c.* 1516, by Raphael of *Andrea Navagero and Agostino Beazzano,* two members of his humanist circle, is a fine psychological study. Navagero on the left is posed with his head twisted sharply, so that the light falls on his neck, while Beazzano on the right inclines his head slightly in an attitude similar to that of the Louvre *Castiglione.* The two men gaze out of the canvas as if they are looking at the viewer. Lorenzo Lotto's *St Jerome* (26) excellently exhibits the quieter atmosphere of his later years. In Saraceni's *St Roch and the Angel* (38) the saint with a dog at his feet lies back gasping while a very earthy angel attends to his wound. This room contains three Caravaggios which are notable examples of his earlier style. The untypical *Mary Magdalene* (40) painted *c.* 1595, shows the saint in the dress of a peasant girl from the campagna. Caravaggio obtains here a fine spatial effect and his handling of the still-life, especially the jewellery on the floor, is highly accomplished. In the marvellous *Rest on the Flight into* 28 *Egypt* (42), *c.* 1596, the earliest of his religious paintings, the figures are studies of humble people set in a brilliantly poetic landscape, with a lovely river scene on the right. The angel's body cuts the picture in half, which is a sign that Caravaggio had not yet mastered all the problems of structure. The youthful *John the Baptist* (44), *c.* 1600, has been well restored and once again stakes its claim, against the version in the Capitoline Picture Gallery, to be the Pio original. The colours of the Doria version are as good and the chiaroscuro on the

28. Caravaggio (1573–1610)
Rest on the Flight into Egypt,
c.1596 oil on canvas
51⅛×63 in. (129×160 cm.)

body of the saint is more pronounced and more powerful. *St Jerome* (46) by Jusepe Ribera, draped in a red mantle, holds a scroll in Hebrew. *Jesus Pays Tribute* (48) is a huge picture with a splendid fish by the Calabian Mattia Preti. Sassoferrato's *Virgin Praying* (53) in brilliant rose and blue is typical of this master from the Marches who painted in the style of Raphael. The *Bust of Olimpia Maldaichini* (I) by Algardi is a penetrating psychological study of the formidable sister-in-law of Innocent X.

Here we enter the Salone Aldobrandini where there are a collection of antique sculpture of the kind thought essential for princely palaces, landscape paintings often hung so high as to be almost invisible and four 16th century Brussels tapestries commemorating the battle of Lepanto after cartoons by Michiel Coxie. Worth noting are *Concert* (103) by Mattia Preti, a massive Caravaggesque canvas, *Erminia meeting Tancredi* (77), an early work of Guercino, and two marble reliefs (II and III) by the French sculptor François Duquesnoy who is considered by some to be greater than Algardi.

Braccio II has pictures by Annibale and Lodovico Carracci, Guercino, Domenico Fetti and Guido Reni, as well as a copy of the Vatican *Aldobrandini Marriage* (140) by Nicolas Poussin. The *Bust of Innocent X* (IV) by Algardi, a bronze head on a porphyry body, is a work of great sincerity and seriousness.

Room I. Giovanni Bellini's signed *Madonna and Child with St John* (172) is disappointing. *The Holy Conversation* (173) by Girolamo Savoldo is splendidly coloured. A glowering indigo sky on the right is balanced by dark trees on the left. A full light falls on the finely model-led figures. The charming 15th century *Marriage of the Virgin* (174) and *Birth of the Virgin* (176) by Giovanni di Paolo are rather early for this Gallery. Boccaccino's *Madonna and Child with Saints* (186) has affinities with Giovanni Bellini. The *Earthly Paradise* (194) by Jacopo Bassano is a delightful landscape with brilliant variations of light and shade. The animals charm Adam and Eve while birds fly over the darkling sky or roost in trees.

Room II. Parmigianino's *Adoration of the Shepherds* (200) is a stylish, impressionistic and, for him, unmannered work, while his *Madonna and Child* (207) is almost classical. *St Jerome* (203) by the Sienese Domenico Beccafumi, in the grand manner, has a fine intens-ity of emotion. The group of paintings (220–223) by Benvenuto Tisi, called Il Garofalo, from Ferrara, have a placid but limited inspiration, elegant colours and delicate romantic backgrounds.

Room III. Thomas de Keyser's *Portrait of a Lady* (237) is a good example of this Amsterdam painter, who first influenced Rembrandt and was later influenced by him. *Mary Magdalene* (258) by Adriaen Isenbrandt of Bruges depicts a little Flemish girl in a red dress with black borders at neck and wrists reading an illuminated missal. The *Holy Family* (260) by Jan ('Velvet') Bruegel is painted, after an en-graving by Dürer, in a highly detailed style with carefully-observed animals. Jan van Scorel's *Agatha van Schoonhoven* (279) a finely-painted, delicate portrait of his mistress, is signed and dated 1523. Pieter ('Hell') Bruegel's *Vision of St John on Patmos* (280) is beauti-fully wrought on copper, but it is sadly defaced by discoloured patches.

Room IV. Six landscapes (281, 283, 286, 298, 299, 301) by the Antwerp painter Jan Frans van Bloemen, called L'Orizzonte, are typical of the Flemish and Dutch painters who worked in Rome in the 17th and 18th centuries producing arcadian and pastoral landscapes. *Portrait of a Franciscan* (291) by Rubens is a robust and incisive painting of a friar in an olive green cassock with brownish lights. Jan ('Velvet') Bruegel's *Earthly Paradise* (295) is full of delightful birds and animals, in particular a noble grey horse who belongs to the Rubens, David, Géricault, De Chirico line. Pieter ('Hell') Bruegel's *Snow Scene* (316) is meticulously painted but it lacks the force and authority of *Battle in the Gulf of Naples* (317) by his father, Pieter 29 Bruegel the Elder, long thought to be a very early work but now dated *c.* 1560. It is interesting to note that the master has given the Neapoli-tan sky an Antwerpian hue.

29. Pieter Bruegel the Elder (*c.*1525/30–1569) *The Battle in the Gulf of Naples,* *c.*1560 oil on panel 16⅛×27⅝ in. (41×70 cm.)

The first Cabinet contains small pictures by Jan ('Velvet') Bruegel, Paul Brill and Herman van Swanevelt, mostly on copper.

Braccio III is most sumptuously decorated with great mirrors in rich gilt frames, with 18th century consoles, settees and gilded chairs. The rich portrait of *Joan of Aragon, Princess Colonna* (337) in the manner of Giulio Romano displays her in a red velvet dress with diaphonous sleeves puffing through the orange lining.

The second Cabinet contains the gem of the Gallery, the *Portrait of*
III *Innocent X* (339) painted by Velazquez in 1650. It is one of the world's great portraits and a masterpiece of psychological penetration. The pontiff is arrayed in purple with cream-coloured frilly apron against a crimson-curtained background and he has a cynical and scornful expression on his greasy face which contrasts markedly with the more benevolent pose and spiritual expression of the Bernini *Bust* (VII) which shares the room. The portrait was called by Reynolds 'the most beautiful picture in Rome'. Beautiful it is, and monumental; it is also implacably objective.

Braccio IV contains landscapes of great importance. There are five by Claude Lorraine, one by his teacher Agostino Tassi, who italianized the realistic northern landscape of Elsheimer, seven by Gaspard Dughet (Poussin), two by Gaspard van Wittel (Vanvitelli), three by J. F. van Bloemen, seven by Herman van Swanevelt, three by Barto-

Iomeo Torregiani and one by Salvator Rosa. The source of all this, curiously enough, is Annibale Carracci, who first created the idealized classical landscape. In his *The Penitent Magdalene* (341) the figure in the lovely blue robe stands against a landscape which looks forward to Claude and Poussin. Claude's *Landscape with a Mill* (343) is almost identical with his *Marriage of Isaac and Rebekah* in the National Gallery, London, and can be dated 1648–1649. A concert and dancing with tambourines is in progress in front of a river running down from a dam. The mill and trees on the left make a typical balance with trees on the right. Mount Soracte is seen in the middle distance. The principal figures are clothed in bright blues, oranges and reds. Two *Landscapes* (340 and 344) by Gaspard Dughet demonstrate his ability to combine the coolness and limpidity of Claude with the solid masses of Poussin. Claude's *Rest During the Flight into Egypt* (346) can be dated about 1639; his *Sacrifice at Delphi* 1650, (348), is more remarkable. A cool yellow light floods the background and a huge pine fills the centre. The main group, red on blue, green on amethyst, brown on olive green, with huge metal urns catching the light, move left under a waving tree. On the bridge, below the pine, piping shepherds and country people lead a garlanded ox towards the shepherds and country people lead a garlanded ox towards the place where another ox is being slaughtered. The whole composition is a wonderful idyll. High up on the wall Salvator Rosa's *Steep Cliffs by the Sea* (349) is a dramatic study of huge rocks forming a bridge, beyond which can be seen the sea with distant mountains in pink and pearly tints. *Mercury Steals away with the Oxen of Apollo* (352) by Claude, datable about 1645, has a fine figure of Apollo fiddling, clad in bronze and seated on a cobalt blue coat, while Mercury nimbly ushers the oxen away. There are a number of lunettes, 1600–1604, by Annibale Carracci and collaborators, of which 356 and 357 are of considerable interest, but *The Flight into Egypt* (359) which is by 30 Carracci alone is a picture of great historical importance. The landscape is solidly built up with repoussoir trees at the side. The large castle in the centre has below it a waterfall which leads down to the figure of Mary who, with Joseph, is moving up the bank towards the left. The ass moves his head away from the line of his body to carry on the diagonal line of the cliff across the river and low down on the right the ferryman, in typical *contrapposto,* indicates how the Holy Family have made their crossing. This is the first of the idealized classic landscapes which were to continue for nearly three centuries as a setting for mythical and religious stories. The tiny *Christ on the Road*

30. Annibale Carracci
(1560–1609)
The Flight into Egypt,
1600–4 oil on canvas
55 × 90½ in.
(139 × 229 cm.)

to Calvary (386) by Adam Elsheimer, painted on copper, has superb trees and a walled city with a night sky in the background. Christ, in a blue robe, carries an immense cross. A fine work by the greatest German painter at the beginning of the 17th century.

The State and Private Apartments, some of which are still lived in by the family, begin with the Winter Garden, containing a 16th century Brussels tapestry, *Allegory of the Month of January,* and proceed to the Fumoir which contains an enchanting polyptych of the early 15th century Tuscan school by (?) the Master of the Bambino Vispo, a triptych of the *Madonna with St John the Baptist and St Bernardino* by the Sienese Sano di Pietro and a tapestry, *February,* continuing the allegories of the months. In the Andrea Doria room is a glass case containing some of the great admiral's possessions and two vivacious tapestries commemorating his victory at the Battle of Lepanto. The Small Dining Room has a bust of *Princess Emily Doria* by Pietro Canonica. The Green Salon contains an *Annunciation* by Filippino Lippi, a fine portrait of *Andrea Doria* by Sebastiano del Piombo, *Gianetto Doria* attributed to Bronzino, but probably by Salviati, and *A Gentlewoman* by Lorenzo Lotto. There are also a magnificent 31 *Deposition, c.* 1485, by Hans Memling, a *Madonna and Saints* by Beccafumi, an 18th century cradle in gilded wood and a fine Tournai tapestry of the middle of the 15th century depicting *The Medieval Legend of Alexander the Great.* The Reception Room has a 17th century Florentine marble table on a carved and gilded wooden base with four dolphins. The vast Ballroom is 17th century and has a rare 'Polish' carpet. A tapestry depicting the *Allegory of Man* is on the wall. The Chapel is a fantastic rococo ensemble with a very rich 17th century altar. There follow three delightful little drawing rooms. The Yellow

31. Hans Memling
(d.1494)
The Deposition,
*c.*1485
oil on panel
$24\frac{3}{4} \times 20\frac{7}{8}$ in.
(68×53 cm.)

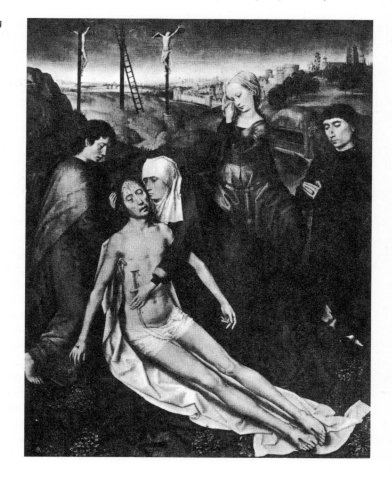

Room is lined with twelve Gobelin tapestries executed by Claude
Audran to the order of Louis XV. The Green Room is completely
furnished and decorated in 18th century Venetian style and there are
three costume pictures in the manner of Pietro Longhi. The Red Room
has four *Allegories of the Elements and Seasons* by Jan ('Velvet')
Bruegel, a portrait of the *Old Pretender* by Alexis Simon Belle, a
curious picture of *Sir Isaac Newton and Lord Gravesend Conversing
with Britannia,* a *Portrait of Count Bjelke* by Joseph Marie Vien, signed
and dated 1757, and the last of the tapestry months, *December.*

The Director is Professor Italo Faldi. The gallery is open Sunday,
Tuesday, Friday and Saturday from 10 a.m. to 1 p.m.

The Colonna Gallery

The Colonna Palace, built by Martin V and reconstructed in 1730 by Niccolò Michetti, is a huge complex running from the Piazza dei Santi Apostoli to the Via della Pilotta, in which street (No. 17) is the Gallery, founded in 1654 by Cardinal Girolamo I Colonna. The building of the Gallery was begun by Antonio Del Grande, continued after his death by Girolamo Fontana and opened by Filippo II Colonna in 1703.

At the entrance are portraits and at the top of the stairs a number of paintings of which *Isabella Colonna-Salviati* (15) attributed to Pompeo Batoni and *Peter's Denial* (20) by Gerrit van Honthorst are worth mentioning.

The Vestibule has a few pictures of interest, particularly *St Julian the Hospitaller* (36) a panel signed by Maestro Jacopo di Sandro, a Florentine artist of the 16th century, *St Andrew* (38) and *St Catherine of Alexandria* (40) by Giulio Romano and *Christ Crowned with Thorns* (41) by Francesco Trevisani.

Hall of the Colonna Bellica. This gets its name from a 16th century *rosso antico* column, the emblem of the family, which is surmounted by a statue of Pallas Athene. On the ceiling are *Marcantonio II Received in Heaven*, escorted by Hercules, and frescoes by Giuseppe Chiari. On the walls: *Portrait of Isabella Colonna and Son* by Pietro Novelli (46) and *Holy Family with St Peter and Donor* (48) by Palma Vecchio, a calm group with a serene landscape. The *Portrait of Lucrezia Tommacelli Colonna* (51) is attributed to Van Dyck. *Holy Family with St James and St Lucy* (53) is typical of the earlier period of the Venetian Bonifazio de'Pitati. Ridolfo Ghirlandaio's *Night* (54) and *Day* (69) are gaily-coloured vulgarizations of the figures on Michelangelo's Medici tombs. Bronzino's signed panel of *Venus and Cupid with a Satyr* (56) is brilliantly chromatic in his best enamelled style. Agostino Carracci's *Cardinal Pompeo Colonna* (57) and Scipione Pulzone's *Pius V* (60) are good portraits, as are Dosso Dossi's *Giacomo Sciarra Colonna* (62) and Lorenzo Lotto's *Cardinal Pompeo Colonna* (64). *Vittoria Colonna* (65), the famous poetess, is elegantly painted in an olive-green dress by Girolamo Muziano of Brescia.

Narcissus at the Fountain (70) is in the manner of Veronese.

Going down seven steps, one broken by a cannon-ball, still there, from the French bombardment of 1849 we reach the Great Hall which 32 is richly decorated. The painting on the ceiling, by Giovanni Coli and Filippo Gherardi, portray the exploits of Marcantonio II Colonna, who commanded the Papal contingent at Lepanto, 1571. This battle was won by Marcantonio or by Andrea Doria, who commanded the Genoese squadron, according to which palace one may happen to be in. The victory is usually credited to Don John of Austria. Salvator Rosa's *Self-portrait as John the Baptist* (73) is a melodramatic but effective work. *A Jolly Fellow* (74) is a genre piece by Dirck van Baburen, a follower of Caravaggio. *Supper in the House of Levi* (75), attributed to Jacopo Bassano, is in harmonious Venetian colours, with a luridly-lit landscape in the background. Tintoretto's *Double Portrait* (79) is divided by a leafy pergola at the back. Crossing the room, Guercino's *Martyrdom of St Emerenzia* (81) is a vigorous painting. P. F. Mola's *Hagar and Ishmael* (82) is in muted colours offset by a stormy sky. *The Family of Alfonso Gonzaga, Count of Novellara* by Scipione Pulzone is a well-organized composition signed and dated 1581. The equestrian portrait of *Carlo Colonna, Duke of Marsi* (84), attributed to Van Dyck, is a fine bravura piece. Crossing the room again, Giovanni Lanfranco's *Magdalene in Glory* (90) is a study in blues and yellows. *Miracle of Our Lady of Succour* (91) by Niccolò l'Alunno of Foligno, a pupil of Carlo Crivelli, has a delightfully naive charm. Above, the Madonna with gilded crown and halo, clad in a blue-green mantle over a pale purple dress sits in an oval halo, surrounded by cherubs with scarlet wings, on a blue cloud. A landscape divides the panel into two parts. Below, there is a tug-of-war for the baby between the agonized mother and a prancing, fairy-tale demon with taloned feet like those of an eagle. Lanfranco's *St Peter Freed from Prison by an Angel* (95) shows the apostle in blue and brown illuminated by the angel's light. *Martyrdom of St Catherine* (96) by Enea Salmeggia is signed and dated 1600. Jusepe Ribera's fine life-like *St Jerome* (102), clothed in a rich red robe, is a splendid anatomical study. Bartolomeo Passarotti's *Family of Ludovico Peracchini* (103) is carefully organized. *The Assumption of the Virgin* (104) may be an early work of Rubens or from his workshop.

Room of the Desks, so-called from the two magnificent desks on each side of the room. That to the left is of ebony from drawings by Carlo Fontana and has 28 ivory bas-reliefs by the brothers Steinhard, the central one depicting the *Last Judgment* of Michelangelo and the remaining 27 reproducing works of Raphael. The desk to the right in sandalwood is decorated with semi-precious stones and, like the first desk, stands on consoles with figures of negroes in ebony and ivory. The frescoes on the ceiling by Sebastiano Ricci depict the *Battle of Lepanto*. Most of the pictures in this room are landscapes, two series being by Gaspard Dughet, pupil and brother-in-law of Poussin (105, 106, 108, 120, 128, 130, 132, 133, 134, 136, 139, 140) and Jan Frans van Bloemen, called L'Orizzonte, with figures by Placido Costanzi (109, 115, 123, 125). Claude's *Ruins of the Palace of the Caesars* (112) has a glowing yellow sky lighting up figures with cows bathing in the river. *Apollo and Daphne* (114) by Nicolas Poussin depicts Daphne on the left in a pale blue cloak. *Noli me tangere* (121) by Lambert Sustris has a marble fountain on the left, a town above it, a farm in the central valley and fantastic hills in the background whose icy blues and greys contrast with the small figures in the foreground. Salvator Rosa's *Coastal Scene* (122) has rocks and trees on the right leading down to an inlet of the sea where a fishing fleet lies at anchor. Michelangelo Cerquozzi's *St John the Baptist* (124) badly needs cleaning, as do many other pictures in this Gallery. Canaletto's small *Church and School of St Roch* is very pleasing. *Joseph Sold by His Brothers* (141) is by the Fleming Nicolas Ryckx.

Room of the Apotheosis of Martin V derives its name from the canvas on the ceiling painted by Benedetto Luti. Above the end wall is Pompeo Batoni's *Time Discovering Truth*. Portraits of *Man of Letters* (143) and *Gentleman* (144) are attributed to Tintoretto. Sassoferrato's *Virgo Purissima* (147) is typically coloured. *Man with Folded Hands* (152) is by Jan Gossaert, called Mabuse. *Portrait of Onofrio Panvinio* (156) the celebrated Augustinian is attributed to Titian. Orazio Borgianni's *St Charles Borromeo* (157) is related to his fine picture in the church of S. Carlino. *Self-portrait* (158) by Francesco Salviati is good. *Old Man at Spinet* (162) by Tintoretto is a fine portrait. Leandro Bassano's *Pietá* (167) is a well-modelled and balanced composition. 33 Paolo Veronese's *Portrait of a Gentleman* (170) is probably the best painting in the Gallery. A youngish man in a slate-blue satin dress and fur-trimmed sleeveless mantle stands before a green curtain draped across the dark grey background.

The Throne Room is arranged, in accordance with the custom of the Old Roman princely families, for a visit from the Pope, for whom is reserved an armchair turned to the wall so that no-one else may sit

III. (opposite) Diego Velazquez (1599–1660) *Innocent X*, 1650
oil on canvas 55⅛ × 47¼ in. (140×120 cm.)

on it. Under the crimson canopy is a 15th century portrait of *Martin V, Oddone Colonna* (199) of the Venetian school. On the walls are a nautical chart (198) presented to Marcantonio II by the Roman people and a parchment diploma (200) given to him by the Roman Senate. There was formerly in this room a large screen with about 30 pictures which have been removed, so causing a gap in the numbering.

Room of Maria Mancini. Francesco Cozza's *Birth of the Virgin* (201) has lovely pastel colours and a charming landscape seen through an arch. In the *Ascension* (203) attributed to Pietro da Cortona, Christ floats above several members of the Colonna family who assisted by angels, have risen from their graves for the occasion. *Resurrected Christ appearing to the Virgin and St John* (206) is a good picture of the school of Roger van der Weyden. Bartolomeo Vivarini's restrained panel of *Madonna Enthroned with Child* (209) is signed and dated 1471. *Madonna and Child with St John Baptist and St Benedict* (210) by Luca Longhi, a 16th century painter from Ravenna, has a delightful landscape. *Madonna and Child* (213) is a panel from Botticelli's workshop. A panel on the same subject (215) by the Florentine Giulio Bugiardini is a simple decorative work. *Portrait of Guidobaldo della Rovere* (216), attributed to Melozzo da Forlì, is a beautifully painted panel of the young Duke of Urbino in a red doublet and buckled cap. *Crucifixion with the Virgin, the Magdalene and St John* (217) by Jacopo Avanzi is a signed panel of the 14th century notable for the grief-stricken faces of the mourners. The *Madonna del Roseto* (221) by Stefano da Zevio has angels above and angel musicians below. *Portrait of Marie Mancini* (224), niece of Cardinal Mazarin and mistress of Louis XIV, who married a Colonna prince, was painted by Caspar Netscher in 1675. *Reconciliation of Jacob and Esau* (226) is attributed to Rubens. The *Seven Joys* (229) and *Seven Sorrows* (231) of the Virgin by Bernard van Orley have seven round miniatures of great beauty around each of the central figures, the first accompanied by a unicorn. The vigorous and vital *Moses with the Tables of the Law* (232) by Guercino portrays with fine lighting a massive figure with an expressive head.

The gallery is open Saturdays only from 9 a.m. to 1 p.m.

32. (opposite above) The Great Hall
33. (opposite below) Paolo Veronese (*c.* 1528–1588)
Portrait of a Gentleman
oil on canvas 48 × 38 in. (122 × 93 cm.)

The Gallery of
the Academy of St Luke

In the 15th century there existed a 'university of painters' who met together in the little church of St Luke on the Esquiline. In 1577 the painter Girolamo Muziano of Brescia obtained from Gregory XIII a letter constituting the Academy of Fine Arts under the patronage of St Luke. A bull of Sixtus V in 1588 consolidated the concessions and privileges of the Academy and succeeding popes, particularly Clement XI, augmented its funds. Federico Zuccari drew up the first statutes and established regular teaching. In 1702 the Clementine Competitions for younger painters, sculptors and architects were inaugurated.

After occupying a number of buildings the Academy, owing to the demolitions made in 1932 to permit the construction of the Via dei Fori Imperiali, moved from its old site to the Palazzo Carpegna on the corner of the Via della Stamperia. The façade looking on to the square is by Giacomo della Porta and assistants. At the end of the entrance hall is a spiral inclined ramp designed by Francesco Borromini to admit to the upper floor people on horseback.

The collection differs markedly from the great private collections of the Borghese, Doria and Colonna families by containing only works by or gifts and bequests from the academicians, many of whom are now forgotten. It does not even have paintings or objects of art from churches. It is therefore a highly specialised collection, mostly of works by minor artists.

Room I. The *Portrait of Clement IX* by G. B. Gaulli, called Il Bacciccia, is not as masterly a composition as the one in the Corsini, but it is a perceptive character-study in warm colours. *The Spinner* by Pier Francesco Mola of Canton Ticino is well-modelled with broad brushwork. *St Jerome* is a workshop copy of Titian's original, 1552, in the Brera, Milan and the fine *Portrait of Marino Corner* is of doubtful authenticity. The *Child* by Raphael is a fresco fragment of a *putto* resembling the one on the right of the prophet Isaiah in S. Agostino and can probably be dated 1512. The *Annunciation to the Shepherds* by Jacopo Bassano is a brilliant painting in strong chiaroscuro with beautifully-modelled figures in the foreground. *Venus with a Mirror* by Carletto Caliari, son of Paolo Veronese, is a stilted picture in the style of his father. Sebastiano Conca's *Vigilance,* a languid allegorical figure, has soft mother-of-pearl tones.

Room II. Paris Bordone's *Seduction* is an elegant work in pleasing colours. The excellent *Portrait of Ippolito Riminaldi* is attributed to Titian. *Judith and Holofernes* by the Venetian G. B. Piazzetta is very dramatic and has a carefully worked-out chiaroscuro. The panel of *Madonna and Child with St Catherine* was formerly attributed to Matteo di Giovanni, but is probably by a Florentine painter. The *Annunciation* by Lorenzo di Credo or his school, is carefully modelled in hard outlines and finely coloured. G. B. Gaulli's *Madonna and Child* is not one of his better paintings but the *Self-portrait* by Federico Zuccari, the first President *(Principe)* of the Academy, is extremely skilful. Bronzino's *Portrait of a Lady* is formal and rather laboured.

Room III. Domenico Pellegrini's *Portrait of Augustus Frederick, Duke of Sussex* and his *Self-portrait,* signed and dated 1827, are competent, if dull, but his *Hebe* is an extravagant neo-classic painting which foreshadows the Victorian academicians. *Portrait of the Miniaturist Marianna Waldstein* by Andrea Appiani, who was so admired by Napoleon that he kissed him on the battlefield of Marengo, is better and more characteristic of Italian neo-classic art. The ladies are represented by a feeble *Self-portrait of Madame Geneviève Brossard de Beaulieu,* a pupil of Greuze, as Contemplation, a drooping *Hope* by Angelica Kauffmann, and a lively *Self-portrait* by the ever- 34 youthful Louise Elisabeth Vigée-Lebrun. The *Portrait of Vincenzo Camuccini,* 1810, by the Viennese Josef Grassi, was for long, and not altogether surprisingly, mistaken for a picture of Lord Byron by Camuccini, who dominated the Academy in the early years of the 19th century.

Room IV. Nicolaes Berchem's *Cattle and Shepherds in the Roman Campagna* is a pleasant Arcadian landscape typical of his Roman period. The six genre pictures of Michael Sweerts, in the *bamboccianti* style, are episodes of everyday life in Rome, finely drawn and well-defined, with an attractive Caravaggesque luminosity. There are two excellent landscapes by Jan Frans van Bloemen, called L'Orizzonte, the most successful of the Flemings who came to live and work in Rome. *Landscape with a Waterfall* was painted under the influence of Dughet while *Landscape with the Colosseum* is a splendid piece of drawing and accurate observation.

Room V. *Tarquin and Lucrece* by Johannes Bilivert, a Fleming born in Florence, is a restrained baroque work. Two *Roman Ruins* in oval

34. Madame Elizabeth
Vigée-Lebrun
(1755–1842)
Self-portrait
oil on canvas

frames by G. P. Pannini are excellent examples of this precise draughtsman and clever colourist who influenced Piranesi, Canaletto and
Hubert Robert. The small *Nymphs crowning Abundance* is a sketch by
Rubens with characteristically swaying and serpentine bodies balanc-
ed by flying *putti* and swirling trees. *Roman Aqueducts* by the Dutch
painter Jan Asselyn is remarkable for its light effects. *Madonna and
Child with Angels* by Sir Anthony van Dyck, a work of his Italian
period, is richly coloured but leans heavily on Rubens for its overall
design. *Susanna and the Elders* by Jacopo Palma the Younger, *White
Horse* by Philips Wouwerman, *Portrait of Admiral Neeuwszoon
Kostenaer*, 1635, by Jan van Mytens, a *Deposition* by Guillaume
Courtois, and *Landscape with Shepherd and Animals*, a huge canvas
by Philipp Peter Roos called Rosa da Tivoli, deserve mention.

　　Room VI. Over the door is *Roman Charity* by Daniel Seiter and the
rest of the room contains a large number of paintings of minor merit
of which it is sufficient to list: *Flagellation of Christ* by the Venetian

Francesco Trevisani, *Battle Scene* by Jean Courtois (Il Borgognone), *Mary Magdalene at the Feet of Christ* and a delicate *Self-portrait* by Benedetto Luti, *Portrait of Anton Raphael Mengs* by Anton von Maron, two *Landscapes* of the Roman Campagna by J. F. van Bloemen, *Seascape with Fishing Boats* by Claude Joseph Vernet in the style of Claude, *View of Tivoli* and *Porto di Ripa Grande* by Gaspard van Wittel (Vanvitelli). There are noteworthy pieces of sculpture: *Self-portrait* and *Bust of Napoleon* by Antonio Canova and *Bust of a Young Girl* by (?) Claude Michel Clodion.

Room VII. Salvator Rosa's *River Anio* is typical of his romantic landscapes. G. B. Gaulli's *Birth of St John the Baptist* is a sketch for his magnificent picture in Santa Maria in Campitelli. *Madonna and Child* by G. B. Salvi, called Il Sassoferrata, is beautifully drawn and coloured and less sentimental than usual. *St Jerome and the Sadducees* may be by Jusepe Ribera but it is more probably by his pupil Hendrik Somer. The oval *Mater Dolorosa* is attributed to Guido Reni.

Room VIII contains terracottas from prize competitions held in the 18th century and plaster casts by Canova and Thorwaldsen.

Room IX is devoted to Italian 20th century painting and sculpture of which the most interesting are *Portrait* by Carlo Carrà, Emilio Greco's *Bust of a Woman,* 1961, and Fausto Pirandello's *Bozzetto,* 1951.

On the staircase there are a number of paintings, plaster casts and terracottas. Of these the huge *Monte Circello* by Giulio Aristide Sartorio, which skilfully depicts the primitive and desolate life of dwellers in the salt marshes, and *Fortune* by Guido Reni are noteworthy.

The Curator is Professor Carlo Pietrangeli.

The gallery is open Monday, Wednesday and Friday from 10 a.m. to 1 p.m. but closed in August.

The Spada Gallery

35 This palace was commissioned by the Apostolic Camera in 1550. It belonged to Cardinal Capoferro, then to the Mignanelli family who sold it to Cardinal Bernardino Spada in 1632. It remained in the hands of the family until 1926 when it was sold to the Italian state. It is now the seat of the Council of State. The façade is by Giulio Mazzoni and it still retains its 16th century appearance. The stucco work consists of heraldic symbols, grotesques and famous figures of Roman history in the niches. The courtyard is also by Mazzoni and is covered with exquisite stucco decorations, delicate festoons, reliefs of tritons and centaurs and acanthus friezes.

About 1635 extensions and restorations were carried out by the great architect Francesco Borromini. His most celebrated addition is 36 the 'perspective' in the garden. Originally it was seen through two wooden gates in the arcade of the left-hand wall and this view has recently been restored which greatly increases its remarkable optical illusion.

The Gallery, on the first floor, consists of four rooms and is entered by a staircase on the left at the back of the palace. The collection was probably started when the family was still living at Brisighella, near Faenza, but it is stamped with the personality of Cardinal Bernardino Spada and is the only one of the smaller patrician collections, once common in Rome, to survive the tempestuous times of the French Revolution and the Risorgimento. The rooms are furnished in the 17th and 18th century styles and the pictures are numbered progressively, beginning from the top of the wall to the right of the entrance to each room. Many of the pictures were recently re-hung to make the more important ones easier to see.

Room I. The furniture, from the end of the 18th century, is of little interest, except for a musical clock in bronze and alabaster, and the Roman sculpture is mediocre. *Landscape in Latium* (2) by Gaspard Dughet, brother-in-law of Nicolas Poussin, is an excellent example of his skill and quiet charm. *The Pillaging of a Village* (3) by Pieter van Laer, called Il Bamboccio, is one of a series of octagonal canvases (the

35. (left) The Spada Gallery
36. (right) Francesco Borromini (1599–1667) The 'perspective'

others are in Room IV) by the founder of the *bamboccianti* group, who painted scenes of Roman plebeian life. The four paintings (9, 17, 26, 36) by Giuseppe Chiari, a faithful pupil of Carlo Maratta, are good examples of the kind of neo-classic art which led on to Anton Raphael Mengs. *The Meeting of Bacchus and Ariadne* (9) is the best and most typical. Guido Reni's *Lucrece* (8) is formally academic and in poor condition, but his *Portrait of Cardinal Bernardino Spada* (25) is 37 magnificent and in a splendid state of preservation. The founder of the gallery is seated in front of a bookcase and is signing offical papers. This study in shades of red was painted about 1630 and the artist's broad handling gives it a stately nobility. Guido Reni's *Judith* (35), executed in 1625, is in poor shape, but it is a fine work and was frequently copied. Domenichino's *Landscape* (24) is an early work but shows the skilful style which, in later years, was to influence Claude. It is interesting to compare Guercino's *Portrait of Cardinal Bernardino Spada* (38) painted in 1631, with that of Guido Reni.

Room II. The two side walls have two fragments of a frieze by Perin del Vaga painted to cover the space below Michelangelo's *Last Judgment* in the Sistine Chapel while the tapestries from Flanders were being woven. The furniture consists of twelve Roman chairs of the first half of the 19th century and two console tables of the 17th century. There are also a late 16th century tabernacle in carved gilt wood

37. Guido Reni (1575–1642)
Cardinal Bernardino Spada (detail)
oil on canvas $11\frac{1}{4} \times 17$ in.
($28 \cdot 6 \times 43 \cdot 2$ cm.)

and a marble copy of the *Head of Laocoön* once attributed to Bernini. *The Visitation* (53) by Andrea del Sarto is an excellent replica on wood of the fresco painted in 1524 for the Chiostro dello Scalzo, Florence. *Portrait of a Musician* (56) painted by Titian about 1515, is an unfinished work of great distinction, damaged by ill-advised cleaning and restoration. The three pictures by Bartolomeo Passarotti, *A Surgeon* (57), *An Astrologer* (60) and *A Botanist* (63) are interesting examples of this minor Bolognese artist. The *Surgeon* and the *Botanist* are wonderfully well-preserved and their vigour, fine brushwork and strong modelling show the painter's transition from Mannerism to something near the classical and natural style of the Carracci. *Portrait of a Cardinal with His Secretary* (61) is attributed to Bartolomeo Cesi, another Bolognese mannerist, who followed the same transition to the style of the Carracci as did Passarotti. *The Crossing of the Red Sea* (65) by Andrea Donducci, called Il Mastelletta, is an early work by this Bolognese painter who belonged to the Carracci school but seems to have derived from Dosso Dossi an element of fantasy. Fiorenzo di Lorenzo's delightful and delicate *St Sebastian* (85) painted about 1475 on wood is a good example of his earlier work.

Room III. The most important pieces of furniture are the four late 17th century console tables of green marble with swags of fruit and garlands of flowers. The two *mappamondi* globes are rare examples of 17th century Dutch cartography, dated 1622 and 1616 and made by Wilhelm Janson. *Landscape* (88) by Niccolò dell'Abbate, a mannerist painter from Modena, who introduced this kind of landscape into France, is a splendid canvas. There is a boar hunt in the foreground, a religious procession, with a greasy pole to celebrate the festival, in the centre and the sea with fairyland cities in the background. Of the two paintings by Pietro Testa, a neurotic painter and engraver from Lucca, *An Allegory of the Massacre of the Innocents* (97) is a masterpiece. It represents St Agnes, surrounded by cherubs, appearing above the scene of the massacre. To the right, under a crag thick with trees, is a boat taking the Holy Family to Egypt. The Christ child holds a cross. In the background are snow-covered mountains. *The Banquet of Antony and Cleopatra* (102) by Francesco Trevisani, who came to Rome with a Venetian background in 1681, is a well-balanced composition. In the foreground is an amusing episode of a dwarf dragging along a dog. Giovanni Battista Gaulli, called Il Bacciccia, a precocious Genoese artist, arrived in Rome as a young man and became a collaborator of Bernini. His greatest work, the fresco in the vault of the nave of the Gesù Church in Rome, was carried out from 1672–1683. The canvas *The Triumph of the Name of Jesus* (108) is a cartoon for the fresco. Naturally, the cartoon is so small that it gives little idea of the grandeur of the magnificent fresco, but it is a fine piece of painting. *The Death of Dido* (109) by Guercino was painted in 1631 and had a tremendous success. It is a grandiose work with a lyrical impulse. Unfortunately he left a good deal of the left-hand side to his apprentices and the deterioration of the paint in this area has affected the balance of the composition. G. B. Gaulli's *Christ and the Woman of Samaria* (115) is a dramatic canvas which reveals his debt to Bernini's revolutionary conception of painting. *St Lucy* (118) by the Florentine artist Francesco Furini is a remarkable example of his brilliant draughtmanship and his titillating sensuality. The soft pearly shoulder of the saint is a masterpiece of suggestiveness. The *Portrait of a Cardinal* (121) attributed to Rubens, must be an early work, if it is by him. The weakness of the modelling suggests that it is not. Annibale Carracci's *Portrait of a Young Man* (124) is a splendid piece of free and unacademic painting. *Oreithyia Abducted by Boreas* (126) by Francesco Solimena, the last great figure of Neapolitan baroque, is a luminous and dramatic work painted about 1701. Worth noting are the magnificent 17th century frames of the two Neapolitan landscapes (131 and 136). Jan ('Velvet') Bruegel's *Landscape with Windmills* (138) is signed and dated 1607 and is a fine example of his meticulous and delicate style.

Room IV. The armchairs and settee are 18th century and the two gilt console tables are 17th century Roman. There are two 16th century stools in the same style as those in Room III. The anonymous

38. Michelangelo Cerquozzi (1602–1660) *Masianello's Revolt*
oil on canvas 37½×52¾ in. (96·8×134 cm.)

Allegory of Architecture (140) may be a satirical squib by Pier Francesco Mola. Orazio Gentileschi's *David* (144) painted under the influence of Caravaggio about 1610, is a fine study of light and shade.
38 *Masianello's Revolt* (149) is the masterpiece of Michelangelo Cerquozzi, a major member of the *bamboccianti* group. The architecture is by his friend Viviano Codazzi. Cerquozzi was famous for his handling of crowds and this is notable in the scene in the market square of Naples where Masianello can be seen in the middle riding a white horse. The *Still-life* (156) by A. Baugin is delightful. One of the only other works by this painter is also a still life, in the Louvre. Orazio Borgianni's *Pietá* (160) painted about 1615 is strikingly similar to Mantegna's *Pietá* in the Brera, Milan. The devoted French follower of Caravaggio, Le Valentin, is represented by a splendid *Portrait of a Woman as Herodias* (165) and a *Holy Family with St John* (169) which is remarkable for its fine colouring and the charming figure of the Virgin.

The Director is Professor Luisa Mortari.

The gallery is open on weekdays from 9.30 a.m. to 4 p.m.; Sundays and Holidays from 10 a.m. to 1 p.m.

The Barracco Museum

The Barracco collection of ancient sculpture is housed in a gem of the Renaissance, the Piccola Farnesina or Farnesina dei Baullari, begun 39 for the Breton prelate Thomas Le Roy by Antonio da Sangallo the Younger in 1523. When Le Roy was ennobled he was permitted to add to his coat of arms the lilies of France, which became confused with the Farnese lilies incorporated into the architectural details and so gave the Farnese name to a building that has nothing to do with the family. The palace was completed in 1546 and was bought by the Commune of Rome in 1887 at a time when there was a good deal of destruction and rebuilding. A new façade was accordingly built by Enrico Gui in 1898–1901.

The collection was formed by a Senator, Baron Giovanni Barracco and presented to the city of Rome in 1902. From the Corso Vittorio Emanuele we enter the elegant Courtyard. On the right is a *Bust of Giovanni Barracco*, 1914, by Giuseppe Mangionello and below an inscription with the name of the founder and the date of the foundation, 1523. Returning through the atrium we mount the stairs and turn to the left into the Loggia, which has 17th century grotesques and landscapes in the lunettes and contains Etruscan art. *Funerary Cippus*

39. The Barracco Museum

40. *Five women prisoners in a palm grove;* Assyrian, 7th century B.C. limestone height 16⅛ in. (41 cm.)

(202) is in the Chiusi style of the 5th century and has scenes of war. Two heads of women, 3rd century, are outstanding. No. 205 in limestone formed part of a tomb-decoration found near Bolsena and No. 204, from a tomb near Orvieto, has a twisted gold necklace and an elaborate hair style. The Vestibule contains reproductions of Mexican, Babylonian and Persian sculpture.

Room I. Assyrian and Phoenician art. Three Assyrian reliefs of the 40 7th century B.C. are noteworthy. Five women prisoners in a palm grove (48), three warriors fleeing through a reed thicket (50), two hunters returning from the chase (49). The relief of a winged deity (47) from the temple of Assurnasipal is from the 9th century B.C. The statue of the Phoenician god Bes (60) was found in a villa in the Alban Hills.

Room II. Egyptian art. Painted stucco head of a mummy (33) is from the Roman era. Fragment of a relief (1) shows the court official Nofer seated before a table with offerings. It is dated 2778–2723 B.C. and is reputed to be the oldest piece of Egyptian sculpture in Rome. *Head of a Youth* (21), possibly Rameses II, is crowned with a blue chaplet. *Sphinx of a Queen* (13), perhaps Hatshepsup, sister of Thutmosis III, is dated 1504–1450 B.C. *Head of a Statue* of a bearded priest wearing a diadem (31) from Roman Egypt, was once thought to be a portrait of Julius Caesar. *Head of a Prince* (15) is of the 18th dynasty. In the centre of the room is a wooden *Head of a Lion* (14),

41. *Stele* of a man on
horseback; Greek,
early 5th century B.C.
marble
height 28¾ in. (73 cm.)

also of the 18th dynasty, in a wonderful state of preservation.

Room III. Greek art to the middle of the 5th century B.C. *(If closed ask attendant to unlock it.)* The lower part of a sepulchral stele (73), a Greek original of the beginning of the 5th century, represents a war- 41 rior with a lance and below him his squire on horseback. *Head of a Priest* (66) is Cypriot art of the 6th century. *Statuette of a Woman* in a chiton (76) is an early 5th century original, probably from the south of Italy. Upper part of a *Statue of Hermes Criophoros* (83) is possibly a copy of a votive bronze by Calamis cast at Tanagra, *c.* 480 B.C. This ram-bearing type of statue is the forerunner of the early Christian 'Good Shepherd' motive. *Statuette of a Woman* in a peplum (77), *c.* 470 B.C. is an Italiote copy of an Olympian statue. Of the group of 5th century statues in Cyprian limestone the most interesting are *Head of a Youth* (70) and *Head of a Bearded Priest* (64) wearing a chaplet and showing traces of colour. The archaic *Head of a Youth* (80) with three rows of curled hair is a Greek original of the late 6th or early 5th century, probably by a sculptor from Samos. *Head of Marsyas* (97) is a free copy of the famous bronze statue of Myron, which was part of the Athene and Marsyas group.

Upstairs is Room IV. Greek art of the 5th and 4th centuries B.C. *Head of Athene* (93) is interesting because the ivory eyes were worked separately and inserted. Upper part of a *Statue of the Amazon of Polycleitus* (102) is a copy of the famous statue in the temple of Diana at Ephesus. *Head of Apollo* (92) is mystic and severe, probably a copy of the bronze statue by Phidias seen by Pausanias near the Parthenon. Statuette of *Hercules* (109) may be a copy, reduced in size, of a work by Polycleitus. In the middle of the room is *Young Athlete Crowning Himself after a Victory* (99), a replica of a lost statue by Polycleitus of which the best existing copy is the Westmacott one in the British Museum. It is possibly a portrait of Kyniskos of Mantinea who won the boxing championship at the Olympic Games.

Room V. Greek art of the 4th and 3rd centuries B.C. *Head of Apollo* (131) is probably a copy of an original by Praxiteles. Above, *Head of an Old Man* (143) may be a portrait of Demosthenes or a Hellenistic Heraclitus. In Glass Case A, upper shelf, are Sumerian bronze statuettes (44, 45) from the 12th dynasty, 2000–1785 B.C. On the other side is a *Bust of Epicurus, c.* 270 B.C. On the facing wall is a *Votive Relief* (129) to Apollo of the beginning of the 4th century. Four young men accompanied by an older man take part in a pilgrimage to Delphi. Apollo is standing, behind him is Artemis and beside her Latona. The men have come to consult the oracle. In Glass Case B bottom shelf is a fine *Krater* (233) of the 4th century from Apulia with volutes representing heads of Medusa. *Head of a Veiled Woman* (132), part of an Attic funerary stele, has a pathetic expression which recalls the work of Scopas. In the centre is a *Wounded Bitch* (139) a marble copy of the celebrated bronze statue by Lysippus, which was kept in the Temple of Jupiter on the Capitol and so prized that its custodians were punishable by death if harm came to it.

Room VI. Hellenistic sculpture. *Archaistic Relief* (176) depicts the cave of Pan. *Relief with Three Maenads* (124) is a reproduction from the time of Trajan of a subject dear to neo-Attic sculptors. *Statuette of Neptune* (151) from an original of the 4th century which showed the god leaning with his right hand on a trident and a dolphin in his left hand. The *Head* (157) at one time thought to be of Alexander the Great is now thought to be of Mithras.

Room VII. Roman art. *Bust of a Young Roman* (190) is an elegant work of the reign of Tiberius. The delightful *Head of a Boy* (194) is possibly identifiable as that of Caius Caesar, nephew of Augustus.

In the Loggia are three 3rd century funerary reliefs (250, 249, 206) from Palmyra.

The Inspector is Professor Carlo Pietrangeli.

The museum is open on weekdays except Monday from 9 a.m. to 2 p.m.; Sundays and Holidays from 9 a.m. to 1 p.m. It is closed in August.

The Museum of Rome

Since 1952, a collection of pictures, sculpture and objects of various kinds, illustrating the history and life of Rome from the Middle Ages to the beginning of the 20th century, has been housed in the Palazzo Braschi, built 1792–1797 by Cosimo Morelli for the nephews of Pius VI, the last palace in Rome to be constructed for a papal family.

On the Ground Floor is a series of rooms surrounding the courtyard. Replicas of works by early Roman marble workers, include the *Tomb of Henry III* from Westminster Abbey. Mediocre paintings and copies of the talking statues (Pasquino, etc.) lead to eight scenes of Roman life: (1) Crib (2) Pipers (3) Wine Cart (4) Notary in a Street (5) Inn (6) Saltarello dancing (7) Lady arriving in sedan chair (8) Apothecary's Shop. The train, 1858, of Pius IX and two railway-carriages, 1851, all constructed in Paris, are splendid relics. Cartoons and satirical sketches of prominent Romans at the turn of the century by Marchetti. The carriage of Cardinal Pecci, later Leo XIII.

Courtyard. A huge and dynamic baroque group *Baptism of Jesus,* 1629–1634 by Francesco Mochi and the Chigi berlin, late 18th century.

Ascending the staircase by Morelli, one of the most beautiful in Rome, we arrive at the First Floor. In Room I are three notable busts. *Carlo Barberini,* brother of Urban VIII, by Francesco Mochi and *Cardinals Francesco and Antonio Barberini* in the manner of Bernini. Room II has an excellent portrait of *Cardinal Giovan Francesco Ginetti* by G. B. Gaulli, called Il Bacciccia, a well-composed and delightfully-coloured picture of *S. Camillo de Lellis* hospitalizing victims of the Tiber floods of 1598, by Pierre Subleyras and a bust of *Clement XIV, c.* 1773, by Christopher Hewetson. Room III has three huge anonymous canvases: *The Tournament of March 5, 1565* was held in the Courtyard of the Belvedere in the Vatican and the *Joust of the Saracen,* a form of tilting at the quintain, was held in Piazza Navona in 1634. *Games at Testaccio* is from the time of Paul III. Room V has frescoes on the ceiling of the *Fable of Psyche* by Ludovico Cardi, removed from the Kaffeehaus of the Palazzo Rospigliosi, and a

42

highly entertaining *Night Festival in Honour of Queen Christina of Sweden* depicting the spectacle arranged for the Queen by the Barberini family on February 26, 1656 during the Roman Carnival. Room V has a very pretty oval stucco ceiling in the form of an umbrella and a bust and portraits of popes. In Room VI are fine fragments of monochrome chiaroscuro frescoes from a 16th century house and in Room VII notable 15th century frescoes representing *Apollo and the Nine Muses* from the hunting lodge of Innocent VIII at Magliana. In Room VIII are *Portrait of Urban VIII* by Pietro da Cortona, *Investiture of Taddeo Barberini as Prefect of Rome* on August 6, 1631 by Agostino Tassi and *Joust of the Saracen at Piazza Navona* on February 25, 1634 by Andrea Sacchi. In Room IX are views of Rome and in Room X six Gobelin tapestries from the first half of the 17th century representing *Child Gardeners*. The Chapel contains a *Tabernacle* by Girolamo da Carpi which Julius III gave to the church of Aracoeli in 1553 and *St Francis Receiving the Stigmata* by Guido Reni. Room XII has the only known portrait of the great engraver· *G. B. Piranesi*, 1779, by Pietro Labruzzi and a *Self-portrait* by Canova. Room XIII has interesting pictures by Ippolito Caffi, one of which, *Panorama of Rome from Monte Mario 1857*, shows how small was the extent of the city at that date. In Room XIV is a fine *Via Capo le Case* by Gaspard van Witte (Vanvitelli) and Room XV has a series of watercolours of people in Roman costumes. Room XVI has a fine floor of flowered Neapolitan tiles, a *Portrait of Benedict XIV and his Secretary* by G. P. Pannini, a *Family Portrait*, probably of the Orsini, painted in 1740 by Marco Benefial, an excellent *Portrait of Pius VI* by Pompeo Batoni and a large *Portrait of John Staples*, set in grand style against Roman ruins, by the same painter. Room XVII is closed. Rooms XVIII to XX have a portrait of *Cardinal Domenico Ginnasi* by Andrea Sacchi and views of Rome in the 17th, 18th and 19th centuries. Room XXI has weights and measures and Room XXII 16th century stalls from the Senate House.

Second Floor. In the anti-camera Room XXIII are three large paintings, 1784, from the Casino of the Villa Borghese by the Scottish painter Gavin Hamilton: *Venus Presents Helen to Paris, Rape of Helen Death of Achilles*. The two following rooms have portraits and views of the 17th and 18th centuries. Room XXVI has fine decorations of Cephalus and Procris on the ceiling. Room XXVII is decorated in the 'Etruscan', that is to say, Pompeian style. There are pictures from the

42. (opposite) The staircase of the Braschi Palace

Rospigliosi Palace illustrating incidents in the Maccarese. Room XXVIII is frescoed with Dionysian motifs. Room XXXI the 'Etruscan Room' has decorations inspired by Greek vases. In Room XXXIII are two gilded mirrors from the Torlonia Palace which was pulled down to make room for the Vittorio Emanuele Monument. Room XXXIV has watercolours of 19th century Rome by Ettore Roesler Franz. Up the wooden stairs are Room XXXV with views by John Ruskin, Samuel Prout, Luigi Vanvitelli and Ippolito Caffi, Room XXXVI with pictures of the Rospigliosi horses and horse racing, Room XXXVII with carnival scenes, festivals and holidays including Ippolito Caffi's amusing *Festival of the Artists at Tor de'Schiavi*, Room XXXVIII with scenes of illuminations and fireworks and two living-rooms with figures.

Descending the staircase we enter Room XLIII with the original model for the Trevi Fountain, 1735, in wood and stucco, Viviano Codazzi's *Arch of Titus* and two sepia washes by Filippo Juvarra. In glass cases are 16 fine miniatures of Rome. Turning to the left and continuing to the end we reach Room XL with a reconstruction of the Alcove of the demolished Torlonia Palace by Filippo Bigioli. In Room XLI are objects belonging to the Università dei Marmorari founded in 1406. In Room XLII are scenes from the lives of Innocent XIII and Pius IX, the latter seen in a picture by Pio Joris walking in the Pincio Gardens. In Rooms XLIV and XLV are views of Rome from the 16th to the 19th centuries and a project for the systemization of Piazza del Popolo by Giuseppe Valadier. Room XLVI has important frescoes and fragments of mosaics from the 12th, 13th and 15th centuries. Room XLVII is an oval decorated in the Chinese style and has gesso busts by Pietro Tenerani of *Princess Vittoria Barberini Colonna* and *Princess Zenaïde Wolkonsky*. Room XLVIII has views of Rome in the 19th century. Room XLIX contains frescoes from demolished churches. Room L contains a number of sentimental and vulgar pictures by Francesco Gai, including a huge canvas of *Princess Elisabetta Brancaccio and her Children*. Room LI has a votive picture offered for the *Liberation of Trastevere from the Plague in 1656*.

The Inspector is Dr Cecilia Pericoli.

The museum is open on weekdays except Monday from 9 a.m. to 2 p.m.; Sundays and Holidays from 9 a.m. to 1 p.m.

V. (opposite) Caravaggio (1573–1610) *Madonna of the Palafrenieri*, 1605–6 oil on canvas 115×83 in. (292×210 cm.) The Borghese Museum and Gallery

The Roman National Museum
Museo delle Terme

The Baths of Diocletian over the centuries suffered great damage, particularly from Sixtus V who, from 1586 to 1589, systematically destroyed one fifth of them to obtain material to build a villa for his sister. With the first restoration of the Baths in 1889 it was decided to house there the collection of sculptures and antiquities which had been amassed since 1870, with the additions of the Kircherian collection formerly in the Collegio Romano and the treasures of the Ludovisi collection acquired later in 1901. The museum occupies a large part of the old Carthusian convent. At the entrance we find seven rooms which surround the right transept of Santa Maria degli Angeli. Four more are near the Frigidarium.

Hall I contains a mosaic with elegant volutes, flowers, birds and animals and on the left three sarcophagi depicting *The Three Graces, A Bacchic Procession* and *The Story of Phaedra.*

Hall II. Against the wall to the right is a plaster reconstruction of part of the temple of Hadrian erected in 141 A.D. by Antoninus Pius in the Piazza di Pietra. There is a fine sarcophagus with standing figures of *Muses* (80711).

Hall III. In the centre of the back wall is a Christian *Sarcophagus* (455) bearing on its tablet the name of Marcus Claudianus with scenes from the Old and New Testaments. Christ is represented without a beard. Against the wall on the right is a large polychrome mosaic in a geometrical style from the beginning of the 3rd century A.D.

Hall IV. In the centre is a Nilotic mosaic from Collemancio near Assisi, with vivacious scenes of pigmies hunting hippopotamuses and crocodiles. An inner mosaic square shows, in a landscape of marshes, pigmies fishing. On the left wall is a large dedicatory inscription of the Baths of Diocletian. A colossal statue (80941) the *Kore* (or *Artemis*) of Ariccia, is a copy of an original by Alcamenes or Cresilas. Against the opposite wall is a reconstruction of a small tetrastyle temple of the Corinthian order dating from the middle of the 2nd century A.D. and found near Torrenova. On the right of the temple is a large sarcophagus (112327) showing a cavalry encounter between Romans and Barbarians and on the left another depicting the meeting of Dionysus and Ariadne.

Hall V. *Group of Mars and Venus* (10522) was erroneously supposed to represent the Emperor Commodus and his wife Crispina. On the left of the group is the shaft of an oriental alabaster column on a beautiful base of white marble found during the building of the new Chamber of Deputies in 1907. On the left of the door leading to the Frigidarium is a marble sarcophagus (115172) with a festive scene of Bacchic *amoretti* playing and dancing.

Hall VI. On the left wall is a copy in plaster of the door of the Temple of Augustus and Rome at Ancyra (Ankara). In the centre is a mosaic with *quadrigae* (cars drawn by four horses) taking part in a race. The charioteers show by their tunics and variously coloured sleeves that they belong to one or other of the four factions of the circus. The winner Aëri, in a green tunic, is shown with a large palm leaf in his left hand. Beyond the mosaic is a large cylindrical drum (54746), Attic art of 1st century B.C., formed of seven marble slabs on which are sculptured in relief the *Dancers of the Via Prenestina* who proceed elegantly in slow rhythm. There are several sarcophagi of which the most notable is one with Bacchic scenes (124736). On the left a seated Silenus merrily raises up the infant Dionysus. On the right the adult Dionysus ying under a bower is uncovered by a Maenad.

Hall VII. In the middle on the left is a rectangular-shaped altar in marble ornamented at the four corners with bulls' heads. On the two ong sides are pleasing festoons of laurel leaves and berries.

Hall VIII, an open space, with the Frigidarium on the left, once occupied by the swimming pools of the Baths, is undergoing restoration. Halls IX, X and XI are closed and, at the time of writing, no date can be given for their re-opening.

The garden is normally entered from Hall X, but at present we have to go through an ante-room and the refreshment bar in order to reach t. In the centre is a colossal marble fountain-basin shaped like a floral calyx. A flight of steps leads down through an arch to the ancient *forica* or latrines of the Baths. Along the curved wall were placed about 30 lavatory holes separated from each other by marble slabs. In the west corner of the garden is the entrance to the museum proper.

In the Entrance Porch, on the left, is a *telamon* in the form of a young beardless satyr, a Roman copy of a Hellenistic original found n 1942, and polychrome mosaics. The Entrance Hall has a mosaic in black and white tesserae of a skeleton with the inscription in Greek know thyself'.

43. *The Tiber
Apollo;*
Greco-Roman
copy,
?2nd century
B.C.

The great Ludovisi Collection, formed by Cardinal Ludovico Ludovisi nephew of Gregory XV, which occupies the small cloister, has been packed up in boxes for a considerable period and at the time of writing there is no information as to when it will be exhibited.

Opposite the entrance to the cloister is the first of eight rooms which contain a selection of the most important sculptures of the museum.

Room I. Floor mosaic of *Four Satyrs and a Head of Pan* in black and white. Large marble basin of a *Fountain* (113189), a fine example of neo-Attic work of the 1st century B.C., is supported by three legs of wild animals and a twisted column. Two quadrangular *Cinerary Urns* (1044, 1039) in the form of small altars have decorations of festoons, fruit and flowers in high relief.

Room II. In an impluvium in the centre is a polychrome mosaic with the head of Oceanus in the middle surrounded by sea-monsters and dolphins. *Torso of Hercules* (106164) is probably a copy of a bronze by Polycleitus. Only the upper part of the head is antique. The *Tiber* 43 *Apollo* (608), a copy of a bronze original by Phidias when young or Calamis, is stained in places by the waters of the Tiber from which it was recovered in 1891. The *Aura* or *Nereid* (124697) is a fragment of a statue, *c.* 400 B.C. found near the Arch of Titus, probably from the acroterion of a temple. *Dancing Girl* (124696) is dressed in a chiton of light material in tiny folds. Dated about the middle of the 5th century B.C., she was found in the Domus Augustana of the Palatine. *Peplophoros* (124667) is a torso of a female, *c.* 480 B.C. and is possibly by an Ionian artist working in Italy. It was found in the Piazza Barberini in 1941. The *Palatine Juno* (51) is finely carved and may be the statue of an empress portrayed in the form of the goddess. *Torso of the Minotaur* (124665) is a powerful study, probably a copy of a figure from a bronze group of the 5th century B.C.

Room III contains the outstanding sculptures. There are two copies of the *Discobolos of Myron*. The one on the right (56039) was found 44 in 1906 on the royal estate of Castel Porziano, the one on the left (126371) is from the Lancellotti Collection and, against the laws of Italy, was sold to Hitler in 1938. It was returned ten years later. Both statues are fine examples of athletic energy. The first is portrayed at the moment after the athlete has passed the discus from his left to his right hand, just when the maximum tension of the body is happening. The Lancellotti copy has the original head, a work of careful and faithful execution, even to the little horns to be seen in the hair above the forehead, and is probably the best existing copy of Myron's master-

piece, delineating as it does the swollen veins and play of tense muscle
45 with a perfection of restraint. *Dying Niobid* (72274) a victim of Apollo
and Artemis, is from the Gardens of Sallust and is probably from a
group containing the fourteen children of Niobe as well as the two
gods who were executing judgment upon them. The beautiful modelling of the adolescent body, the girl's tragic attitude and the head
thrown back in agony from the pain of the arrow in her back have won
great admiration for this figure, *c.* 440 B.C. ever since it was discovered
in 1906. The treatment of the draperies suggests a sculptor from the
Ionian islands, though some scholars consider it a Roman copy. *Venus
of Cyrene* (72115) was found in the Baths of Cyrene in 1913. The
goddess is rising from the sea and is presumably lifting her arms to
squeeze the water from her hair. The ivory patina of the Parian marble
adds to the beauty of the body, by whose right side is a dolphin with a
small fish in its mouth, making a fine contrast with the contours of the
youthful Venus. The slightly formal treatment of the figure suggests a
Peloponnesian original of the 4th century, but some scholars consider
it to be a much later work by a sculptor from one of the Greek cities of
Asia Minor. *Ephebus of Subiaco* (1075) a nude youth about to touch
the ground with his left knee, is a fine study in anatomy. A copy of a
4th century original from Nero's villa at Subiaco it probably formed
part of another Niobid group. *Torso Valentini,* in the museum since
1949, is a finely finished, naturalistic piece of sculpture akin to works
of Myron dating from the first half of the 5th century B.C. *Young Man
Leaning on a Spear* (1049) is a bronze in the same pose as the Alexander the Great of Lysippus. It may represent Pollux after his victory in a
boxing match over Amycus, King of the Bebryces or, more probably,
Demetrius I Soter of Syria who came to Rome as a hostage in 175 B.C.
46 The tangled hair, deep-set eyes, furrowed brow, disdainful mouth and
massive body suggest a prince. As a portrait it is an exciting mixture
of realism and idealism. *Boxer* (1055) is in bronze, a little over life
size, sitting with his legs apart and torso bent forward. He shows signs
of injury from his opponent, the coarse, short nose is flattened and
his mouth is open as if the clotted blood in his nose prevented him
from breathing properly. It is a work of almost brutal realism by Apollonius son of Nestor, whose signature is on the Belvedere torso in the
Vatican. *Apollo of Anzio* (121302) is an excellent copy of a bronze
47 by an unknown master of the 4th century B.C. *Young Girl* (50170)
also found at Anzio, is generally regarded as a masterpiece of early
Hellenistic art, though it may be a copy. She carries a salver with a
roll of cloth, a laurel twig and a box on it. The sweet disorder of her

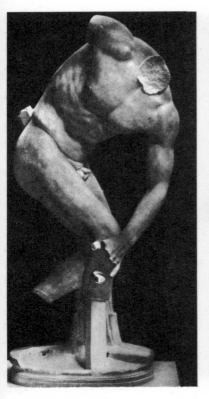

44. (left *Discobolos of Myron,* Lancellotti copy, ?1st century B.C. marble height 60 in. (152 cm.)
45. (right) *Dying Niobid, c.* 440 B.C. marble height 59⅛ in. (150 cm.)

dress has been explained in a number of ways, but never convincingly. The female *Head* (124679) belongs to a figure found in 1929 at Butrinto in Albania. The best of the mosaics is a whirling wheel with fourteen spokes like curved rays.

Room IV. The beautifully modelled *Charis* (607) found in 1862 on the Palatine and attributed to Callimachus, is dressed in a chiton whose folds and wrinkles are minutely carved. *Dancer* (108596) from Hadrian's Villa near Tivoli rests lightly on the tip of her left foot as if she were beginning a pirouette. The group of an *Amazon on Horseback* (124678) is a Pergamene work showing the female warrior attacking a Galatian. *Child Satyr* (499) is a Hellenistic work with a head copied from a similar statue in Florence. The child twists his

46. (left) Apollonius son of Nestor, *Boxer, c.* 50 B.C.
bronze height 50⅜ in. (127 cm.)
47. (right) *Young Girl of Anzio, c.* 250 B.C.
marble height 66⅞ in. (169 cm.)

body round sharply to laugh with pleasure at his tail, which he has
just discovered. The *Muse,* or *Nymph* (12) seated on a rock was found
in the stadium of the Palatine. *Tyche* (121987) the goddess of a sea-
port, is accompanied by a charming child merman shouting and pointing at some distant object. The *Muse* (124722) like its counterpart
No. 12 was found in the stadium of the Palatine. They may have formed part of a 3rd century group by Philiscus of Rhodes. At the end, two
statues of a crouching *Venus* (108597, 60750) belong to the type
made famous in the 4th century by the sculptor Doidalsas of Bithynia
and the painter Camiros. On the wall is a mosaic of a large round shield
with volutes and a head of Medusa in the middle.
    Room V. The marble altar (417) with plane-tree branches sur-

mounted by a bull's head was found during the demolition of the Apollo theatre near the Ponte Sant'Angelo. The altar to the left is in two parts, an ossuary on top and a cippus below. On the cippus are a wedding ceremony, figures of maenads dancing and *camilli* carrying fruit for sacrifice and a large half-open umbrella. The delicacy of the reliefs reminds one of the work of Agostino di Duccio.

Room VI. *Augustus as Pontifex Maximus* (56230) found in 1910 in the Via Labicana is an excellent portrait. The head, which was worked apart from the body and inserted later, is particularly fine. *Head of an Old Woman* (124493) is a severely realistic work of the first period of the Empire. The *Head of Nero* (618) is the best portrait of him that we know. *Bust of the Chief Vestal* (639) from the House of the Vestals in the Forum is important because it provides us with an exact record of the clothes worn by the vestals.

Room VII. In the middle is an *Altar from Ostia* dated October 1, 124 A.D. with reliefs of the origins of Rome: Romulus and Remus, cupids carrying the arms of Mars, Mars and Rhea Silvia and a youthful Hymen. *Head of a Maiden* (1043) has the hair parted in the middle, several rows of curls above the temples, two thick curls on each side of the neck and a knot of hair on the nape, the height of fashion in the time of Claudius. *Head of Sabina* (629) wife of Hadrian, is an exquisite work. Her hair is elaborately dressed and her painted eyes have the pupils cut in a halfmoon line. The refined *Head of Hadrian* (124491) is one of the best portraits of the emperor known to us. *Head of Vespasian* (330), full of life and vigour, is one of the finest Roman portraits in existence.

Room VIII. The *Sarcophagus of Acilia* (126372) a mutilated work of the 3rd century A.D. has figures in high relief probably representing philosophers and poets in a flamboyant, almost baroque, style. The female head has hairdressing typical of the period. The *Sarcophagus* (125802) opposite has pastoral scenes on the front, a lion tearing a lamb to pieces on the sides and chariots on the top border. *Head of a Young Girl* (1119) formed part of a high relief and is notable for its tenderness and refinement. *Head of Gallienus* (644) is modelled with vivid realism.

From the corridor we go up the stairs to the long gallery containing the stuccoes from a Roman house in the precincts of the Villa Farnesina. A door in the middle of the wall leads into a room containing the frescoes of the Villa of Livia, wife of the Emperor Augustus, at Prima 48 Porta, transferred to the museum in 1951. The four walls are decorated with a continuous picture of an orchard of fruit and flowers, a master-

48. Decoration of the Villa of Livia fresco height 118⅜ in. (299·7 cm.)

piece of the second period of Roman painting. Birds flit from branch to branch and the trellis work on the wall gives the impression of separating us from the flowers and trees in the grass border.

We now return to the Room of the Farnesina Stuccoes which were discovered in 1879. The first stuccoed ceiling comes from a small room (Cubiculum B) and depicts a landscape with buildings and a bridge, an initiation scene of the cult of Dionysus and a Bacchic orgy. In the centre ceiling (Cubiculum E) there are dancing figures, the Hours preparing the chariot of the sun for Phäethon and architectural scenes. In the third ceiling (Cubiculum D) are ornamental borders of spirals and cupids and a small square picture of a drunken Silenus.

At the end of the room we enter the Halls of the Mural Painting. Hall I contains paintings (removed from Cubiculum E) in the second Pompeian style. Hall II contains magnificent paintings from Cubiculum B. The background colour is cinnabar red. The picture in the central frame represents the nymph Leucothea fondling the infant Dionysus. On the left wall Aphrodite is enthroned while Eros, standing before her, holds in his right hand his mother's sceptre. Hall III contains a 28 feet wide frieze on a black background from the large room C. The frieze represents, according to Loewy, the Egyptian king Bocchoris, famed for his wise judgments. In the middle is the *Tiber Bacchus* a graceful, youthful figure of the 2nd century B.C. Hall IV contains paintings from Cubiculum D. On the widest wall is Aphrodite, to whom a girl is making an offering. The border has delightful women and nymphs in the Egyptian style and love scenes. On a column is scratched the name of the painter, Seleucis. Hall V contains fragmentary pictures. On the landing are two rooms with mosaics from the Villa Ruffinella near Tusculum, from Genazzano, and from the Villa of Septimius Severus at Baccano.

Descending the stairs we enter the Michelangelo Cloister which was built in 1565, a year after his death. One cypress, in iron bands, was planted at that time. Few of the exhibits merit attention. At the end of Wing I is a *Statue of a Woman* (68) in an attitude of prayer, who may be Faustina the younger. The head is from another statue. Wing II has a large fragment of a granite slab (52045) with Egyptian deities in sunken relief from the temple of Isis and Serapis in the Campus Martius and *Lid of a Sarcophagus* (61586) portraying a boy with nude torso lying on a bed, while a snake glides towards the egg he is holding in his left hand. At the angle of Wings II and III are two large pilasters (1023, 1036) with fragments of the accounts of the *ludi saeculares* celebrated in the reigns of Augustus and Septimius Severus. Between them is a Nilotic mosaic (171) of pigmies hunting crocodile and hippopotamus and two women fleeing in terror.

From Wing IV we re-enter the corridor. At the end on the left are five rooms devoted to minor sculpture. Room I has *Roman Girl as Diana* (108518), a life-size statue from Ostia and *Relief with Figures of the Hesperides* (124543), a damaged slab of Pentelic marble with three young women, neo-Attic work probably of the 1st century A.D. Room 2 temporarily houses the only object from the Ludovisi Collection which has not been packed into a box, the three-sided relief known as the 'Ludovisi Throne' (8750). This was found in the neigh- 49 bourhood of the Gardens of Sallust in 1887. A young woman, presumably Aphrodite, is rising from the waves, assisted by two women, who are standing on the shingle of a beach and holding out a cloth which covers the beautiful body of the goddess below the waist. These may be the Fates or simply the handmaidens of Aphrodite, whose long, wet hair clings round her neck while her face glows with new-found life. The vertical folds of the garments of the women attendants reveal, in subtle modelling, the bodies beneath. The figures are shown in gradually receding depth which enables the arms of the three women to weave a fine sculptural pattern. On the left side is a nude female of great beauty playing a double flute. On the right is a young woman wrapped in a cloak, seated on a folded cushion, taking incense from a box to throw on to a brazier. This relief, dated *c.* 470–460 B.C., is probably by an Ionian Greek working in Italy. It is perhaps the finest piece of antique sculpture in Rome.

Room 3 has a good *Dionysus* (622) from Hadrian's Villa, a copy of

49. *The Ludovisi Throne, c.*470–60 B.C.
marble height 33½ in. (84 cm.)

a bronze statue of the 4th century B.C., a headless *Athene* (108595), also from Hadrian's Villa and an *Apollo* or *Eros* (75675) from the Palazzo Chigi, a careful copy of a Hellenistic bronze.

Room 4. The relief of a *Maenad* (126375) holding a goat by the horn is a fine example of the period of Hadrian. *Sleeping Hermaphrodite* (1087) is a copy of an original of the 2nd century B.C. Apart from the boyish hips the body is mainly feminine. This type of statue was popular because the dual nature of the hermaphrodite also symbolized fertility. *Head of a Sleeping Nymph* (1194) is a fine study in serenity. *Head of a Dying Persian* (603) is a work of astonishing realism in the Pergamene style of the first half of the 2nd century B.C.

Room 5 is devoted to statues in coloured marbles of which the huge *Seated Goddess* (124495) is the most typical. *Equestrian Statue* (115164) of a small boy is delightful. The head, hands and legs of the boy are of *lunense* marble, while his body and that of the horse are of alabaster. The group was reconstructed from a hundred fragments found in the Borgo Acilio in 1928.

The museum is open on weekdays except Monday from 9.30 a.m. to 4 p.m.; Sundays and Holidays from 9.30 a.m. to 1 p.m.

The Borghese Museum
and Gallery

The Borghese Gallery owes its existence to Cardinal Scipione Cafarelli 50
Borghese, nephew of Paul V. Known as 'Rome's delight' because of
his elegant manners and sumptuous banquets, he was also a great
collector of art. The Borghese Palace in the Campus Martius already
contained important works of art when Scipione Borghese commissioned the Dutch architect Jan van Santen (known in Italy as Giovanni
Vasanzio) of Utrecht to erect a richly decorated villa in the family vineyards outside the Porta Pinciana. His intention was twofold, to create
a building to house the treasures which Paul V's generosity had enabled him to accumulate and to have a suburban villa in which he
could entertain. Van Santen, with the assistance of Flaminio Ponzio,
began work in 1613 and finished in 1616. The vineyards were turned
into formal terraces, with secret gardens, beds of rare flowers and
splendid trees arranged in symmetrical avenues.

50. The Borghese Museum and Gallery

51. Johannes Wilhelm Baur (d.1640) *View of the Borghese Villa*, 1636
watercolour on parchment 11 × 17 in. (30 × 45 cm.)

The Cardinal commissioned many works by contemporary artists but he also wished to have a representative collection of earlier masters and called on the generosity of his friends from whom he received, among other gifts, Veronese's *The Preaching of John the Baptist* sent by the Patriarch of Aquileia. He also did not scruple to force minor clergy and friars to sell him masterpieces housed in convents and
51 churches. In 1633 Johannes Wilhelm Baur painted the watercolour (now in Room XIX) showing the exterior ornamentation of the villa, and in 1650 Jacopo Manilli gave a detailed description of its contents and its interior decoration. It was only partially decorated at that time but there are still four small rooms on the top floor with the original painted ceilings.

In 1624–1625 Giovanni Lanfranco frescoed the ceiling of the great loggia giving on to the gardens, but the villa, as we see it today, was refurbished in the middle of the 18th century by Prince Marcantonio Borghese, who appointed Antonio Asprucci as architect and instructed him to engage all the best decorators to complete the Cardinal's original project. Asprucci selected a great masterpiece for each room of the ground floor and arranged for the ceiling to corres-
52 pond, e.g. Bernini's *Apollo and Daphne* has the *Metamorphoses* by

52. (left) Gian Lorenzo Bernini (1598–1680) *Apollo and Daphne*, 1622–25 marble height 95 in. (243 cm.)
53. (right) Correggio (1494 or 1489–1534) *Danäe, c.*1530 oil on canvas 24×76 in. (60·9×193 cm.)

Pietro Angeletti on the ceiling. By so doing he altered the careful arrangements made by Bernini to have his works seen from the correct angle. Asprucci also indulged in fashionable decoration in Room IV, the Egyptian Room, which was considered so representative of modern taste that it was reproduced in engravings. He also designed the Entrance Hall to give the illusion of space annihilating and bursting the walls, though he carefully subordinated the decoration to the architectonic whole in the other rooms. The profusion of many-coloured marbles is a sufficient indication of Marcantonio's wealth.

Unfortunately Marcantonio's son Camillo, owing to his allegiance to Napoleon and his marriage to Napoleon's sister Pauline, broke up part of the collection, selling several important pictures and receiving the fief of Leucadio in Piedmont in exchange for the delivery in Paris of two hundred pieces of classical sculpture, many of which are now exhibited in the Louvre. Camillo, however, was not entirely a depredator and later he tried to make amends by acquiring Correggio's *Danäe* 53 and by placing Canova's portrait of his wife as Venus Victrix in the collection. He also had erected the little temple of Aesculapius, whose grace is still reflected in the tiny lake nearby, constructed the grandiose Propilei giving access to the Porta del Popolo and the Arco Romano at the entrance to the Lake Garden, planned the amphitheatre of the Piazza di Siena and renovated the English gardens which had been laid out by the Scottish painter Jacob More in 1773.

The last renovation of the Villa was undertaken in 1833 by Francesco Borghese who increased the classical collection and created the museum; he also brought from the family estate near Tusculum five large mosaics with gladiators and hunting scenes which decorate the floor of the Entrance Hall. He also set up a trust to protect the treasures. In 1891 the pictures, which had been in the Borghese Palace for nearly three hundred years were brought to the Villa. In 1892, owing to a financial disaster, the family had to sell objects which were not on the trust list and finally the Villa and its contents were sold to the State in 1902.

Although the great park has suffered from unfortunate alterations it still has an aristocratic air and the private character of the Villa and its collections remains unchanged. It is indeed still possible to recon- struct in imagination the magnificent style in which the Roman princes lived and entertained.

The Ground Floor contains the museum; Roman numerals are used for the sculpture and Arabic numerals for the pictures. We enter a Vestibule with examples of Roman sculpture and a useful coffee and snack bar on the right and proceed to the Entrance Hall which is remarkable for its size, rich decoration and statuary. The ceiling frescoes, 1774, are by the Sicilian Mariano Rossi and represent Marcus Furius Camillus breaking off peace negotiations with Brennus. The decoration includes amusing grotesques by Pietro Rotati and twelve Caesars in the niches by G. B. della Porta. The animal decorations by Wenceslas Peter are famous. The high relief on the wall facing the entrance is an antique restored in the 18th century and represents Marcus Curtius leaping into the chasm. On the floor are five fragments of 4th century mosaics from Torrenuova depicting fights between gladiators and wild animals. The sculpture is of small importance.

Room I is decorated by G. B. Marchetti, the paintings are by Domenico de Angelis and the bas-reliefs by Vincenzo Pacetti. The plaster model of Jean Antoine Houdon's *St John the Baptist,* 1764– 1768, reveals his feeling for naturalness and his precise control of the sculptural form. Pietro Bracci's bust of *Clement XII* shows fine psycho-

V. (opposite above) Dosso Dossi (*c.* 1479/90–1542) *The Enchantress Circe, c.* 1530 oil on canvas 69¼ × 68½ in. (175 × 173 cm.)
VI. (opposite below) *Sarcophagus of the Spouses, c.* 530 B.C. terracotta height 55⅛ in. (140 cm.)

logical penetration and masterly treatment of the surface. In the centre
is Antonio Canova's virtuoso marvel, *Pauline Borghese*, sister of
Napoleon, as *Venus Victrix, c. 1806*. His domination of the material
and his lightness of touch, coupled with the beauty of his model,
enabled him to free himself from his obsession with the ideal world
and classical rules, and produce a masterpiece.

Room II. The picture in the centre of the ceiling by Francesco
Caccianiga represents *The Fall of Phäethon* and the ornamentation is
by Luigi Agricola. The centrepiece is Gian Lorenzo Bernini's *David*, 56
1623–1624, the psychological masterpiece of the Borghese statues.
Feet set wide, he twists to get the maximum impetus into his shot, his
tense mouth and strained features emphasizing his superhuman pur-
pose and iron will. He looks towards his adversary and past the
spectator, who must stand in front of the base to see David as Bernini
intended him to be seen. The *Landscape with a Stag Hunt* by Niccolò
dell'Abbate of Modena is a remarkable excursion into fantasy. Worth
noting are Guido Reni's *Moses with the Tables of the Law*, painted
under Caravaggio's influence with fine effects of light and colour, and
(CXXXII) a rare green porphyry amphora, 1787, by Antoine Guillome
Grandjacquet.

Room III is decorated by Giovan Battista Marchetti, one of the
principal assistants to the architect Asprucci, and the *Metamorphosis
of Daphne* by Pietro Angeletti in the middle of the ceiling is an accom-
paniment to Bernini's *Apollo and Daphne* group, 1622–1625. This 52
like the other Bernini works was originally placed against a wall and
should be viewed as one comes through the door. His stupendous,
breath-taking technique enabled him to cut the marble as if it were
butter and at the same time achieve the most delicate effects. The god
has just caught up with the nymph who is uttering a soundless
scream. Still running she takes root and shoots out leaves and tendrils.
Apollo, modelled shamelessly on the Apollo Belvedere, is taken aback
and pauses as he is about to grasp Daphne. The light, airy suppleness
of this group, with contrasting planes culminating at the apex, are unequalled in Bernini's work. We then pass through a little chapel to
Room IV, which is known as the Hall of the Emperors, because of
the eighteen 17th century busts in porphyry and alabaster round the
walls. The ornamentation of the ceiling is by Marchetti and Domenico

54. (opposite above) Domenichino (1581–1641) *Diana Hunting*, 1618
oil on canvas 88⅝×126 in. (223×320 cm.)
55. (opposite below) Jacopo Bassano (*c.*1510/18–1592) *The Last Supper*
oil on canvas 66⅛×106¼ in. (168×270 cm.)

56. Gian Lorenzo Bernini (1598–1680)
David, 1623–24 marble

de Angelis painted the three canvases of the *Story of Galatea.* The polychrome effect created by the many kinds of marble, the floor and walls, the tables, columns and amphoras gathered together in this room, make it one of the most sumptuous examples of Italian 18th century taste. On the right is Bernini's *Neptune,* originally commissioned for Cardinal Montalto's villa on the Esquiline hill, a bronze variant, produced about 1620, of the *Neptune and Triton* group now in the Victoria and Albert Museum, London. Of far greater importance is Bernini's *The Rape of Proserpine,* 1621–1622. Here again Bernini's technique is fantastic and he cuts the marble so as to give it at times the effect of clay modelling and at times of bronze. Pluto, like Apollo, has just snatched the unwilling girl who struggles and cries in vain. The hand of Pluto sinking into Proserpine's soft flesh is a miracle of virtuosity. At the far end of the room is a bronze copy (CCXLIX) by Antonio Susini, signed and dated 1613, of the group known as the Farnese Bull now at the National Museum of Naples. Another 17th century work is a herm of Bacchus (CXXXXV) with a bronze head in archaic style, often taken for an original antique.

The ceiling of Room V is painted by Marchetti and Nicola Buonvicini and portrays the myth of Hermaphrodite and Salmacis. It contains among other late statuary a *Sleeping Hermaphrodite,* a poor copy of the Hellenistic original, which once belonged to the Borghese collection, was sold by Prince Camillo to Napoleon and is now in the

Louvre. Over the doors are four competent but unimaginative land-scapes by the Antwerp painter Paul Brill.

The ceiling of Room VI is ornamented by Marchetti and *The Banquet of the Gods* in the centre is the work of the Lyonnais painter Laurence Pecheux. There are two works by G. L. Bernini. The group of *Aeneas and Anchises* was at one time attributed to his father Pietro, but we now know that it was commissioned by Scipione Borghese in 1618 and completed, probably with his father's advice, by Gian Lorenzo in 1619. The vertical build-up of the composition, which is meant to be seen from all sides, is in the Mannerist tradition, but the play of muscles and sinews under the skin is typical of Gian Lorenzo's personal style. The figure of *Truth*, 1646–1652, was begun when the sculptor had fallen out of favour, after the death of Urban VIII. It was intended to be part of a large group entitled *Truth Revealed by Time*.

The decoration of Room VII is by G. B. Marchetti in the Egyptian style. The various Egyptian episodes are painted by Tommaso Conca from Gaeta. The statue of a youth astride a dolphin (CC) of Hadrian's period, with a satyr's head added later, was probably part of a fountain and is interesting because of its connection with the statue of Jonah designed by Raphael and executed by Lorenzetto in the Chigi chapel of S. Maria del Popolo. A statue of a young girl in a *peplos* (CCXVI) is an original work of the Peloponnesian school, 5th century B.C. The antique head, much restored, is from another statue.

Room VIII has on the ceiling a *Sacrifice of Silenus* and scenes of satyrs painted by Tommaso Conca. In the centre is a *Dancing Satyr*, a fine copy of a bronze original by Lysippus, the first Greek sculptor to use casts from life. Thorwaldsen added the forearms and the clappers, with no justification. The satyr was probably holding a double tibia. There are pictures of interest by Gerrit van Honthorst (a charming *Concert*), Dirck van Baburen, Perin del Vaga and Lelio Orsi. Giorgio Vasari's *The Nativity* is better than many of his works, but it shows how badly the great historian of Italian art painted.

We now return to Room IV where a door in the left-hand corner leads to the staircase and the Gallery on the first floor. In the Entrance Room Luca Cambiaso's *Venus and Cupid at Sea* recalls in its clarity some of the luminosity and chromatic skill of Veronese.

Room IX. Anton de Maron, a Viennese, painted the ceiling between 1784 and 1786 with five scenes from the story of Dido and Aeneas. The fine white marble fireplace is by Vincenzo Pacetti. The inner part is lined with majolica tiles depicting the dragon and eagle, the Borghese armorial bearings. The delightful *Crucifixion with Sts*

Jerome and Christopher by Pinturicchio is preserved in its original frame and in perfect condition. Every detail of the landscape is painted, as if by a miniaturist, with freshness and delicacy. Saint Christopher in his glowing golden tunic leans on a flowering stick and stands in a stream where fish swim by in an aqueous paradise. Raphael's *Portrait of Man*, 1502–1504, is a virile, austere work with characteristics of his Umbrian origins, but it cannot compare with the *Portrait of a Lady with a Unicorn*, 1505–1506. Formerly the lady wore a cloak and bore the wheel and palm of St Catherine, but a restoration in 1935 revealed her to be holding a unicorn, the symbol of chastity. An infra-red photograph, on the left, shows that the lady was originally older and that the unicorn developed from a calf. The chartreuse green of the bodice, the crimson velvet sleeves, the brilliant handling of the jewelled pendant and the grace of the lady combine to make this pic-

57 ture one of the most enjoyable of Raphael's works. The *Deposition* of Raphael (actually an Entombment) was commissioned by Atlanta Baglioni of Perugia to commemorate the death of her son in a struggle for the mastery of the city. It is signed and dated 1517 and is the most ambitious of his Florentine works. The separate figures are powerfully drawn and the body of Christ, although influenced by Michelangelo's *Pietà* (itself derived from an antique sarcophagus) has a tender relaxation which contrasts markedly with the violent movement of the bodies around. The predella of this panel is in the Vatican gallery. Fra Bartolomeo della Porta's *The Holy Family* is a solid construction with a landscape reminiscent of Leonardo. The circular *Madonna and Child* by Sandro Botticelli is grouped in a harmonious and natural way, but it is an inferior work and suggests the presence of collaborators. Lorenzo di Credi's delicate *Madonna and Child with St John* reveals in the sky-blue gown of the Madonna and in the loving care with which the pot of flowers is treated his tenderness and precision.

Room X. *The Labours of Hercules* were painted on the ceiling in 1786 by Christopher Unterbergher. The decoration is by Marchetti. In the centre of the room is *The Gipsy Girl* by (?) Tiburzio Vergelli, put together from ancient fragments in the 16th century. Sodoma's *The Holy Family* is a latish work, *c.* 1525–1530, in which blue-green tones contrast with the red of the Virgin's gown. The Spanish painter Alonso Berruguete spent fourteen years in Italy and it is sad that his *Madonna with St Elizabeth and the Two Holy Children* is in such a bad state of preservation. Andrea del Sarto's *Madonna and Child with St John*, *c.* 1519, in spite of too frequent repairs, impresses by its modelling, equilibrium of composition and harmonious colours. The head of the

57. Raphael (1483–1520) *Deposition,* 1517
oil on panel 72½ × 69¼ in. (184 × 176 cm.)

Madonna seems to recall Leonardo's *Virgin of the Rocks.* The *Portrait of Cardinal Marcello Cervini degli Spanocchi,* probably by the Florentine Francesco Salviati, is an impressive meditation on a theme of Raphael, with refined and elegant colours. Andrea del Brescianino's skilful and decorative *Venus with Two Cupids* is set in a niche to give it a classical architectural background. Paul V thought so highly of Marco d'Oggiono's *The Redeemer in the Act of Blessing* that he kept it in his bedroom until he gave it to Scipione Borghese in 1611. Albrecht Dürer's *Portrait of a Man* dated 1505 is a good character study but not one of his most distinguished works. The *Venus and Cupid* by Lucas Cranach the Elder contrasts to its advantage with Andrea del

58. Girolamo Savoldo
(active 1508–after
1548) *Tobias and the
Angel*, c.1540
oil on canvas
48⅜ × 37½ in.
(123 × 95 cm.)

Brescianino's work. It is dated 1531. The typical Nordic nude, with slim hips and a slightly distended stomach, wears a most elegant bronze-red velvet hat which considerably increases her erotic attraction. She is accompanied by a Cupid carrying a honeycomb who seems horribly bored by a number of bees. The Latin text indicates that pleasure is mixed with pain, an ancient Theocritan concept dear to the medieval mind. Angelo Bronzino's early *St John the Baptist* is disturbingly contorted and counterpoised. The stone-coloured flesh with a blue loin cloth is striking, as is the saint's oval face, but the restlessness of the picture makes it an unsatisfactory whole. Andrea Solario's *Christ Bearing the Cross* has a distinctly Flemish flavour.

Room XI. Lorenzo Lotto's *Self-portrait, c.* 1530, a noble work, has a sombre unity of shades of black, relieved by the white lace cuffs and the melancholy head bathed in light. The fallen rose petals under his hand hide a small skull which adds to the solemnity of the atmosphere, itself somewhat enlivened by a lyrical landscape seen through the window on the left. Jacopo Palma the Elder's *Madonna and Child with Saints, c.* 1512, is a serene and finely-coloured picture with a superb portrait of a devout person in the left-hand corner. Jacopo Zucchi's two pictures on copper brilliantly express the riches of the sea (perhaps also the recent discovery of America) and the Creation. Girolamo Savoldo's *Portrait of a Young Man* is remarkable for a Caravaggesque graduation of the shadows from one surface to an-

other. Savoldo's *Tobias and the Angel, c.* 1540, a late work of the 58
Brescian master, is notable for the superb figure of the Angel who,
borne by his great silvery wings, alights on a rock. His blue and rose
costume is set off by the orange-gold one of the kneeling Tobias. In
Lorenzo Lotto's *Holy Conversation* the crude and clashing reds, blues
and greens show the influence of German painting.

Room XII. Pietro da Cortona's *Portrait of Marcello Sacchetti* demon-
strates by the solidity of the figure and the high relief of the caryatid
his architectonic qualities, while the *Madonna and Child* by Pompeo
Batoni, the chief rival of Anton Raphael Mengs, is a charming and
delicate work with beautifully-balanced colours. *A Sibyl* by Domenichino, painted for Scipione Borghese, shows the Bolognese master
at his best. Mouth open, as if prophesying or singing, with a scroll of
music in her hand and a viol behind her, she wears a mantle of red
brocade over her gold-embroidered gown and a white bodice under-
neath. Annibale Carracci's *Head of a Laughing Youth,* which shows
traces of the original charcoal sketch, has a gaiety and vigour which
are anything but academic.

Room XIII. The four small panels by Bacchiacca illustrating *The
Story of St Joseph,* 1516–1518, in a style resembling that of Perugino
contrast sharply with the tremendous Michelangesque pyramid which
Pellegrino Tibaldi has built up in his *Adoration of the Holy Child, The
Blessed Virgin with St John* by Giulio Romano is striking. The deriva-
tion from Raphael is obvious but the two children, St John is hand-
ing a small bird to Jesus, are beautifully executed.

Room XIV was in the 16th century an open loggia and its ceiling
was frescoed by Giovanni Lanfranco, 1624–1625. An enormous
illusionist cornice is carried by stone-coloured caryatids between
which the sky is seen. The representation of the Gods on Olympus is
grandiose but highly decorative. In 1786 the loggia was closed and
the fresco restored, unfortunately with some damage to the colouring.
Spaced along the wall are four circular canvases, *c.* 1622, by
Francesco Albani depicting *Stories of Love.* These tondi show considerable ingenuity and their decorative charm made them so famous
that they were copied well into the 18th century. Rather too high up
on the wall is *Rinaldo and Armida* by Alessandro Tiarini, whose notable foreshortenings, coupled with rhetorical and dramatic effects,
greatly impressed his contemporaries. The first of the six paintings by
Caravaggio, *St John the Baptist, c.* 1605, was so frequently repainted
in the 19th century that it is irreparably damaged. On an easel is the
View of the Borghese Villa, 1636, by Johannes Wilhelm Baur showing 51

the building in its original state, with statues and the double staircase
54 which was destroyed by Asprucci. Domenichino's *Diana Hunting,*
1618, was painted for Cardinal Pietro Aldobrandini but it so fascinated
Scipione Borghese that he had it removed by force from the artist's
studio. The sunlit landscape, the elegantly grouped figures and the
refined colours make this work superior to most of Domenichino's
large frescoes. On an easel is Caravaggio's *St Jerome, c.* 1604, painted
in such a flowing and lucid style that it has caused critics (probably
wrongly) to doubt its authenticity. The early pictures *A Boy with a*
Basket of Fruit and *The Ailing Bacchus,* both *c.* 1592, are remarkable
for their treatment of fruit and leaves, a novelty in Italian painting at
that time. The sick Bacchus is often held to be a self-portrait of Caravaggio when suffering from malaria. His *David with the Head of*
Goliath, 1605–1606, also contains a self-portrait, Goliath, of a very
different kind. The curious colouring is reminiscent of Savoldo. The
IV *Madonna of the Palafrenieri,* 1605–1606, was painted for the Con-
fraternity of the Palafrenieri (Papal Grooms) who intended it for an
altar in St Peter's. It was refused by the Canons who were horrified by
the picture's outspoken realism. The power of the composition, the
revolutionary treatment of light and shade, the profoundly human
study of ordinary people and the solid modelling of the Virgin and
Child make this one of Caravaggio's greatest achievements. The serpent which the Madonna crushes underfoot is a symbol of heresy.

The sculpture in this room is of particular interest, showing as it
does various phases of Bernini's development. *The Goat Amalthea*
with the Infant Jupiter and a Faun, 1615, was completed when he was
sixteen. It was long mistaken for an antique and it was doubtless inspired by some Hellenistic work. The two busts of *Cardinal Scipione*
Borghese have an interesting history. The magnificent original
(CCLXV) was executed in 1632 but, when it was nearly finished, the
marble cracked across the forehead and Bernini was forced to make a
copy secretly in a fortnight or, according to some, three days – a stag-
gering performance – but the copy lacks the vigour and spontaneity of
the original, where the half-open mouth and expressive gaze show
the Cardinal in animated conversation. The small *Bust of Paul V,* 1618,
is a treasure and it is interesting to compare his blank eyes with the
sparkling ones of the Cardinal. The base is modern. CCLXIX *The*
Model for the Equestrian Statue of Louis XIV of France, c. 1670, has a
sad history. The monument was to have been erected in Versailles, but
when the King saw the statue he banished it to the uttermost corner
of the garden and later wanted to break it up. In 1688 Girardon

changed the headgear and turned the rock beneath the horse into flames in order to alter the group into one of Marcus Curtius. How different from these works of Bernini is *Sleep*, in *nero antico*, by his great rival, the Bolognese Alessandro Algardi. The sleeping boy crowned with poppy heads, a dormouse fast asleep at his side, is a charming example of classical realism.

Room XV has a large canvas of *Aeneas Fleeing from the Fire of Troy*, 1598, by Federico Barocci. This melodramatic work is notable for the appearance of Trajan's column in burning Troy. *Mourning over the Body of Christ, c.* 1605–1606, by Peter Paul Rubens is an early work, full of expressive warmth, painted during his second visit to Rome. The overall brownish tone is relieved by the fine red of Saint John's robe, the gleaming golden hair of Mary Magdalene and her sage-green cloak. Of the three Bernini portraits the *Self-portrait* No. 554, *c.* 1623, is the best. The careful brushwork and sober expression suggest the influence of Andrea Sacchi, while the *Self-portrait* No. 545, *c.* 1635, shows darker colours and a more unified composition which may have been due to the influence of Velazquez. In his *Portrait of Monsignor Clemente Merlini*, Andrea Sacchi (the rival and opponent of Bernini and Pietro de Cortona) shows great mastery of the classical style which he learnt from the Bolognese school of the Carracci. The Auditor of the Sacred Rota is portrayed against a massive background of bookcase and books; his humorous, almost quizzical, smile illuminates his face, which stands out against the darkness of the background and his clothes, while his short expressive hands add patches of light to the predominantly dark tones of the picture.

In the little corridor there is a charmingly-coloured panel of *Tobias and the Angel* by the Emilian artist Raffaelino da Reggio. Room XVI, like Room XV, is decorated by Marchetti. Savoldo's *Venus Asleep* has a fine landscape which, illuminated by the setting sun, provides a background for the pale, sleeping figure. The fresh contrasting colours of Jacopo Bassano's *Adoration of the Shepherds* and the elegant linear rhythms make this picture both attractive and satisfying. His *Last Supper* is considered by some to be his masterpiece. The grandeur of the composition, built up to the figure of Christ, and the brilliant painting of the objects on the table, atone for the over-crowded scene. Bassano's *Adoration of the Magi* is exquisitely coloured in tones that recall Tintoretto and El Greco; indeed the painting was formerly attributed to the latter.

Room XVII. Scarsellino's panel of *Madonna and Child with Saints* is curiously interesting, in that it appears to represent a family scene set in the Po valley, with burning stubble in the distance lighting up the landscape. Garofolo's *Madonna and Child with Two Saints* and Scarsellino's *Diana and Endymion* are good examples of these Ferrarese painters. Francesco Francia's three pictures, *Madonna and Child, St Francis* and *St Stephen*, are representative of the serene and graceful style of this Bolognese master. The large panel by Ortolano, another Ferrarese painter, depicting *Christ Taken from the Cross, c.* 1521, is composed of a statuesque group of figures against a background which is an admirable example of the landscape painting of the period. There is also a deliciously archaic *Doubting Thomas* by Lodovico Mazzolini. The figures are set against a landscape from fairyland and the light sprinkling of gold accentuates the fabulous atmosphere.

Room XVIII contains most of the pictures of the foreign schools. An early Rubens of *Susanna and the Elders* is colourful but immature. *View of a Port* by Paul Brill, one of his best works, *The Visit of the Blessed Virgin to St Elizabeth* by Marten Mandekens, *The Guardroom* by Peter Codde and Franck Francken's *An Antiquary's Shop* are worth noting.

It is necessary to go back through Room XVI to reach Room XIX, which is frescoed by the Scottish painter Gavin Hamilton, who helped Prince Marcantonio in 1794 to redecorate the Villa. The subject of the frescoes is *Episodes from the Life of Paris.* In the corners of the room are two portrait busts by Algardi of which that of *Cardinal Ginnasi* is particularly fine. The bust of *Vincenza Danesi* is a notable psychological study, but the careful observation is somewhat fragmented and it does not have the sensibility and solidity of the Cardinal. Outstanding among the six works of the Ferrarese master, Dosso Dossi, is
V *The Enchantress Circe, c.* 1530. The witch wears a brocaded costume of deep crimson, hyacinth blue and opalescent green. Behind her is a dream landscape lit by a lurid glow and peopled by reclining figures. Her gesture of lighting a brand from the embers of a brazier provides the limiting line of the central triangle, which is topped by her golden, tasselled turban. Out of this magic world the enchantress looks into an unfathomable distance. *Apollo and Daphne,* contemporary with *Circe,* is another fantastic picture in which the minute figure of Daphne is seen on the left vanishing into a laurel grove. *Diana and Callisto* and the paintings of his brother Battista are inferior works. Pordenone's *Judith* is a fine harmony of colour and structure. Correggio's magnificently lyrical *Danäe, c.* 1530, was painted for the coronation in
53 Bologna of the Emperor Charles V, to whom the Duke of Mantua in-

ended to give it. It travelled to Prague, to Stockholm, to Rome with Queen Christina of Sweden, to London and to Paris. Finally it was bought in 1824, for 285 English pounds by Prince Camillo Borghese who added it to the collection in 1827. Like all the great oil paintings of Correggio this work has a tender and voluptuous quality, indeed Danäe herself is so seductive that she might have been painted by Boucher. The cloud above the bed has a ripe golden colour and the landscape seen through the window takes on a golden hue. Parmigianino's *Portrait of a Man* is analytically penetrating but the very limited range of colour makes the picture dull.

Room XX has a ceiling depicting the story of Psyche and Eros by Francesco Novelli and a fireplace of white marble and red porphyry by Agostino Penna dated 1782. *Holy Conversation* by Jacopo Palma the Elder is brightly-coloured. Above are two figures of a *Singer* and a *Flautist, c.* 1510, attributed to Giorgione, but more probably by one of his followers. Giovanni Bellini's *Madonna and Child, c.* 1508, is an intimate and moving work. The group is pyramidal in structure and backed on the left by a straight emerald green curtain. A slender tree stands out in front of a landscape of mountains and clouds. Titian's early masterpiece *Sacred and Profane Love, c.* 1515, has been interpreted in many ways, but it would appear that the picture represents the two aspects of Venus. Curiously enough it is the nude figure that dominates the picture while the clothed figure has a more worldly aspect. The two women meet at a Fountain of Love but the reliefs offer difficulties. A man is being scourged and an unbridled horse, the symbol of sensuous possession, is being led away. In contrast to these restless images, the superb landscape is serene and peaceful in the evening light. Titian's *St Dominic, c.* 1565, or *St Vincent Ferrer* as some think, has the appearance of a portrait. The colour is sombre and the effect conveyed is that of an intelligent and suffering human being. *The Portrait of a Man, c.* 1474, by Antonello da Messina is a marvel. 59 The expression of the face, the slant of the eyes, the humorous and self-satisfied line of the lips, the simple geometry of the head are magnificent. As a combination of psychology and technique it is unequalled for its time except by other portraits by the same artist. Vittore Carpaccio's *Courtesan, c.* 1495–1500, or more properly, Portrait of a Venetian Woman, is in such bad condition that it does small justice to this brilliant painter. Titian's wonderful *Venus Blindfolding Cupid, c.* 1565, was somehow mixed up in the ancient inventories with The Three Graces, which is not surprising as it is a most mysterious picture. It probably represents an initiation into Love. The colour and com-

59. (left) Antonello da Messina (*c.*1430–1479) *Portrait of a Man, c.*1474
oil on panel 11¾×9½ in. (30×24 cm.)
60. (right) Paolo Veronese (*c.*1528–1588) *St Anthony Preaching to the Fishes*
(detail), *c.*1580 oil on canvas 44⅛×61¾ in. (112×157 cm.)

position are formidable – the painter was 88 – and the blue, rose and
violet in the foreground contrast with the distant landscape lit by a
fiery sky. The two pictures by Veronese are excellent examples of his
work. *The Preaching of St John the Baptist* is early and unfinished,
but the fresh crystalline colours, lemon yellow, copper, aquamarine,
rose, green and violet and the elegant figures form a superbly decorative whole. *St Anthony Preaching to the Fishes, c.* 1580, is a splendid
poetic composition. The colours are deeper and more subtle, particularly in the magnificent seascape. The dramatic figure on the cliff
pointing into the infinity of the sky, the sea boiling with fish, the group
of listeners in semi-oriental garb, the distant town and the overall
luminosity are unforgettable. Titian's *The Scourging of Christ, c.* 1560,
is a coarsely painted work in which the hands of assistants are apparent, but the sense of suffering which appears in the face of Christ is
authentic.

The Director is Professor Paola della Pergola.

The museum is open on weekdays except Monday: May 2 to
September 30 from 9 a.m. to 4 p.m.; October 1 to April 30 from 9.30
a.m. to 4 p.m.; Sundays and Holidays from 9 a.m. to 1 p.m.

The National Etruscan Museum of the Villa Giulia

The Villa Giulia has housed since 1889 collections of pre-Roman antiquities from Latium, Umbria and southern Etruria. The Villa was built 1551–1553 by a number of architects for Julius III, the last Renaissance pope, who used it for entertainment on a grandiose scale. The overall design is probably by Vignola, in spite of Vasari's claim to have been the author. The screen above the nymphaeum is by Ammanati and the elegant nymphaeum itself was mainly built by him, with the assistance of Baronio. The façade embodies two different orders, Tuscan on the ground floor and Composite above. The large entrance door, in *rozzo bugnato*, leads to a pillared atrium of the Corinthian order and thence to a semicircular portico with Ionic columns, the vault of which has frescoes of children and birds. The Courtyard, with long walls and Ionic columns, leads to the Loggia, decorated in stucco by Ammanati. Two curved staircases lead down to the first floor of the Nymphaeum, the lower floor of which is entered through a room under the Loggia. The gardens on both sides of the courtyard from part of the architectural whole. To the right is a 19th century reconstruction of the Temple of Aletrium (Alatri).

Except for the special collections, the museum is arranged regionally, with large maps, plans and explanatory material illustrating and describing each area. This method has the defect that nowhere is there a chronological survey of Etruscan Art. It is, of course, true that

61. The National Etruscan Museum of the Villa Giulia

Etruscan art was static and archaizing and that Etruscan civilization was the sum of its parts, which were the individual cities and centres, but some general guidance would be helpful to most visitors.

On the left of the entrance is a room with ceiling frescoes by Taddeo Zuccari or Prospero Fontana. Here are exhibited objects recently discovered in two temples at Pyrgi, on the coast about 30 miles north-west of Rome. Of special interest is a fine fictile of the War of the Giants.

The museum proper begins with five rooms containing finds from Vulci. Room 1 contains two very important statues in nenfro, a soft stone of volcanic origin, one is a vigorous centaur in archaic Greek style of the Peloponnese but with strong Etruscan characteristics, c. 600 B.C., and the other a youth riding a sea-monster of which the front part is missing, from the middle of the 6th century B.C. Room 2. The Guglielmi Altar and a small pediment showing Dionysus flanked by a panther and Ariadne holding a thyrsus, with Cupid and a swan on her left, are interesting. Room 3 contains material from the Iron Age cemeteries of Osteria and Cavalupo of the kind called Villanovan. In Cases 1, 2 and 3 are a number of funerary urns, called 'hut-urns' because they are miniature reproductions of Villanovan-type dwellings. On the top shelf of Case 2 is a fine Nuragic warrior in bronze, wearing a conical cap. Room 4. Showcase 1 has a group of black-figured Attic vases, one with scenes of boxing (bottom shelf), and an exquisite embossed plaque (middle shelf) in bronze lamina with Achilles and Troilus, all from the Tomb of the Warrior at Osteria. In Case 6 is a large black-figured Attic hydria (spheroid jar with three handles) with five women at a fountain and above them a scene with a quadriga. In Case 8 is an Attic rhyton (drinking vessel) in the shape of a female head with earrings. Room 5. Cases 1–3 contain votive objects including little clay models of buildings. In Case 4 is an antefix with a circular nimbus showing traces of blue and red. In the centre of the room a stairway leads down to an important reconstruction of a tomb from the Maroi tumulus at Caere (Cerveteri). There are two chambers containing beds against the side walls, and a number of funerary objects, belongings of the dead. Showcase 6 (middle shelf) has a bronze model of a farm cart with yoke, from Bolsena. Room 6 has material from Visentium (Bisenzio). Case 2 (top shelf) has a bronze carriage and a bronze ladle from a tomb at Olmo Bello and a bronze receptacle (bottom shelf) decorated on top with figurines of a chained bear and men dancing.

In Room 7 are temporarily arranged the famous painted terracotta

62. (left) *Centaur* from Vulci, *c.* 600 B.C.
nenfro height 30⅜ in. (77 cm.)
63. (right) *Head of Hermes, c.* 500 B.C.
terracotta height 14⅝ in. (37 cm.)

sculptures from the temple of Apollo at Veii. On the right, Case 1 bottom shelf, there is a superb male head, probably of Hermes. In the 63
centre of the room is a splendid antefix from the roof of the temple of
Apollo in the shape of a ferocious Gorgon. Towards the back of the
room, facing one another as they must originally have been, are the
magnificent statues of Apollo and Hercules, which probably adorned 64
the central beam of the temple. These masterpieces of Etruscan art can
be dated around the end of the 6th century B.C., as can the goddess
and child discovered under the altar by Professor M. Pallottino when
he was excavating the temple. The main group probably represented
the struggle between Apollo and Hercules for the Arcadian Stag,
which took place in the presence of Hermes and Artemis, and may be
by Vulca, the only Etruscan sculptor known by name, who is mentioned by Pliny. In Case 3, middle shelf, is a votive statuette of Aeneas
carrying on his shoulders his father Anchises. In Case 4, middle shelf,
is the Head known as the 'Malavolta' in which some see a strange 65
affinity with the figure of *St George* by Donatello, now in the Bargello
Museum, Florence. Datable from the latter part of the 5th century B.C.

it is one of the most beautiful works in the classical Greek style to come out of Etruria.

Room 8 contains material from Caere (Cerveteri), the largest and richest city of maritime Etruria. There are a number of antefixes in Cases 1, 2 and 3, those of a Silenus and a Maenad being noteworthy. In Case 4, top shelf, are a superb masculine head from the temple of Manganello, one of the most important portraits of the latest period of Etruscan art, c. 80 B.C., and a beautifully-modelled head of a young boy from the same temple. In the centre of the room is a large sarcophagus of the middle of the 6th century B.C. with orientalizing feline shapes on the front and two pairs of lions on the cover.

VI   Room 9 contains the *Sarcophagus of the Spouses* from the second half of the 6th century B.C. The young couple recline, according to the Etruscan fashion, on a banqueting couch in a beautifully balanced group. Etruscan ladies participated in banquets, as we see, and were very emancipated, which greatly shocked the Greeks and Romans. Ionic influence is apparent in the faces of the spouses, as it is in the head of the Veii Apollo, and a word must be said here about the so-called 'archaic smile' which is produced by drawing the eyes and mouth as if they were in independent planes.

At the top of a flight of steps Room 10 exhibits material from the cemeteries which formed a ring round Caere. Case 2 contains a jug in the black glossy pottery called bucchero (top shelf) with incised decoration of two winged horses and a hind, and a large Corinthian krater (middle shelf) with warriors on horseback, chariots and animals. Case 3 (top shelf) has a superb group of buccheri with incised and plastic decorations. Case 6 (middle shelf) has two interesting vases of Egyptian majolica, one in the shape of a female figure, the other in the shape of a baboon. The star-shaped case has in Arm 7 a Laconian goblet (top shelf) with Gods of the Winds and Harpies. Arm 10 has a black-figured hydria with a scene of a warrior leaving home. Case 13, top shelf, has two amphoras of Nicosthenes with satyrs and maenads dancing. Arm 16 has an amphora (middle shelf) by Nicosthenes with Centaurs, Lapiths and Bacchic scenes. In Case 18 is a red-figured Attic pelike depicting Hercules and Old Age. In Case 19 are (top shelf) a large kylix signed by Epictetus showing Leda and the Swan with Hercules and two warriors fighting in the background, and a red-figured Attic psykter (global vase with cylindrical support) with Theseus fighting the Minotaur on one side and a divinity seated on a

64. (opposite) *Apollo of Veii, c.*500 B.C.
terracotta height 69 in. (175 cm.)

TEMPLA DOMVM EXPOSITIS.VICOS FORA MOENIA PONTES:
VIRGINEAM TREVII QVOD REPARARIS AQVAM.
PRISCA LICET NAVTIS STATVAS DARE COMMODA PORTVS:
ET VATICANVM CINGERE SIXTE IVGVM.
PLVS TAMEN VRBS DEBET: NAM QVAE SQVALORE LATEBAT:
CERNITVR IN CELEBRI BIBLIOTHECA LOCO.

throne on the other side. Case 20 has a large, red-figured Attic krater with a warrior running on the body of the krater and on the neck athletes and Hercules struggling with Cycnus. The work is attributed to the Master of Berlin. Cases 21–25 have Faliscan and Etruscan vases.

We now go up the stairs to the Upper Floor where are several 'Antiquariums'. The majority of the objects in these rooms are from the Kircherian Collection. Room 11 has in Case 2 (lower shelf) an embossed bronze mask of Acheloüs. Room 12, Case 3 (upper shelf) has a remarkable bronze 4th century group of a peasant guiding two yokes of oxen which pull a plough, known as *The Ploughman of Arezzo*. Rooms 13–14 have a fine collection of bronze statuettes, armour, mirrors, candelabra and cylindrical-shaped cistae. In Room 15, Case 4 (upper shelf) is the Chigi Vase from Formello (Veii), *c.* 66 650–625 B.C., the finest known example of protocorinthian manufacture. There are three figured bands of exquisite workmanship in reds, browns and whites, portraying a lion-hunt, a hare-hunt, hoplite warriors and chariots. On the left a piper is keeping the hoplites in step. Room 16 has balsam-holders and Etruscan and Attic vases. Room 17 has in Central Case 1 (lower shelf) two fine plates with fish decoration and Italiote vases and in Case 5 (lower shelf) a series of Etruscan and Roman masks of characters in plays. Room 18 has five funerary urns of the 3rd and 2nd centuries from Chiusi of which the most interesting has a banquet bed, in front of which are two young men standing on a stool. They are perhaps servants of the dead man on the lid.

The Castellani Collection was put together by Augusto Castellani, who came from a family of goldsmiths famous in Rome in the 18th century, and presented by him to the Italian State in 1919. It is housed in the semi-circle of Rooms 19–23. The collection is vast and only a few items can be mentioned. In Case 3, central shelf, are two hydriai from Caere, one with Hercules and Eurystheus and the other with the Rape of Europa. The lay-out of the scenes is spacious and balanced and the colour construction in Ionian style. Case 4, middle shelf, has a fine black-figured Attic goblet decorated by warriors fighting. Case 7, middle shelf, has two amphoras with large handles, both red and black figured. Case 8 has a series of red-figured goblets, one depicting Ulysses and his companions leaving the cave of Polyphemus. Case 9 continues the series. On the lower shelf is a hydria whose shoulders

VII. (opposite) Melozzo da Forlì (1438–1494) *Sixtus IV Nominating Platina Prefect of the Vatican Library*, 1477
fresco transferred to canvas The Vatican Picture Gallery

 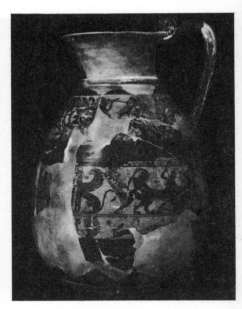

65. (left) *Head of a Youth*, called 'Malavolta', *c.* 430 B.C.
terracotta height 7⅞ in. (20 cm.)
66. (right) *The Chigi Vase;* Protocorinthian, *c.* 640 B.C.
terracotta height 11¼ in. (28·5 cm.)

are decorated by Hercules struggling against the Nemean lion. Case
10, lower shelf, has a pelike with Dionysus between a young girl with
a pitcher and a satyr. On the other side is a group of satyrs and
maenads. Case 11 has a series of Faliscan, Apulian and Campanian
vases. Case 12 contains vases made in Volsinii with characteristic
silvery dressing and decoration in relief. Room 24 leads from the
Castellani Collection to the Faliscan, Latin and Umbrian sections.

Room 25 has urns, vases and tomb material from the Ager Capenas
and the Ager Faliscus. Showcase 1, upper shelf, has an Etrusco-
Campanian plate of the middle of the 3rd century B.C. decorated with
bands of rosettes and ivy leaves. In the centre is a war elephant with
its calf. On the back of the elephant is a crenallated tower with two
brown-skinned warriors. On the elephant's neck is a driver with a
Phrygian cap, which suggests that the group was inspired by the
elephants used by Pyrrhus against the Romans. In Case 4, top shelf,
is a large impasto cup on an openwork stand with a handle which
represents two pairs of horses facing each other and held by a

charioteer. Room 26 Case 2 has a kylix portraying Dionysus, with a thyrsus in his left hand, kissing and embracing Ariadne. Case 3 has in the centre a crematory bronze tomb in the shape of a house and on the end shelf of Case 5 is a large Faliscan krater with beautiful handles joined to the vase by animals. It is decorated in superb polychrome, on one side with a scene of the abduction of Cephalus by Eos and on the other Boreas abducting Oreithyia, who has been surprised in the bath. Room 27 Case 1, top shelf centre, has a black-figured kylix with a figure seated on a bed playing a lyre and, outside, Dionysus seated among dancing maenads. Case 2, middle shelf, has two rhytons, one in the shape of an astragal with a lion and a cupid in the upper part and the other in the shape of a dog's head with a banquet scene on the neck, which are masterpieces of Greek art of the first half of the 5th century B.C. The first is signed by Syriscos. Case 3 has a red-figured bell-shaped krater of the middle of the 5th century B.C. with girls dancing and on the top shelf left a bell-shaped krater from southern Italy with scenes of the destruction of Troy. Room 28 has in Case 1 a krater with Hercules and the Nemean lion on one side and athletes on the other. Case 3 has a red-figured bell krater with the entry of Hercules into Olympus. On the top shelf is a Faliscan kylix with Apollo on a mule and in the centre two large terracotta jugs with rich decoration.

Room 29 has on two levels sculptures and terracottas from temples near Falerii Veteres. On the wall above left are gable tiles and an open-work cornice together with a decorative cover-slab from the Sassi Caduti temple, on the right is part of the decoration of the Temple of Apollo at Lo Scasato with remarkable antefixes of the Asian Artemis and winged figures. Large figured terracottas which decorated the pediments of the two temples are seen on the lower part of the trellis screen. Upper part of a nude statue of Apollo (2670) with the head looking upwards and to the right and the upper part of a young man who could be Mercury (2686) are very fine, as is the head of a young man looking upwards and bent slightly to the left. In the glass cases are excellent examples of temple decoration in the form of antefixes of heads of Maenads, Silenus and Gorgons. In Case 3 an acroterion from Sassi Caduti shows an early 5th century group of warriors fighting. One has fallen on one knee and is so accurately modelled that his armour can be minutely studied. There are also in Case 4, from the larger temple at Vignale, three female heads, a portrait of a young man on the lower shelf beside a female head modelled in delicate style and on the top shelf a fine male portrait. In Case 5 is a female head from

Celle in peperino with large curls bound by a crown of bronze leaves.

Room 30 contains material from the Temple of Diana at Nemi including in Case 4 a fragment of a frieze in gilded bronze hung upside down and a terracotta model of the pediment of the temple. Room 31 has a fine entablature slab, hung upside down on the trellis, from the Temple of Juno Sospita in Civita Lavinia and in Case 1 a large antefix of a Maenad's head with a diadem, earrings and double necklace from the same temple. Room 32 contains material from the Mater Matuta Temple at Satricum. Case 3 has a fictile head of a dead warrior who has a reddish-yellow face and a dull buff helmet, and the head of a warrior with an Attic helmet of checkerboard pattern. In other Cases are votive objects.

Room 33 contains the fabulous treasures of Praeneste, mostly from the 7th century B.C. Barberini and Bernardini tombs. The Barberini Collection, acquired by the State in 1908 can be divided into two main groups, the contents of a large tomb of the orientalizing period and the contents of tombs of 4th–2nd centuries B.C. The Bernardini Tomb, discovered in 1876, corresponds in style and contents with the Regolini-Galassi tomb in the Vatican. The 7th century tombs contained a mixture of gold and silver ornaments, bronzes and ivories by Egyptian, Assyrian and Greek craftsmen. Case 2, top shelf centre, has a large breastplate or fibula from the Barberini Tomb which has feline heads at each corner. The central cylinder supports twelve chimeras and the two external spaces are each ornamented by 25 sphinxes. All the figures except the corner ones are in hammered gold plate ornamented with granulated lines. Case 3 centre has a fine golden clasp and a gilded silver goblet with Egyptian decoration showing Pharaoh in triumph and an Assyrian king's hunt. On the top shelf there is a silver sword sheath and an ivory plaque in low relief shows a boat and oarsmen among lotus plants. On centre shelf (b) is a golden skyphos (drinking cup) surmounted by two sphinxes and a large breastplate in thin gold plate decorated with lions, chimeras and harpies. All these are from the Barberini Tomb. With Case 5 begin the objects from the Bernardini Tomb. On the top shelf left are a strigil with a female-figure handle, a wooden cosmetics box, a quadrangular bronze cista with an acrobat on top as handle and another with a handle of two bearded warriors holding a dead companion. On the middle shelf left is the Mirror of Praeneste with Hercules and two Centaurs and in the centre an Etruscan mirror with the scene of a conversation. On the top shelf middle is a cylindrical cista with handle formed by a pair of winged genii and another with handle formed by two Amazons who support

67. *The Ficorini Cista, c.* 300 B.C.
bronze height 29⅛ in. (74 cm.)

a dead companion. On the bottom shelf is a cista with a handle formed
by Peleus and Atalanta fighting. The crowning masterpiece is the
Ficoroni Cista on the top shelf far right, the largest and most beautiful 67
yet discovered. The lid is decorated with a scene of a boar and stag
hunt and the handle consists of Dionysus between two satyrs. On the
body of the cista is the scene of the boxing match between Pollux and
Amycus, King of the Bebryces. The huge leonine claw feet are typically Etruscan. The names of the maker and the buyer of the cista are
recorded in archaic Latin. It is a work of the end of the 4th century B.C.

Room 34 contains in Case 2 a red-figured Attic krater, signed by
Pampheios showing in the medallion Ulysses escaping from the cave
of the Cyclops; a pair of gold earrings of great richness; a necklace of
three golden chains with three bullae in sheet gold; a rhyton in the
shape of a double-faced herm of Satyr and Maenad and an Etruscan
mirror; all from Todi. There are also a beautiful bronze female head
from Cagli (Case 3) and parts of a small cask with embossed bands
from Gualdo Tadino (Case 4).

The Director is Dr Mario Moretti.

The museum is open on weekdays except Monday from 9 a.m. to
4 p.m.; Sundays and Holidays from 9 a.m. to 1 p.m.

The National Gallery of Modern Art

68 The Palace of Fine Arts, in which the works of Italian painters and sculptors of the 19th and 20th centuries are housed, was built by Cesare Bazzani in 1911 and enlarged by the same architect in 1933. The history of the collection begins with the National Exhibition of Art held in 1883 in a building specially constructed in the Via Nazionale. In addition to purchases, many legacies have enriched the collection.

Behind the Entrance Hall are two large rooms in which general exhibitions, one-man shows or retrospective exhibitions are regularly arranged.

Room I (Corridor) contains 18th century neo-classic works, together with paintings that show the first glimpses of romanticism, as does Room II. *The Temptation of St Anthony* by Giuseppe Bison is an elegant composition. The *Double Portrait* is by Teodoro Matteini, a pupil of Batoni. The portraits of *Cardinal Vicar Count Malvezzi* and *Cardinal Vicar della Somaglia, 1786*, by another pupil of Batoni,

Gaspare Landi, have a lightness of brushwork and, in the case of the first, a witty, even malicious, touch. The three *Landscapes,* executed in encaustic technique, are by an amateur, Marianna Dionigi.

Room II. *Portrait of an Officer of the Papal Guard* is by Vincenzo Camuccini, President of the Academy of St Luke in the early years of the 19th century and a leader of neo-classicism. *Portrait of Vincenzo* 69 *Monti,* the poet, by Andrea Appiani, who was a great favourite of Napoleon and admired by Stendhal, is an elegant and vigorous work. Filippo Agricola's *Portrait of Costanza Perticari,* Monti's daughter, is also excellent. *Still-life* by Vincenzo Podesti is a brilliant study of receding planes of perspective. There are also interesting portraits by Francesco Podesti of Ancona, Adeodata Malatesta from Modena, the Venetians Michelangelo Grigoletti and Natale Schiavone, and Gaetano Forti, all of which show romantic tendencies.

Room III. *Lamb with Rosary,* 1840, by Tommaso Minardi is a pretty piece with a self-satisfied child and an even more self-satisfied lamb. *Portrait of Field-Marshal Prince Alexander Bariatinsky,* 1837, at the age of 20, is by Emile-Jean Horace Vernet, the French military and sporting painter. *View of the Royal Palace in Florence,* 1827, is by Giovanni Migliari, for many years decorator of the Scala Theatre in Milan. Eliseo Sala's *Portrait of a Lady* is a gay work showing her in blue with a lace fichu and grey fur cuffs. There are also portraits by Pier Celestino Gilardi and *Blind Homer with the Shepherd Glaucus* by Tommaso Minardi. The sculpture in this room is of considerable im-

68. The National Gallery of Modern Art

69. Andrea Appiani (1754–1817)
Vincenzo Monti, 1805–10 oil on canvas
$29\frac{1}{2} \times 23\frac{5}{8}$ in. (75×60 cm.)

portance. Two portraits by Pietro Tenerani, a pupil of Thorwaldsen, *Pelligrino Rossi* seated and *Princess Wolkonsky*, are faultless and frigid, yet psychologically penetrating. Lorenzo Bartolini's *Count Guelfo Trotti Estense Mosti* is a sensitive portrait of an aristocratic invalid.

Room IV. The group of four pictures by Domenico Induno indicates his interest in popular narrative art and his well-designed portraits. Of the nineteen pictures by the Neapolitan Giacomo Gigante, *Gulf of Naples, Coast at Sorrento* (watercolour), and *Coast of Ischia* best display his keen sense of observation and his mastery of light effects. *Castel dell'Ovo, Naples* is by Anton van Pitloo who taught and influenced Gigante. A clear morning light illuminates Filippo Palizzi's *View of Valetta, Malta. Landscape* and *Azalea* by Massimo d'Azeglio show him to have been much greater as a writer and politician than as a painter. Giovanni Carnevali, called Il Piccio, was an original artist with a great sense of colour, as can be seen in his fluidly painted *Biblical Scenes.* His *Portrait of a Man Writing* is admirable in pose and expression and has a fine harmony of greens, greys and reds.

Rooms V and VI contain about 150 pictures by Filippo Palizzi. His work could be much better appreciated if there were only fifteen, but the conditions of the bequest make this impossible. *Source of the Molina at Cava,* 1857, *Two White Calves,* 1859, *Small Donkey Facing Front, Friends in the Stable,* 1866 and *Lamb,* 1873, illustrate the freshness and richness of his colours and his simple, idyllic attitude to the countryside.

Room VII. Of the five pictures by Gioacchino Toma *Luisa Sanfelice in Prison* is the most interesting. He was a great constructor of interiors with an architectonic vision and he here depicts a girl who was condemned to death in Naples because of her lover's misdemeanours. She claimed to be pregnant, but this was proved to be untrue and she was executed on September 11, 1800. Federico Rossano's *The Banks of the Seine* is delicately coloured. Michele Cammarano, a Garibaldino as many of these painters were, exhibited in Paris in 1870 and became a friend of Courbet. His *Café in Piazza San Marco, Venice* is a brilliant, impressionistic nocturne in which the red cloak, the cream dress and pale trousers are lit up against a background of shiny blacks and greys. Domenico Morelli, who revolutionized Neapolitan painting, is well represented. His *Embalming of the Body of Christ* is dramatic and vigorous, with a chiaroscuro and contrasting effects of light that recall Caravaggio. His *Portrait of Bernardo Celentano,* the painter, is a fine, quizzical picture of a dandy. Giovanni (Nino) Costa fought in defence of Rome in 1849. In 1860 he went to Florence to meet the 'Macchiaioli' and introduced their techniques to Rome. He was influenced by Corot and was received in 1863 by Lord Leighton in London, where he left a number of pictures. *Women Loading Wood on a Ship at Anzio,* 1852, an early work, decorative and full of.somewhat naïve charm, shows that he was moving in the same direction as the 'Macchiaioli' before he had met them. His tiny *Ripa Grande 1848* is excellent. Edoardo Dalbono's *The Terrace* is accomplished and amusing.

Room VIII contains works of the 'Macchiaioli', a group of artists in sympathy with the French impressionist movement who worked mainly in Florence 1850–1865. They exploited the individual blob of paint. Giovanni Abati's most characteristic work is his *Oxen on the Beach.* Raffaello Sernesi belonged to the second phase of the 'macchia'. He died of wounds at an early age fighting with Garibaldi and therefore had a small output. *Sunlit Roofs* shows his purity of form and gift of portraying diffused light. Odoardo Borrani was particularly successful with small pictures such as *The River Mugnone* with its bright colours and limpid atmospheric effects. Giovanni Fattori has often been regarded as the leader of the movement, but this is not strictly correct, although he is probably the best. Having fought in the rising of 1848–1849 he was a specialist in battles and military subjects, but he is outstanding in pictures like *Portrait of my First Wife,* an intense and austere work, and *Portrait of Patrizio Senese,* a brilliant study in blacks and greens. Silvestro Lega was a revolutionary, a conspirator and a man of action. His *The Visit,* 1868, is beautifully composed in refined colouring, with figures in expressive attitudes in sombre clothes. Adriano Cecioni was the theorist of the group and *Interior with the Figure of a Woman* is remarkable for its fine draughtsmanship. Telemaco Signorini was a writer and a wit as well as an excellent painter. He was the real leader of the 'Macchiaioli' movement. Unfortunately his masterpiece *Madwomen in San Bonifacio* has been removed to Venice. His *Summer Rain at Settignano* and *Houses at Nettuno* are noteworthy. Giovanni Boldini's *Interior with Figure* is very witty. Vito d'Ancona's *Lady with Sunshade* is amusingly portrayed from the back. Sculpture: Adriano Cecioni's *Mother* is a huge and magnificent attempt at realistic jollity; Valmore Gemignani's *Portrait of Giovanni Fattori* is very successful.

Room IX. In the centre is Federico Faruffini's *Virgin of the Nile* which shows how he was caught in the transition from decadent academicism to naturalistic realism. Bernardo Celantano's sketch for *The Council of Ten* is much better than the pretentious original in

Room XI. In the alcove are a number of pictures by Ippolito Caffi who continued in Venice the panoramic tradition. His *Cagliari, 1853,* is particularly good.

Room XI contains huge historical diploma pieces, all remarkably unsuccessful. *The Sicilian Vespers* by Francesco Hayez is the most famous. Trained in the neo-classic style he was later stirred by historical events such as this. He was a fine draughtsman with an excellent sense of formal values and a good portraitist, but this huge canvas is flat, melodramatic and conventional. Bernardo Celentano's *Portrait of a Woman, 1859,* is expressive and richly coloured.

Room XII is devoted to works by Domenico Morelli.

Room XIII. Domenico Morelli's *Portrait of Signora Teresa Oneto* is a grandiose piece, with the lady wearing an ivory satin evening gown seated against a damask background. His *Temptation of St Anthony* is so melodramatic as to be ridiculous.

Room XIV. Federico Podesti's large *Triumph of Venus* is in neo-classical style with marked archaizing tendencies.

Room XV contains a number of enormous canvases including Giovanni Fattori's *Battle of Custoza, 1880,* and Michele Cammarano's *The 24th June at San Martino. The Corpse of Luciano Manaro* by Eleuterio Pagliano is a simple and sincere record of a patriot and soldier who died after a battle in the arms of the painter. Fine brushwork, harmonious and varied colours, together with the vigorous modelling of the figures, make this a considerable achievement.

Room XVI. Antonio Fontanesi of Turin saw an exhibition of Corot in Paris in 1855 which greatly impressed him. He was also influenced by Constable and Gainsborough. A Garibaldino, he taught in Tokyo from 1877 to 1879. His *Diana Bathing* has fine effects of light mirrored in the river. He was particularly fond of country scenes with trees and there are two examples of these, *Women at the Spring* and *At the Fountain. The Pussino Valley* by Vittorio Avondo was painted under the influence of Fontanesi. Giacomo Favretto, a Venetian, specialized in views and portraits. *Awaiting the Newly-married Couple* has pure pictorial values which enable it to transcend genre art. Every particular of the view and the figures has been carefully studied. The colouring is notable for the sombre tones of the standing water of the *rio,* the velvety blacks of the gondola and its cabin, the bright tones of light on the house and the red of the headdresses. *After the Bath* is a simple domestic episode transformed into a brilliant colour study. The immediacy of this work is notable. The three pictures by Tranquillo Cremona are remarkable for their delicate colouring.

70. Giovanni Segantini (1858–1899) *At the Fence,* 1885–86
oil on canvas 66⅞×153⅛ in. (170×389 cm.)

Room XVII is dedicated to the works of the sculptor Medardo
Rosso. Donated by his son the collection covers the period 1881 to
1906. From 1890 to 1910 he enjoyed a European reputation second
only to Rodin, who was considerably influenced by him. Later he sank
into obscurity but is now again recognized as being a great and
original sculptor. His *Bersagliere with his Girl under a Street Lamp,*
1881, is a study in light effects and is richly pictorial. He broke away
from three-dimensional sculpture in favour of rendering plastically his
own impressions of the subject. Works like *Woman Laughing,* 1882,
are realistic but one moves quickly on to the *Veiled Woman,* 1893,
where the forms are almost dissolved in light. In *Ecce Puer,* 1906, the
extreme of dissolution is reached.

Room XVIII. In *Quiet* by Eugenio Gignous a diffused light bathes
the greens and browns of the landscape. Giovanni Segantini was a
'divisionist', a kind of neo-impressionist. He lived in the mountains
and painted Alpine scenes with great brilliance. His *At the Fence* is a 70
long realistic landscape with light from the right falling on cows and
women in the foreground. In the dark background on the left are
snowy mountains. The light effects at a high altitude are remarkably
portrayed. *Dahlias* by Gaetano Previati and two *Views of Capri,* 1868,
by Guglielmo Ciardi are noteworthy.

Room XIX. Mosè Bianchi was fascinated by the lagoons of Venice
as can be seen from his *Canal at Chioggia.* Emilio Gola's *Landscape,*
where a solitary woman blends into the woodland and the stream's
reflected colours, shows his interest in light and mobility in the open
air. The *Upper Biellese,* 1887, by Lorenzo Delleani has been called

'conventional and vulgar', but to others it is the best Italian mountain scene of the century. The cows at pasture in the foreground are finely coloured and a subtly painted mist pervades the top third of the picture except for a crag on the right. There are a number of elegiac paintings of lagoons by Pietro Fragiacomo.

Rooms XX, XXI and XXII have pictures by Bonomi, Previati and Italico Brass, whose *Puppets* is excellent, and (XXII) sculptures by Rodin, *Bust of the Sculptor Dalou* and *The Age of Bronze.*

Room XXIII. Ettore Tito was a painter of genre scenes, portraits, lagoons and Alpine landscapes. He was best at anecdotal pieces such as his overcrowded and fussy, but colourful, *Old Fishmarket.* Luigi Nono's *Refugium Peccatorum* overplays the pathos of a genre scene while *The Heir* by the Neapolitan Teofilo Patini is a precise and realistic picture of utter desolation.

Room XXIV. *Little House at Montmartre* is a good example of the work of Federico Zandomeneghi, who has been called, rather unfairly, 'a Toulouse-Lautrec manqué'. He was actually more influenced by his friend Degas. Three splendid portraits by Giovanni Boldini, *Marchese Casati, Mademoiselle Lanthelme,* 1907, and *Giuseppe Verdi,* 1886, are excellent examples of the bravura technique of this virtuoso painter who spent most of his working life in Paris. The *Verdi* is a pastel in a mixture of greys and blacks that recall Whistler, who 71 influenced him considerably. *Races at the Bois de Boulogne* by Giuseppe de Nittis, who was at first one of the 'Macchiaioli', is a brilliant and intense impressionistic work in pastel on three panels, where the influence of Degas and Renoir is clearly seen. *The Little English Girl* and *Woman on the Beach* are in his earlier manner.

Room XXV has a number of vivid landscapes and seascapes by Gaetano Esposito, Francesco Lo Jacono and Edoardo Dalbono. *The Vow* (and ten studies for the picture) by Francesco Paolo Michetti from the Abruzzi, is in a tragic D'Annunzian style. His *Little Shepherdess* is a harmonious and bucolic picture from his native mountains.

Room XXVI. *Solitude* is by the Sicilian Francesco Lo Jacono. Antonio Mancini travelled as a mountebank until he took up painting in Naples with Michetti as his master. His earlier works *The Little Invalid* and *The Matchseller,* both 1878, have a fine total harmony, but in his late work his exuberant sense of colour runs riot as can be seen in the *Portrait of Lydia.*

Rooms XXVII, XXVIII and XXIX contain pictures by minor artists, but have some good paintings such as the Venetian landscapes by Luigi Serra of Bologna and the vigorous *The Hawser* by Ettore Tito.

71. Giuseppe De Nittis (1846–1884)
central panel from *Races at the Bois
de Boulogne,* 1881 pastel $77\frac{1}{8} \times 75\frac{1}{4}$ in.
(196×191 cm.)

Room XXX is devoted to a 'divisionist' painter Gaetano Previati. His efforts to translate light and shade into colour and so achieve a mystical luminosity of religious intensity are not entirely successful.

Room XXXI has prints and engravings by foreign masters including Hokusai, Gillray, Hogarth, Cruickshank, Rowlandson and Goya.

Room XXXII contains excellent 19th century graphic art from the Luigi Sprovieri collection, mostly by French artists.

Room XXXIII contains interesting realistic paintings by Luigi Levi (Ulvi Liegi); *Old Women,* 1927, by Felice Casorati and a *Portrait of H.R.H. the Duchess of Genoa,* 1904, by the society sculptor Pietro Canonica. Outside in the garden is Emile-Antoine Bourdelle's *Hercules the Archer.*

Room XXXIV contains pictures by foreign painters. Worth notice are: *Irene* by Ignacio Zuloaga, *Portrait of A. Mancini* by John Singer Sargent, *Visit of Condolence* by Christian Krogh, *At the door of the Granary* by Anders Zorn and *Boys Bathing* by Sir Frank Brangwyn.

Room XXXV is devoted to the work of Vincenzo Gemito the Neapolitan sculptor which oscillates between a remembered classicism and a wish to create popular realist art. The best are *Portrait of Anna Gemito* in terracotta, *Small Bust of Charles V, The Little Fisherman* and *The Water Seller.*

The thirty-two rooms which contain the 20th century Italian and foreign painting and sculpture have been closed for re-organization. It is hoped that they will be re-opened sometime in 1968.

The Director is Dr Palma Bucarelli.

The gallery is open on weekdays except Mondays from 9 a.m. to 2 p.m.; Sundays and Holidays from 9.30 a.m. to 1 p.m.

The National Military and Art Museum
Castel Sant'Angelo

72 This museum was inaugurated in 1925 in the Castel Sant'Angelo. The military collections give a survey of the instruments of war from early times to the present day and there are notable examples of antique furniture and tapestries. Some of the paintings and frescoes are of considerable importance.

The castle retains the circular design of Hadrian's Mausoleum begun by him in 135 A.D. and finished in 139 by Antoninus Pius. We enter by the bronze doors in the south side, pass into the Courtyard of the Saviour and proceed to the Entrance Vestibule. In the centre are four models of the castle, the first is an archaeological reconstruction of the Mausoleum, the second shows what remains of the original building, the third and fourth are reproductions of the castle as it was in the times of Alexander VI and Urban VIII. On the right begins the spiral ramp, 148 yards long, which leads to the funerary chamber of Hadrian. The ramp was richly decorated and traces of the mosaic ornamentation remain. Above are four ventilators, one of which was converted into the Sammalo Prison described by Benvenuto Cellini.

At the end of Hadrian's ramp we turn into the Staircase of Alexander VI which cuts diametrically across the circular building, greatly

72. Castel Sant'Angelo

altering the interior of the square base. By way of a bridge built in 1822 by Valadier the staircase passes over the sepulchral cella and brings us to the Courtyard of Honour, known as the Courtyard of the Angel from the marble angel sheathing his sword by Guglielmo della Porta (or Raffaello da Montelupo). On the right of the courtyard are a series of small rooms of which the first (14) is a reconstruction of a guard-room. The next five contain collections of arms and armour, from the Stone Age to the 19th century.

Across the courtyard are the two Halls of Clement VIII which have been closed for two or three years for re-arrangement of the armoury and the historical museum of the castle. The Hall of Justice, where important trials were held, has also been closed for a considerable time. The Hall of Apollo (19) dates from the reign of Paul III and owes its name to the grotesques by Luzio Luzzi of Todi representing mytho-logical episodes. It contains a fine marble fireplace and rare Renais-sance arms and armour which are clearly labelled. Particularly worthy of notice are two Lansquenet swords, used during the sack of Rome, 1527, and found during excavations of the castle, and a rare pair of 18th century pistols, chiselled in gold and silver and bearing the signature of the famous Neapolitan goldsmith Michele Battista. A door on the right leads into the Chapel of Leo X. On the altar is a *Madonna and Child* by Raffaello da Montelupo and at the side a small and delicately painted triptych by Andrea da Velletri. At the time of writing the Rooms of Clement VII are closed for restoration.

A passage on the right leads into the Courtyard of the Well, named after the beautiful marble wellhead with the Borgia arms on the left. A small staircase leads to the Bathroom of Clement VII (27) decorated with grotesques in the Pompeian style by Giulio Romano. On the right side of the courtyard, at a lower level, are a series of cells known as the Historical Prisons (30) where, according to popular belief, Giordano Bruno, Cardinal Carafa, Lucrezia Patroni and Beatrice Cenci were confined. On the wall of the last cell is a charcoal drawing of Christ, possibly executed by Benvenuto Cellini during his imprisonment there. Further on, at the same level, are two large underground oil stores and five grain silos.

We return to the courtyard and take the staircase (33) to the Loggia of Paul III, built by Antonio da Sangallo the Younger in 1543, and the semi-circular Gallery of Pius IV from both of which there are splendid views of Rome. On the right are a number of rooms once used by courtesans and later turned into political prison cells. The first room (36) is a reconstruction of a political prison of the time of Gregory

XVI and the others contain uniforms, decorations and medals, chiefly from the various Italian states into which Italy was formerly divided. From the attractive vestibule by Antonio da Sangallo we reach the Loggia of Julius II, an elegant construction by Bramante, 1505, which has a fine view of the Ponte Sant'Angelo. A staircase leads to the Papal Apartments.

The Pauline Hall or Hall of the Council is covered with brilliant polychromatic decorations by Perin del Vaga and his twenty-eight assistants, among whom was Domenico Beccafumi. The grotesques are by Giovanni da Udine and the huge figures of the Archangel Michael and the Emperor Hadrian by Pellegrino Tibaldi, one of the leading Mannerists of the late 16th century. The chiaroscuri are by Polidoro da Caravaggio and the fine stuccoes by Girolamo da Sermoneta and Baccio (or Raffaello) da Montelupo. The beautiful marble floor contains the coat-of-arms of Innocent XIII who restored the room.

The Perseus Room derives its name from the frieze by Perin del Vaga and assistants. Perseus is again to be seen on the richly ornamented ceiling, intaglio work of the 16th century. The furniture forms part of the donation of the Contini-Bonacossi family. In the right-hand corner is a *Statuette of a Saint* attributed to Jacopo della Quercia. From the left, there is a polyptych of *Madonna and Child Enthroned with Saints, c.* 1475, by the Zavattari brothers, a *Madonna* of the 14th century Florentine school, a Brussels tapestry with an episode from the life of Julius Caesar and a plaster cast of a *Bust of Paul III* by Guglielmo della Porta. At the back is a good *Madonna Between SS. Roch and Sebastian* attributed to Lorenzo Lotto.

The Room of Cupid and Psyche is so called from the frieze by Perin de Vaga illustrating in seventeen episodes the story from the *Golden Ass* of Apuleius. The ceiling of carved and gilded wooden squares and the large Farnese bed, complete with canopy and bed-linen of needlepoint lace, are fine examples of 16th century work. The excellent *Madonna* by Bartolomeo Montagna is in poor condition owing to constant restoration. The two panels *The Redeemer* and a grimacing *St Onuphrius, c.* 1493, are late works of Carlo Crivelli, in a good state 73 of preservation. *St Jerome, c.* 1508, by Lorenzo Lotto lacks the lyric impulse of his Louvre painting of the saint, but it is a fine picture and has a minutely observed landscape. *Christ Carrying the Cross* is by Paris Bordone and *Silenus Teaching Bacchus* in the manner of Jacob Jordaens.

Returning to the Pauline Hall and passing through the Pompeian

73. Lorenzo Lotto (*c.*1480–1556)
*St Jerome, c.*1508 oil on panel
31½ × 28 in. (80 × 71 cm.)

Corridor, decorated with grotesques by Luzio Luzzi, we arrive at The Library where the ceiling is richly decorated with frescoes by Luzio Luzzi and stuccoes by Girolamo Sicciolante da Sermoneta. The marble chimneypiece is by Raffaello da Montelupo and there is some good 15th century furniture.

At the time of writing the Adrianeo Room and the Room of the Festoons, which contain good pictures, frescoes and furniture are closed for restoration, as are the Cagliostro Room, the small Dolphin and Salamander Room and the Room of the Stork.

Returning to the Library we pass into the circular Treasure Chamber which contained also the secret archives of the Popes, housed in the Renaissance walnut cupboards that line the walls. In the centre of the room are three 14th century treasure chests.

A short Roman staircase leads to the Round Hall and the Hall of the Columns. At the top of the staircase is the Terrace, the setting of the last act of Puccini's *Tosca.* Dominating everything is the huge bronze angel sheathing his sword, 1753, by Peter van Verschaffelt.

On the way back to the entrance there are a number of rooms and passages of small interest. On the left of the Courtyard of the Saviour is the Antiquarium (74–76) containing architectural and sculptural fragments found in the castle.

The Director is Major-General Proto Cadoni.

The Castel is open on weekdays except Monday from 9.30 a.m. to 4 p.m.; Sundays and Holidays from 9 a.m. to 1.30 p.m.

The Vatican Museums and Galleries

The great collections of art accumulated by Popes, Cardinals and others are housed in the Vatican Palace which covers an area of thirteen-and-a-half acres, excluding the gardens. The halls, rooms, galleries and chapels number altogether around 14,000. The huge complex of buildings was begun in the 14th century and is still being enlarged.

The entrance hall, in the Viale Vaticano, leads to a Double Staircase by G. Momo with a bronze balustrade by A. Maraini. This staircase has two spiral ramps, one for going up and the other for coming down. There is also a lift. The Ambulatory at the top of the staircase has a post office where postcards and Vatican stamps are sold. Passing through the turnstiles and proceeding up the steps we reach a semicircular hall with mosaics from Hadrian's Villa. On the left of the open courtyard is the entrance known as the *Quattro Cancelli* (Four Gates) which gives access to the museums. In front a passage-way leads to the Picture Gallery.

I The Vatican Picture Gallery

The Picture Gallery (Pinacoteca Vaticana) owes its origin to Pius VI who formed a collection of pictures assembled from the various museums and from the library. In accordance with the Treaty of Tolentino, 1797, the Pope was forced by Napoleon to surrender the best works to France, the pictures alone numbering one hundred. At the instigation of the Congress of Vienna, Antonio Canova and Gaetano Martini were sent off to Paris as Pontifical Commissioners and by 1816 succeeded in recovering 77 pictures. These were placed by Pius VII in the Borgia Rooms which thus became the first premises of the Picture Gallery. After many transferences and vicissitudes the collection was housed in the present building, built in Lombard Renaissance style by Luca Beltrami, which was opened in 1932 by Pius XI. The original collection has been augmented by 270 paintings from the old Pinacoteca and 183 from the storehouses, the Sacristy of St Peter's, the Vatican apartments and the Papal Palace at Castel Gandolfo. From

1960 onwards a collection of contemporary artists has been formed.

Room I. The pictures are not arranged in correct numerical order. They are mostly on wood and are Byzantine or derive from that school. From the left, *St Francis and Four Episodes in his Life* (23) belongs to the School of Giunta Pisano and can probably be dated around the middle of the 13th century. *The Twelve Feasts of the Church* (24), of the Cretan School, portray six festivals in lively narrative and vivacious colour. Vitale di Bologna's *Madonna and Child* (17) signed by the painter, is a delicate and serene, but much repainted work of the 14th century on a gilded Gothic background. *Madonna and Child with SS Onuphrius, Nicolas of Bari, Bartholomew and John the Evangelist* (9), a fine polyptych by the Florentine Giovanni Bonsi, is signed and dated 1371. *St Francis of Assisi* (2) is a crude but vigorous portrait by a contemporary, Margheritone d'Arezzo. The important *Last Judgment* (526) by Johannes and Nicolaus, a large signed altarpiece of the Roman Benedictine School, is dated towards the end of the 11th century. The unusual round shape is divided into zones separated by bands with inscriptions in Leonine verse. In the predella, paradise is seen on the left as a city of jewelled walls. Between the windows is a gay gilded panel of *Madonna and Child with Saints in Adoration* (13–15) by the 14th century Florentine painter Giovanni del Biondo. The *Madonna and Child* (2139) by Sassetta is a little masterpiece of linear design by this exquisite Sienese painter. In the centre of the room is the cope of Boniface VIII, a fine example of 13th century *opus Anglicanum* embroidery.

Room II. In the centre is the puzzling *Stefaneschi Triptych* painted, it is said, by Giotto and his assistants at the request of Cardinal Jacopo Caetani Stefaneschi for the jubilee proclaimed by Boniface VIII in the year 1300 and intended for the *confessio* of Old St Peter's. The panels are painted on both sides, as is the predella. In the central panel Christ is enthroned, surrounded by angels, with the donor, Cardinal Stefaneschi, kneeling at His feet. The martyrdom of St Peter is on the left and that of St Paul on the right. On the back St Peter is represented on a Cosmatesque throne, while Stefaneschi, kneeling on the left, holds up a miniature reproduction of the triptych and a bishop, on the right, holds out a book. Part of the predella has been lost. Some authorities date this work as late as 1330 and ascribe it wholly to Giotto's workshop, possibly with the assistance of Taddeo Gaddi. Nos. 124–132 form a group by the Sienese Giovanni di Paolo, of which the delicate *Annunciation* dated 1445 and a charming, almost surrealist, *Nativity* 74 are outstanding. The panels 147–50 and 158–161 of the *Story of St*

74. (left) Giovanni di Paolo (14th and 15th century) *Annunciation,* 1445
oil on panel height 26 in. (66 cm.)
75. (right) Fra Angelico (*c.*1387 or ? *c.*1400–1455) *Virgin Between St Dominic and St Catherine of Alexandria* oil on panel 9 × 7⅛ in. (23 × 18 cm.)

Stephen are by Ambrogio Lorenzetti (or possibly Bernardo Daddi) and are remarkable for their chromatic harmony. Simone Martini, in his refined *Redeemer in the Act of Blessing* (165) is still influenced by the Greek Byzantine style. Bernardo Daddi's *Madonna of the Magnificat* (174) is a magnificent piece of 14th century stylization. Lorenzo Monaco in *The Acts of Charity* (196–201) shows a fresh charm and sensitive colouring.

Room III. Fra Filippo Lippi's *Coronation of the Madonna* displays his pure line and fondness for subtle combinations of colours. Much finer is Fra Angelico's *The Virgin Between St Dominic and St Catherine of Alexandria,* where his delicate miniaturism, light colours, powerful modelling and refinement of design, worked out according to a rigorous perspective, demonstrate his profound skill and his joyful religious faith. The predella with *Stories of St Nicholas* is remarkable for the strange, twisted rocks which go back to Hellenistic painting. There is, on the left, a similar series of *Miracles of St Nicholas* (247–50), *c.* 1425, by Gentile da Fabriano. This splendid painter from the Marches,

a master of the courtly International Gothic style, can produce start-
ling dramatic effects as in the shipwreck episode, where a mermaid
seems to be swimming away from under the ship. Benozzo Gozzoli's
Madonna of the Girdle (262) represents the Virgin in the act of
bestowing the girdle on St Thomas. Like Gentile da Fabriano, this
ornamental painter is a master of narrative, though his work is transi-
tional between the Gothic and Renaissance styles. The figures in the
predella, grouped in shining buildings or luminous landscapes, are
harmonious and elegant.

Room IV is notable for frescoes by Melozzo da Forlì of angel-
musicians, in bold foreshortening, with upturned glowing faces. These
come from the great fresco of the Ascension from the Basilica of SS.
Apostoli. Sadly little is left of the work of this fresh and vigorous painter who was so highly thought of by his 15th century contemporaries.
His masterpiece is the fresco (transferred to canvas) showing *Sixtus*   VII
IV Nominating Platina Prefect of the Vatican Library. The Pope is seen
conferring the post of Librarian on the humanist Bartolomeo Platina,
in the presence of Cardinal Giuliano della Rovere (afterwards Julius
II), his brother Giovanni and Girolamo and Raffaele Riario. Here a
recession of pillars and arches creates a space for the protagonists.
The powerful portraits are vigorously painted and the figures carefully
posed and modelled. The colours have a profundity and intensity of
tone which enable the figures to stand out against the sumptuous
architectural background, masterly for its spatial organization. There
are also two pictures by Melozzo's pupil Marco Palmezzano. The
great tapestry, the earliest copy of Leonardo da Vinci's *Last Supper,*
was woven in Brussels for Francis I of France and given to Clement
VII in 1533.

Room V. Francesco Cossa's *Miracles of St Vincent Ferrer* (286),
painted 1474, was the predella of a huge altarpiece intended for the
Griffoni chapel in San Petronio, Bologna. The central piece is in the
National Gallery, London and the lateral pieces in the Brera, Milan.
This pupil of Cosmè Tura had great gifts of monumental composition
and his figures are modelled with the strength of a sculptor. The colours achieve an effect of enamel and precious stones and the diffused
light reveals Cossa's debt to Piero della Francesca. Also in this room
are a harsh *Pietà* by Lucas Cranach and a *Madonna Venerated by the
Auditors of the Rota* by Antoniazzo Romano, a follower of Melozzo,
who set up a school in Rome.

Room VI. This contains altarpieces and polyptychs of the 15th
century. Carlo Crivelli's *Madonna and Child* (297) is a typically

elaborate and luxuriant work, with the appearance of coloured marble, signed Venice 1482. The *Pietà* (300) is over-dramatic and the expressions of the mourners are too contorted and agonized. His style is harsh and linear, because of northern influences, but he is usually saved by his genius for decoration and his strong visual imagery. His brother Vittore Crivelli worked in a similar but less intense manner, as can be seen from the *Madonna and Saints* dated 1481. Carlo's follower Niccolò l'Alunno carried his master's tendency to exaggerate agony to an almost comic extent, as is evident in his enormous *Crucifixion* (299). Antonio Vivarini, in contrast, seems staid and archaic. The elaborate Gothic frame, however, enhances the elegant modulations of colour in his *St Anthony Abbot and Other Saints* signed and dated 1469. The Abbot is carved in high relief and the other saints are in gilded niches

Room VII has good examples of the Umbrian school of the 15th century. Pinturicchio's *Coronation of the Virgin* (312) is a grand composition by this gay and decorative painter. There are gold metal studs with a large central boss in the oval bordered by angels, which contrast with the more sober scene below and the rural landscape. Lo Spagna's *Adoration of the Magi* (316) is a dignified and modest work of this little-known Spaniard, which is notable for finesse of modelling and charming grouping of the figures. It is known as the 'Madonna della Spineta' because it comes from the Convent of the Riformati della Spineta, near Todi. *The Virgin Enthroned with Saints* by Perugino, known as 'The Altarpiece of the Decemviri', a latish work of 1495, is well-composed with strong, warm colours, precise drawing and graceful modelling, but the drooping postures of the saints suggest a failing of vigour and inventiveness. In the three little pictures (from a predella) of *St Benedict, St Flavia* and *St Placidus*, the green, blue and red of St Flavia's garments make a pleasant contrast to the dark tones of the other saints. Perugino's *Resurrection*, painted in 1502, has two figures of sleeping soliders which may be the work of his pupil Raphael.

Room VIII, the main hall of the Gallery, is devoted to Raphael. *The Coronation of the Blessed Virgin* was commissioned in 1503 by Maddalena degli Oddi for the family chapel in the church of S. Francesco at Perugia. At twenty Raphael was a master of the traditional Perugine styles and in this composition he attempts greater things. He was unable to handle satisfactorily the division of the picture into two parts by a band of cloud, but the naturalness of the figures and the variety of expression on the faces of the onlookers show that he had already

76. Raphael (1483–1520)
The Madonna of Foligno, 1512
oil on panel transferred to canvas
126×76⅜ in. (320×194 cm.)

outstripped his master Perugino. *The Madonna of Foligno* was paint- 76
ed in 1512 for the high altar of Santa Maria in Aracoeli. It was commissioned by Sigismondo de'Conti (the incisively painted kneeling
figure in red) after a thunderbolt had fallen on his house at Foligno
and left it miraculously undamaged. Here the cloud does not break the
continuity of the picture: the richly-modelled Madonna sits on it, holding her child, with perfect naturalness. In the foreground a delightful
child-angel holds a slab which probably contains the vow of the
donor. On the right St Jerome brings forward Sigismondo while on
the left St Francis kneels in adoration and the Baptist in his customary
brown smock points to the Virgin who sits in front of a sun-like sphere
surrounded by cherubs peeping out from the clouds. In the background is a feathery, vibrant view of Foligno, illuminated by a rainbow
which encircles the flaming thunderbolt. The predella in chiaroscuro,
depicting the three theological virtues, belongs to the *Entombment* in
the Borghese Gallery. *The Transfiguration* is at once a great masterpiece and a problem. Christ, Moses and Elijah appear floating in glory

above the hill. By means of an ingenious use of light and shade, the three figures dressed in white have an opalescent glow. Raphael was very slow in the execution of this picture, which had been ordered in 1516–1517 by Cardinal Giulio de'Medici for the Cathedral in Narbonne. He tried to finish the face of Christ on his deathbed and the masterpiece was carried over his coffin at his funeral in 1520. The picture is divided into two parts owing to the fact that Raphael portrayed under the Transfiguration a scene which follows immediately after in the bible text, that is, the healing of a youth possessed of a devil. On the hill a symbolic, visionary event is taking place; below there is a crowded, noisy human scene. It is known that Giulio Romano was paid for this picture in 1526. Raphael's responsibility for its design has never been questioned and he quite certainly painted the head of the apostle Andrew, but it appears that the upper part of the picture was finished by Giovan Francesco Penni and the lower part, including the landscape, by Giulio Romano. The tapestries around the walls, ordered by Leo X in 1515, were woven in Brussels by Pieter van Aelst and portray ten scenes from the *Acts of the Apostles.* The cartoons for seven of them are in the hall of the Victoria and Albert Museum, London, which is curiously enough almost exactly the same size as the Sistine Chapel for which they were intended and where the tapestries were first hung in 1519. They have borders of grotesque ornamentation by Giovanni da Udine. The subjects are: (A) *Blinding of Elymas,* (B) *Conversion of St Paul,* (C) *Stoning of St Stephen,* (D) *St Peter Healing the Lame Man,* (E) *Death of Ananias,* (F) *Delivery of the Keys,* (G) *Miraculous Draught of Fishes,* (H) *St Paul Preaching at Athens,* (I) *The Sacrifice of Lystra,* (L) *St Paul in Prison.* The most famous is *The Miraculous Draught of Fishes.* Peter and Andrew, in a flat-bottomed boat filled with fish are worshipping Christ. In a second boat the athletic sons of Zebedee strain their bodies, in splendid foreshortening, to draw in the net. In the foreground is a group of screaming herons and in the distance on the left a lovely township. The cartoons for these tapestries were executed in sized watercolours when Raphael was at the height of his powers and are most eminent examples of what is called The Grand Manner.

77   Room IX. Leonardo da Vinci's *St Jerome, c.* 1482, a monochrome of brown on brown, is unfinished, but the intelligence in the saint's sunken eyes, the anguished vigour of his ascetic body and his grand gesture make the painting important. Lorenzo di Credi's *Madonna and Child* has hard outlines but its primary colours are attractive. The *Pietà*

77. Leonardo da Vinci (1452–1519)
*St Jerome, c.*1482 oil on panel
40½×29½ in. (102×749 cm.)

by Giovanni Bellini was painted about 1478 as part of the great altarpiece intended for the Church of S. Francesco in Pesaro. The drawing
is still hard, in the style of Mantegna, but the colours blend enchant-
ingly and anticipate the great colour-symphonies of his pupil Titian.
    Room X. Titian's altarpiece of the *Madonna di S. Niccolò dei Frari,*
painted about 1528 for the Venetian church, is sadly damaged and
has been much repainted in the upper part. The lower part, showing
the saints is, however, masterly. The splendid chasuble of St Nicholas
and the various shades of greens and gold, combined with a dynamic
use of space, give the picture a monumental air. The pictures by
Veronese, an *Allegory* (346) high on the wall and *St Helena* (352)
are worth noting. The saint is portrayed in a richly-brocaded dress and
rose velvet mantle. Sebastiano del Piombo's *St Bernard Victorious
over a Demon* (350) is grim and sombre, but not dull. In great contrast
is Paris Bordone's lively and colourful *St George and the Dragon* (354).
Garofalo's *Virgin and Sibyl Appearing to Augustus* (355) is well composed and coloured and has some good portraits. *The Coronation of
the Madonna with Saints* (359) was commissioned by the nuns of
Monteluce near Perugia in 1505. But Raphael kept delaying the
execution of the order and it was eventually painted after his death,
in accordance with his designs, by Giulio Romano (upper part) and
Giovan Francesco Penni (lower part). This large, rather gaudy, work

is similar in composition to the *Coronation* in Room VIII, both being divided into two halves by a cloud.

Room XI. Giorgio Vasari's *The Stoning of St Stephen* (363) is a bombastic piece of mannerist nonsense. Annibale Carracci's *Holy Trinity with the Dead Christ* (1249) is somewhat disorderly in construction; the colours are sombre but the figures finely executed. *The Annunciation* (365) by the Cavalier d'Arpino, dated 1606, is typically simpering and mannered. Girolamo Muziano of Brescia's *Resurrection of Lazarus* (368) is a large diploma piece which made him famous because it was praised by Michelangelo. Much more attractive is the lively and homely triptych of the *Assumption and Saints* (372) by Cola dell'Amatrice, a painter from the Abruzzi, which is signed and dated 1515. The five paintings by Federico Barocci are of interest, particularly the graceful *Madonna of the Cherries* (377), and the tempestuous *Blessed Michelina* (378), as examples of Counter-Reformation art. Fra Bartolomeo della Porta and Raphael collaborate in *St Peter* (356) and *St Paul* (362), an unusual combination.

Room XII. *The Martyrdom of St Processus and St Martinianus* (381) by Jean de Boulogne, called Il Valentin, a devoted follower of Caravaggio, is confused by excessive detail. Andrea Sacchi's *Vision of St Romuald* (382), *c.* 1638, is his masterpiece. Using a variety of white tones, this leader of the new Bolognese classicism presents the saint under the shadow of a magnificent tree, recounting his dream of the ladder leading to heaven to a group of Camaldolese monks, whose expressive faces deserve close study. Of the Guercino pictures in this room *Doubting Thomas* (383) and *Magdalene with Angels* (391) are finely-balanced works both in colour and composition. Domenichino's *Last Communion of St Jerome* (384) shows admirable composition, dramatic poignancy and unexpectedly refined colours. It is signed and dated 1614. *The Denial of St Peter* (385) by an unknown, possibly Dutch, follower of Caravaggio, is luminous and expressive. The most important picture in the room is Caravaggio's *Deposition,* 1602–1604, commissioned by Francesco Vittrice for the family chapel in the Chiesa Nuova, a stupendous, almost classical work, illuminated from above and full of action. The movement is diagonal, the corner of the grave-stone emphasizing the effect, the figures are rendered with intense feeling, the emphatic gesture of Maria de Cleofa contrasting with the heavy Michelangesque body of Christ, and the colours are well harmonized. The three pictures by Guido Reni are excellent examples of his work. *The Crucifixion of St Peter* (387) is a carefully built-up composition with lighting reminiscent of Caravaggio; *The Virgin in*

Glory with St Thomas and St Jerome (389) is more typical of himself; but it is *St Matthew* (395), with its fine draughtsmanship and almost Venetian sensibility of colour that captures the attention.

Room XIII. Sassoferrata's *Madonna and Child* (396) is archaic in style and colouring and is completely dwarfed by Carlo Maratta's huge ten-foot canvas (397) on the same subject. The latter is a model for the mosaic in the Quirinal courtyard. Orazio Gentileschi, an intelligent follower of Caravaggio who died in London, is represented by *Judith* (1059) where the play of light produces translucent effects on the richly-coloured costumes. Anthony van Dyck's sentimental picture of *St Francis Xavier* was painted about 1621–1623 during a visit to Rome. Of the three pictures by Pier Francesco Mola of Canton Ticino, the *Vision of St Bruno* (1931) has a striking dramatic quality. Pietro da Cortona's *Madonna Appearing to St Francis* is a good example of the work of this great decorator. Jusepe Ribera's powerful *Martyrdom of St Laurence* (judged by some to be by his Dutch pupil Hendrik Somer) is thickly painted in dark colours, while Pompeo Batoni, in his *Madonna Appearing to St John Nepomuc* (415) has kept the baroque form but livened it with 18th century grace.

Room XIV. A miscellaneous collection of which the paintings of flowers framing sacred pictures by the Dutch Jesuit Daniel Seghers are the most interesting. Pietro da Cortona's jolly *Satyr Tamed by Cupid* (748) has a wide romantic landscape and Donato Creti's *Astronomical Observations* (432–39) show the interest aroused in the early 18th century by scientific discoveries. Room XV is devoted to portraits. Titian's early *Doge Niccolò Marcello* is a finely-coloured free copy of a picture by Gentile Bellini. The court portrait of *George* 78 *IV* by Sir Thomas Lawrence is a glittering, elegant and sumptuous piece of adulation. It was given to Pius VII by the English King. Carlo Maratta's splendid portrait of *Clement IX* (460), signed and dated 79 1669, is in a very different style. The lucid, fluent brushwork and the penetrating psychology bring out the sensitive hands and searching glance of the Rospigliosi pope. It rivals, perhaps surpasses, the portrait of Clement IX by G. B. Gaulli (Il Bacciccia) in the Corsini Gallery. 10 It is interesting to recall that by 1680 Maratta was regarded as the greatest painter of the age. In a different style again is the portrait of *Benedict XIV* (458) by the Bolognese Giuseppe Maria Crespi, who cleverly catches, against a grandiose background, the witty spirit which lights up the somewhat pudgy features of the Lambertini pope.

Room XVI contains 19th century painting and sculpture of which *St Mark's, Venice* (3358) by Ippolito Caffi from Belluno, who cleverly

78. (left) Sir Thomas Lawrence (1769–1830) *George IV*
oil on canvas 115×80¼ in. (292×204 cm.)
79. (right) Carlo Maratta (1625–1713) *Clement IX*, 1669
oil on canvas

continued the panoramic tradition of Canaletto and Guardi, is the most interesting.

Room XVII is notable for the Bergamesque sculptor Giacomo Manzù's miniature study of *John XXIII* (3345), and for a bronze *Thinker* by Rodin. Félix Edouard Vallaton, a Swiss painter from Lausanne, combines in his *Lunch on the Grass* (3391) intimate realism with a disciplined sense of form and fresh colouring.

Room XVIII is devoted to contemporary art. There is a good piece of sculpture by Ossip Zadkine, *Man with Guitar* (3451), also landscapes by Mario Sironi, Ardengo Soffici, Ottone Rosai and No. 3362, Carlo Carrà's *La Darsena at Venice*, 1938. No. 3363 is a good *Still-life*, 1951, by Filippo De Pisis and there is an even better one, 1957, of jugs and pots against a pale blue background by the Bolognese Giorgio Morandi. Maurice Utrillo is well represented by his *Church of St Ausonne, Angoulême* (3368) and Giorgio De Chirico, in his later manner, shows us (3371) *Milan Cathedral from the Rooftops*, 1932.

II The Museums of Antiquities

These contain the largest collections of antique sculpture in the world and they will soon be increased by the Lateran collections for which a new building is now being constructed. The contents were originally assembled by the Renaissance popes, in particular Julius II. In succeeding years many of the exhibits were dispersed, but were reassembled and strengthened by the popes of the late 18th century and 19th century, particularly Clement XIV, Pius VI, Pius VII and Gregory XVI.

A The Egyptian Museum

At the time of writing this museum, which occupies rooms in the lower floor of the Belvedere Pavilion, is closed for re-organization and no definite date can be given for its re-opening.

B The Pio-Clementine Museum

This is approached through the Hall of the Greek Cross at the top of the Simonetti Staircase. In the floor of the Hall, between two granite sphinxes, is a coloured Mosaic representing a Basket of Flowers, 2nd century A.D., in the middle another, a shield with the head of Minerva and the Phases of the Moon, 3rd century A.D. *Sarcophagus* (566) of Constantia, daughter of Constantine, is in porphyry with figures from Christian symbolism: children bearing grapes, peacocks and a ram. *Sarcophagus* (589) also in porphyry, is that of St Helena, mother of Constantine. It is decorated in high relief with Roman horsemen in triumphal procession, barbarian prisoners and fallen soldiers. At the head of the cavalry there is a figure, possibly the Emperor himself, trampling on a dead enemy.

The Circular Hall is covered by a cupola imitating that of the Pantheon. In the floor is the great polychrome Mosaic of Otricoli, divided into sections, representing a battle between Greeks and Centaurs and groups of Tritons and Nereids. In the centre is an enormous porphyry bowl found in the Golden House of Nero. From the right: *Jupiter of Otricoli* (539) is a colossal head of serene beauty, a copy of an original attributed to Bryaxis, 4th century B.C. *Female Divinity* (542), perhaps Demeter, is copied from a Greek original of the late 5th century B.C. The curves of her body contrast with the vertical folds of the heavy peplos. *Hercules* (544), a colossal statue in gilded bronze standing about 11 feet 9 inches high, found in the ruins of the Theatre of Pompey, is an early imperial replica of a Greek original in the style of Scopas. *Juno* (546), the so-called Barberini

Hera, is a Roman copy of an original of the 5th century B.C. by Agora-critus. The arms are restored. *Seated Statue* (548) of an emperor, pos-sibly Galba or Nerva, is a work of the 1st century A.D. *Juno Sospita* (552) is from Lanuvium, Roman work of the 2nd century A.D. with Italic elements.

The Hall of the Muses with a ceiling decorated with frescoes by Sebastiano Conca, is an octagon with a vestibule at either end. First Vestibule contains a *Herm of Pericles* (525), replica of a 5th century B.C. original by Cresilas. The general is in a Corinthian helmet which emphasizes his pear-shaped head. The Octagon is a magnificent room with sixteen columns of Carrara marble. Around the walls are the statues of the *Nine Muses* and *Apollo*, found near Tivoli and sup-posedly copies of bronze originals of the 3rd century B.C. From the right, *Apollo Musagetes* (516) in a long robe and carrying a cither decorated with the flaying of Marsyas, is an impressive figure. The Muses alternate with herms of poets, philosophers, the Seven Sages and other personages, some of which were found together with the muses. *Antisthenes* is a fine baroque portrait, from the middle Hel-lenistic period, of the founder of the Cynic school. Second Vestibule contains a *Relief* (489) of a Pyrrhic dance, a neo-attic copy of an Attic work of the 4th century B.C.

The Hall of the Animals was organized by Pius VI to contain animal statues, for the most part by the 18th century sculptor F. A. Franzoni. Some are from antique fragments, others are entirely Franzoni's own work. On the floor are three Mosaics of the 2nd century A.D.: *Falcon Devouring a Hare* with ornamentation of marsh birds in black and white and two framed polychrome *Still-lifes*. In the section on the right is a *Sow* (10) with a litter of twelve, Roman work, perhaps of the Augustan period. The colossal *Head of a Camel* (25) is a fountain-head, copy of a Hellenistic original of the 2nd century B.C. *Statue of Meleager* (40) with his dog and the head of a boar is a replica of an original by Scopas of the 4th century B.C. The finely-proportioned figure stands in an attitude of classical repose. The much-restored *Triton Abducting a Nereid* (62), with cupids, is an exquisite, almost rococo, example of late Hellenistic work. The so-called triton is really a marine centaur. In the section on the left is a group of *Mithras Slay-ing the Bull* (150) of the 2nd century A.D. On the wall behind are two coloured *Mosaics* (138, 152) depicting *Bull Attacked by a Lion* and *Landscape with Goats*. The first is a lively and dramatic scene, the second peaceful and pastoral. Both are set in rugged landscapes.

The Gallery of Statues penetrates into and forms part of the Belve-

80. (left) *Apollo Sauroctonos;* Roman copy, ?1st century B.C. marble
81. (right) *Cnidian Venus;* Roman copy, ?1st century B.C. marble

dere Pavilion, built by Innocent VIII in 1487. From the right: *Eros of Centocelle* (250) also known as the Genius of the Vatican, is probably a statue of Thanatos, the god of death, from an original bronze of the 4th century B.C., possibly by Cephisodotus. *Bust of a Triton* (253), a copy of a Hellenistic original of the 2nd century B.C., has an affinity with the Pergamene school. *Apollo Sauroctonos* (264) is an elegant 80 copy of the celebrated bronze by Praxiteles, depicting the god contemplating a lizard which he is about to kill with a dart. *Amazon* (265) from the Villa Mattei is possibly a copy of one of the Amazons of Ephesus by Phidias, the head being a copy of one by Cresilas. It is badly restored and the figure probably leant on a lance. *Poseidippus* (271) and (?) *Menander* (390), comic poets, form a pair, copies of originals of 3rd century B.C. *Apollo Citharoedus* (395) is probably a copy of a Peloponnesian original of the beginning of the 5th century B.C. *Resting Satyr* (406) is one of a number of copies of an original by Praxiteles. The *Barberini Candelabra* (412, 413) from Hadrian's Villa, are exceptionally fine Roman work in neo-Attic style of the 2nd century A.D. In low relief on the right are Mars, Minerva and Venus and, on the left, Jupiter, Juno and Mercury. *Sleeping Ariadne* (414) is a reconstructed cast of a Hellenistic original, *c.* 240 B.C. The rock on which the figure rests is wrongly restored, making the head too high. The composition is based on a spiral movement which undulates from the feet and crossed legs to the beautiful curve of the right arm.

The Gallery of Busts is divided into three small rooms. Room 1. From the right: *Caracalla* (292), *Head of Octavian* (273) as a boy, *Julius Caesar* (3) and a *Portrait Group* (388) of (?) Cato and Porcia, probably from a tomb of the 1st century B.C., are of interest. In the middle, left, is a *Column* (389) of the Augustan era, with three dancing Hours, found near the Ara Pacis. Room 3. In a niche is a seated statue of *Zeus* (326) called Jupiter Verospi, a copy of a Hellenistic original. The lower part is a restoration.

Opposite the entrance to the Gallery of Busts, to the right is the Mask Room, square with columns of oriental alabaster reconstructed from fragments, according to the orders of Pius VI. On the floor are four small polychrome mosaics from Hadrian's Villa dating from the 2nd century A.D. Three depict theatrical masks and one a landscape. On the end wall is an important copy, restored with a head from an-
81 other statue, of the *Cnidian Venus* (474) by Praxiteles, executed about 340 B.C. Her lips are parted in a gentle smile and she stands in a graceful pose, one hand in front of her making the so-called 'gesture of modesty' and the other holding her draperies, which rest on a hydria (pitcher), indicating that she is about to take a bath. The *Three Graces* (433) may perhaps be a Hellenistic original of the 2nd century B.C.

We now return to the Hall of the Animals and enter the Octagonal Courtyard of the Belvedere, which was constructed by Giacomo da Pietrasanti from designs by Bramante. Here Julius II placed his classical collection. The Courtyard was rebuilt in its present form by Michelangelo Simonetti in 1773. Flanking the doorway are two *Molossian Hounds*, of the school of Pergamum.
82   On the right is the Cabinet of Laocoön. Laocoön, a Trojan priest of Apollo, and his two sons are seen in the coils of two serpents sent by the god to crush him. The group illustrates an episode in Virgil's *Aeneid*, Book II, and was discovered in 1506 on the site of Nero's Golden House on the Colle Oppio. It was at once identified as a sculpture mentioned by Pliny, the work of three sculptors from Rhodes, Agesander, Polydorus and Athenodorus. The group was wrongly

VIII. (opposite) *Fibula from the Regolini-Galassi Tomb, c.* 650 B.C. gold length 12⅝ in. (32 cm.) The Etruscan Museum of the Vatican

restored by G. A. Montorsoli about 1533 according to the plaster model (176) in a niche in the next room. It was immensely admired in the Renaissance and in the 19th century and was analyzed at length by Winckelmann and Lessing. Byron acutely describes it as 'Laocoön's torture dignifying pain'. The recent reconstruction has restored the right arm found by Pollak in 1906 and removed the right arm of the younger son. The group is a virtuoso study of pain rising in a crescendo from the boy on the right to the screaming agony of Laocoön's face. It should be seen from a central point as it it were a relief. It is now dated by most authorities about 150 B.C., along with the Sperlonga sculptures found in 1957, which show the same Pergamene influence.

We next enter the Cabinet of Apollo, containing the *Apollo Belve-* 83 *dere* (92), which came into the possession of Julius II before he became pope. Copied by Bernini and admired by Winckelmann it became one of the most famous works of art in the world. It is a copy of a bronze original of the late 4th century, possibly by Leochares. The god has just shot an arrow and his gaze follows its flight. The elegant modelling of the body has surface weaknesses and probably does not convey the mastery of the original.

The Cabinet of Canova contains three statues by Antonio Canova placed there by Pius VI to fill the gap left by the antique sculptures that had been removed to Paris after the Treaty of Tolentino. Canova aimed at sublimity, dignity and grace and generally achieved the third, even if his charm is sometimes rather sugary. *Perseus* (32) is an elegant and fashionably academic work of 1800, clearly showing the immense influence which the Apollo Belvedere had on neo-classic European art of the early 19th century. The two boxers (33, 33A) *Creugas* and *Damoxenes* have some nobility but are over-dramatized. In the niche in the next room is the group of *Venus Felix and Cupid*. The body is copied from the *Venus of Cnidos* while the head is a portrait of a Roman lady of the 2nd century A.D. Against the wall is a *Sarcophagus* (49) with a battle of the Amazons, Achilles and Penthesilea being grouped in the centre.

The Cabinet of Hermes contains a *Hermes* (53) previously thought

82. (opposite above left) *Laocoön, c.*150 B.C. marble height 72½ in. (184 cm.)
83. (opposite above right) *Apollo Belvedere;* Roman copy, ?1st century B.C. marble height 88¼ in. (223 cm.)
84. (opposite below left) *Augustus of the Prima Porta, c.*23 B.C. painted marble 80¼ in. (204 cm.)
85. (opposite below right) *Mars of Todi,* first half of the 4th century B.C. bronze height 55⅞ in. (141 cm.)

to be Antinoüs. The figure probably shows Hermes in the form of Psychopompos, the conductor of souls to Hades, and may be a copy of an original by Praxiteles.

The exit, between the Cabinets of Apollo and Canova, leads into the Round Vestibule. On the left is the Cabinet of the Apoxymenos containing the statue of an athlete scraping the oil from his forearm with a strigil which was found in Trastevere in 1849. This is the only copy known of a famous bronze by Lysippus executed c. 330 B.C. This statue proves Pliny's statement that Lysippus introduced a new system of proportion, making the head smaller and the limbs, particularly the legs, longer. There is also a new sense of movement, due to the fact that the trunk, head and limbs all face in slightly different directions. This enables the statue to be seen from more than one point of view. On the wall to the left is an altar of the 1st century A.D. with a sacrificial procession including three bulls, followed by four figures carrying the household gods *(lares)* and by priestly officials known as Vicomagistri. The *Altar of Augustus* (1155) dedicated in 12 B.C. is notable for the representation of the prodigious sow of Laurentum, which was found by Aeneas with thirty piglings.

It should be remarked that many of the statues in the open air are discoloured with dirt and badly looked-after.

We return to the Round Vestibule opening off the Cabinet of Hermes and enter the Vestibule of the Torso. The *Belvedere Torso* was found in the Campo dei Fiori in the time of Julius II and was greatly admired by Michelangelo, on whom it had a strong influence, and Raphael. It bears the signature of Apollonius, son of Nestor, an Athenian sculptor of the 1st century B.C., whose signature is also on 46 the *Boxer* in the Museo delle Terme. Some think that this Apollonius was a copyist and that the original of the Torso can be dated about 150 B.C. The figure is sitting on a leopard hide and is remarkable for the impression of movement (the head must have been turned sharply to the left), the powerful articulation of the limbs and the rich modelling of the flesh. Against the wall is a *Sarcophagus*, in peperino, of L. Cornelius Scipio Barbatus, Consul in 298 B.C., the first of the family to be buried in the Tomb of the Scipios on the Appian Way. It is in the form of a Doric altar and the archaic inscription, in Saturnian verse, is thought by some to be by Ennius.

C The Chiaramonti Museum

A steep flight of steps decorated in Pompeian style leads from the Vestibule of the Torso to the gallery, 980 feet long, which forms the first part of the museum. The gallery is named after its founder Pius VII (Chiaramonti) and is divided into 59 sections numbered with Roman numerals (odd numbers on the left, even numbers on the right). The gallery was originally arranged according to Canova's advice, but subsequent additions have produced overcrowding and, indeed, confusion. It will therefore be sufficient to mention the outstanding objects. Section XVI. *Head of Athena* (3) copy of a Greek original of the 5th century B.C., has eyes restored with remarkable skill. The Greek sculptors often added the eyes separately using ivory or grey stone for the whites and semi-precious stones for the pupils. XIX. *Portrait of a Roman* (13) is a realistic representation of an unknown man at the time of the end of the Republic. XXIII. *Penelope* (16) is a fragment of a woman seated in a meditative attitude, with her legs crossed and her head resting on the back of her right hand. Under the chair is a large work-basket. The plastic treatment of the folds of her dress suggests an Ionic archetype of the period 470–460 B.C. XXVII. *Head* (21) from a Palmyran relief in limestone is characteristic of Syro-Roman art in the years of the city's greatest prosperity, 130–270 A.D. XXXI. *Relief of the Three Graces* (2) is an early copy of a Greek original c. 470 B.C. *Relief with Horseman* (17) is a copy of a Greek original of the 5th century B.C. XLIII. Statuette of *Ulysses* (19), part of a group of Ulysses offering wine to Polyphemus, is probably a Roman copy of a Greek original of the 3rd century B.C. XLVII. *Portrait of a Lady* (15) is a statue of one of the Julio-Claudian family, with the hairstyle fashionable during the reign of Augustus.

To the right is the entrance to the New Wing (Braccio Nuovo) constructed 1817–1822 by Raffaele Stern. It is a noble hall 230 feet long and 26 feet wide, with a barrel vault coffered in the classical style and an apse in the middle with antique columns of marble and granite. The floor is inlaid with mosaics of the 2nd century A.D. from a Roman villa at Tor Marancia, outside the Gate of St Sebastian. On the right: *Silenus Carrying the Infant Dionysus* (11), a realistic and harmonious composition, is a replica of an original by Lysippus. The *Augustus of the Prima Porta* (14) found in 1863 in Livia's villa *'ad gallinas albas'* on the Via Flaminia is probably the best portrait of Augustus in existence. The emperor, aged about forty, is wearing a cuirass over his toga. He holds a sceptre in his left hand and his raised right hand shows that he is in the act of speaking to his troops. The head is a fine character study and the pose is full of authority. The armour is decorated in relief with scenes that date the statue. Beneath the divinities of the sky and the chariot of the Sun, the Parthian King Phraates IV is restoring to a young official (? Tiberius) in 20 B.C. the eagles lost by Crassus at Carrhae in 53 B.C. The small cupid riding a dolphin, a support for the emperor's right leg, is a symbol of Venus, the fabled ancestor of the *gens Julia*. In the last niche is the figure of *Mnemosyne* (23), the mother of the Muses, a copy of an original of the 3rd century B.C. by Philiscus of Rhodes.

In the rectangular recess opposite the apse are: *A Bust of Julius Caesar* in the centre and at the six sides tombstones found near the Mausoleum of Augustus. Five belong to the Julian family and one to that of Vespasian. Continuing along the gallery there is a *Portrait Bust* (53) of an unknown Roman of the Augustan period, a masterpiece of realism. On the opposite wall the statue of *Demosthenes* (64), an excellent copy of an original by Polyeuctes which was erected in Athens in memory of the great orator in 280 B.C., is a fine example of a complete portrait, in which the whole figure plays its part in the characterization. The slightly inclined head, the hooded eyes, the tensed body all combine to express the personality of Demosthenes. The hands were originally clasped tightly together. Some can see in the mouth indications of the stutter which afflicted the orator. A *Wounded Amazon* (67) with arms and feet added by Thorwaldsen, may be a copy of the statue with which Polycleitus won the competition for the Temple of Diana at Ephesus. Also on the left is a fine *Artemis* (85) wearing a robe that reaches the ground, a copy of an original of the 4th century B.C.

In the apse: A severely realistic *Bust of a Man* (89) of the late Republican era, who may be Mark Antony and a *Bust* (94) of Marcus Aurelius as a young man. In the centre is *The Nile* (106) a splendid Hellenistic work, found in 1513 near the Temple of Isis in the Campus Martius. The river god, portrayed as a vigorous man, leans his elbow on a sphinx. He is holding a cornucopia of grapes and a sheaf of corn, symbolizing the fertility of the river. Clambering over him are sixteen children, greatly restored, supposed to represent the 16 cubits which the Nile rises when in flood, the period of maximum yield. On the base is a Nilotic scene of pigmies hunting crocodiles and hippopotamuses. There are also an ibis, an ichneumon and lotus pods, characteristic of the Nilotic fauna and flora. We proceed along the gallery to the *Giustiniani Athena* (111), a copy in Parian marble of a bronze of the 4th century attributed to the Argive sculptor Euphranor. The goddess stands in an attitude of pensive concentration. *Resting Satyr* (117) is a copy of the famous statue of Praxiteles, but inferior to that in the Capitoline Museum. The *Bust of Philip the Arabian* (121), Emperor from 244–249 A.D., is a revealing portrait of an artful and shifty character. The *Doryphoros* (123) or Spear-bearer, is a copy of the famous bronze of Polycleitus, described by Pliny as his 'canon' from which other artists derived their knowledge. Polycleitus was a great student of the proportions and structure of the body as can be seen from the harmonious and balanced pose of this athlete.

We now return to the end of the New Wing, go (right) through the corridor of the Library and up two flights of the Simonetti Stairs to the Hall of the Chariot, a circular domed room designed by G. Camporese in Carrara marble for Pius VI as a setting for the *biga*, a racing chariot with two horses, from which it takes its name. The chariot, dating from the 1st century B.C., was reconstructed in 1788 by F. A. Franzoni from ancient fragments. Only the body of the chariot and part of the right-hand horse are original. The body of the chariot was long used in the Middle Ages as the episcopal throne of San Marco. Along the wall, from the left: *Discobolos* (618) is a copy of Myron's work with a modern head. *Discobolos* (615), from a bronze original by Naucides, is represented measuring out the ground in paces. *Statue* (612) of a 1st century Roman, wearing a voluminous toga, in the act of sacrifice, is finely wrought. A bearded *Statue of Dionysus* (608), a Greek inscription giving it the name of Sardanapalus was added later, is majestic and full of humanity. Its simplicity and directness suggest an original of the 4th century B.C.

The landing outside leads, right, to the Gallery of the Candelabra which takes its name from the splendid pairs of marble candelabra of the imperial era placed on either side of the arches which divide the room into six sections. Section I. *Sarcophagus* (20) of a small boy, a gracious Hellenistic work, shows him reclining with a book and his pet dog lying beside him scratching itself. The pair of candelabra (32, 39) with Bacchic rites came from Otricoli. Section II. *Pan* (10), extracting a thorn from a satyr's foot, is a replica of a Hellenistic original of the 2nd century B.C. *Diana of the Ephesians* (22) is of the 3rd century A.D. The candelabra (44, 51), from a Roman villa, were used in the churches of S. Agnese fuori le Mura and S. Costanza. Section III. The candelabra (24, 25) came from S. Agnese. Section IV. Small *Satyrs* (37, 40) are playfully looking at their tails. *Statue* (38) is of an old fisherman, a realistic work of the Pergamene school, 3rd century B.C. *Tyche of Antioch* (49), a 'Personification' of the city, is a Roman copy of a bronze by Eutychides, which must be dated after 300 B.C., the time when Antioch was founded. She is seated, wearing a castle-crown, on a rock, with one foot resting on the shoulder of a youth who is swimming below her, personifying the river Orontes. *Boy with a Goose* (66) is a copy of a bronze by Boëthus of Chalcedon. *Sarcophagus* (85) with the slaughter of the Niobids is a good work of the 2nd century A.D. Section V. *Statue of a Girl* (5), a Roman copy of a Peloponnesian bronze of the 5th century B.C., represents an athlete victorious in the Olympic games in the act of running, with her right foot passing the winning-post. The tree-trunk was added by the copyist. The candelabrum (24) from Otricoli has divinities on the base and two doves on the spiral stem. Section VI. *Statuette* (5) of a woman wearing a cloak, is a copy of a Hellenistic original of the 3rd century B.C. *Persian Fighting* (32) is copied from one of the original bronzes, given by Attalus I of Pergamum to the Athenians, which were placed on the Acropolis of Athens, 3rd century B.C.

We return to the landing outside the Hall of the Chariot.

D The Etruscan Museum
This is reached from the landing outside the Hall of the Chariot, by turning to the left and ascending the staircase to a door on the right. The museum was founded by Gregory XVI in 1837 and enlarged in the reigns of Pius XI and Pius XII. In addition to Etruscan art it contains outstanding examples of Greek art. Room 1. *Sarcophagi:* (27) from Tuscania with slaughter of the Niobids, has on the cover a reclining woman with an expression of surprise. (74) from Tarquinia, has mythological scenes from the Oresteia, 1st century B.C. (59) from Caere (Cerveteri) has a wedding procession; some colour still remains on the frieze and the face of the dead man, 5th century B.C. There are also four mummies from the Egyptian Museum. Room 2 contains the famous treasures from the Regolini-Galassi Tomb. The frescoed frieze of *Moses, Aaron and Pharaoh* is by Federico Barocci and Federico Zuccari. The tomb, named after its discoverers, was opened in 1836 and the objects found in the tumulus at Caere, *c.* 650 B.C., were in an unusually good state of preservation. They are arranged in the central case and in Cases A–K. Apparently three people were buried in the tomb, a woman of high rank and two men, one cremated. Cases A–C contain the ornaments and equipment of the woman. Case A. Gold fibula (1) with ornamental motifs ranging from linear designs to rows of animals adorned with 'granulation'. The large disc is decorated with five lions inside a double border of interweaving arches and palms. The thin convex lamina below has 55 figurines alternating with leaping lion-cubs. The pattern is of Assiro-Phoenician origin but the superlative workmanship is Etruscan. There are also bracelets (3, 4),

VIII

mirrors (2), a breastplate in relief (28) and a vast necklace (66). Case B contains ivories, cups, plates and silver ornaments of the orientalizing period. Case C contains the famous Libation Bowl (20207) with six handles in the form of animals and a reconstructed chair and footstool (217). Case D contains the equipment of the cremated man, who was probably a lucumo, or priest-king. His Cremation Urn is surmounted by a headless lion. Stand E holds the reconstructed *Biga* of the lucumo. Cases F–K contain the equipment of the second man who was probably a warrior prince. Case F has a bronze incense-burner in the shape of a wagon (240), shields, daggers, etc. Case G contains two five-handled libation bowls (307, 308), a bronze stand with repoussé figures (303) and a large bronze bowl (305). Case I contains small, elegant plates of Eastern origin (20366-8), a silver drinking cup (20365) and a bronze bowl (20369). Stand H holds the Funeral Chariot and the bronze bed of the buried man. Case K has pottery and bucchero bowls. Case L has equipment from tombs near the Regolini-Galassi site including black-figured urns and bucchero vases in relief. Case M has similar material including a bucchero vase from Caere (20235) from the end of the 7th century in the shape of a stylized charioteer attached to the handle with a vertical tape, driving two enormously lengthened crowned beasts (? protomes of horses). Cases O and P contain ceramics from other tombs in the necropolis.

The first section of Room 3 is under reconstruction. There remain: in Case I a bronze incense-burner from Vulci of the end of the 6th century B.C. The tripod has arches ornamented with palm leaves surmounted by figures of Hercules, Hera and panthers. On a stand to the right is a bronze *Statuette of a Boy* (12107) from Lake Trasimeno, wearing a large necklace from which is suspended a bulla (amulet). He has a bird in his left hand. This is a votive offering dating from the middle of the 2nd century B.C. Case H has fine bronzes, incense-burners, tripods, buckles, jars, etc. In Case K is a Mirror from Vulci (12241) ringed by a border of ivy, with Eros winged like an angel carrying away Cephalus, a delicate work of the middle of the 5th century B.C. Also in Case K is a fine oval cista (12259) of the 3rd century B.C. with a battle between Greeks and Amazons, the handle being formed by a nymph and a satyr riding on swans. Case L has a Mirror (12242) engraved with Hercules and Atlas, derived from a Greek model of the 5th century B.C., and another Mirror (12645) from Vulci of the beginning of the 3rd century B.C. portraying Usil, the sun-god, standing between Nethuns and Thesan. At the end of the room is the *Mars of Todi*, a large bronze statue in armour from the first half of the

4th century B.C., which was a votive offering. The five parts of the badly-proportioned statue are ill-related, the face is expressionless and the body is rigidly encased in a cuirass, which seems to be the main interest of the sculptor. The statue has a vaguely Attic quality but it is ridiculous to describe it as having been inspired by Greek art of the 5th century as is often done. On the breastplate is an inscription in Umbrian saying that it was dedicated by Ahal Trutitis. The helmet is modern. Room 4 contains cinerary urns, many surmounted with figures. The most notable is a well-preserved *Alabaster Urn* (13887) of 2nd century B.C. with a relief of the chariot race between Pelops and Oenomaus, King of Pisa.

Room 5, the Guglielmi Room, is named after Benedetto Guglielmi who gave a collection of objects from Vulci to Pius XI in 1937. In Case A are bronze objects including large candelabra with figures on top. In Cases B and C are black-figured hydrias. In Case F, far end of middle shelf, is a bucchero jar from the 6th century B.C. with incised decoration and an inscription. In Case G are fragments of gold filigree ornaments. On separate pillars are: Stand I, an incense-burner, or table lamp, in the form of a bronze figure of a youth, with a double-corded necklace and an egg in one hand and a cup in the other standing on a tripod ornamented with seated fawns, *c.* 500 B.C.; on Stand K a red-figured hydria perhaps painted by the Athenian Euthimides, *c.* 520 B.C. Room 6 contains a collection of jewellery, mostly from Vulci. Case A has gold pins, necklaces and rings. Case B. Seals, rings, etc. Case C. Larger ornaments: Bullae, pendants, brooches and fragments of ornamental jewellery that adorned statue No. 10, 5th to 4th centuries B.C. Also coronets and diadems used as funerary wreaths. Case E. Fine bangles and gold sprays. Case F. Elegant leaf-sprays of gold. Case G. Rings and necklaces with amethyst pomegranate drops. Room 7 contains terracottas: cinerary urns, Villanovan vases, antefixes, statues, votive objects and so on. In Case F is a vigorous polychrome *Pegasus* (14130) an acroterion from Caere of the beginning of the 5th century B.C. It probably ornamented the frontal extremity of a temple and is an important testimony to the ability of the Etruscans to portray animals. In Case K, top shelf centre, is a *Female Bust* (14107) of the beginning of the 1st century B.C. which may be considered as a forerunner of the naturalistic portrait-busts of the Augustan era. Case M contains an *Urn, c.* 100 B.C., from Tuscania with the dying Adonis reclining on a *kline*.

Room 8 is in three sections. Section I: In Cases A, B and C are antefixes and friezes in terracotta; armour in bronze and iron; bronze weights, one in the shape of a pig; helmets, rings, pins, keys and other objects in common use. In Case D are statuettes in bronze and terracotta, ivory and bone objects In Case F and G are antefixes and architectonic friezes in terracotta. On the left wall is the tail of a dolphin in bronze (15057). On the right wall are three plaques of the Labours of Hercules: the fights against the Nemean lion, the Lernaean hydra and the Cretan bull. Section II. On the right, fragment of a bronze male torso larger than life-size. Case L. Alabaster phials of the Greek classical period and the Hellenistic era. Case M contains an important collection of Roman glass. Section III. Bronze head (15054) of a woman, 1st to 2nd century B.C. Head of an emperor (15032) wearing a laurel crown, 3rd century A.D. and a fragment of a bronze portrait-statue of a Roman from the beginning of the Empire. Room 9 houses the Falcioni collection containing very fine objects of bronze, gold and terracotta in excellent condition, for the most part from the neighbourhood of Viterbo. Room 10 has fragments of a large bronze statue (15058) possibly Neptune.

Rooms 11 and 12 contain the Greek Originals. 11 contains *Nymphs Dancing* (1345), an Attic relief of the 4th century B.C.; fragment of a relief with a horse (1900) 5th century B.C.; and a relief with two divinities (799), probably Zeus and Hera. 12 has the important *Palestrita Stele* (559), a sepulchral relief from Attica datable *c.* 440 B.C. A young athlete is represented in profile with a youthful attendant who offers him a strigil and a flask of oil. The relief is low but has a fine linear rhythm. Fragment of a *Horse's Head* (1016) may be one of Athena's horses from the west pediment of the Parthenon. *Head of Erichthonius* (1013) is from one of the metopes of the Parthenon. *Head of a Goddess* (905) is part of an acrolith of the 5th century from Southern Italy or Sicily. On the head was a helmet probably of bronze, the wig, the eyebrows and eyelashes made of strips in bronze and the eyes of polished grey stone in which were set pupils of precious stones. The ears probably had gold earrings.

Passing through a corridor (13) which turns to the left and ends on a landing we proceed down the Staircase of the Assyrian Reliefs and turn to the right into Rooms 14–16 which include a curving room (15) overlooking the Courtyard of the Fir Cone. These rooms, very recently re-arranged, contain a collection of Greek, Italiote and Etruscan vases. In Room 14 are examples of Italiote vases and other products of Magna Graecia. The most interesting, on a stand at the end of the room, is a *Krater* from Paestum (17370) of *c.* 375 B.C. with red figures on black representing three young men seated on a triclinium playing

86. *Amphora of Exekias, c.* 540–530 B.C.

kottabos, a game of Siciliote origin. Room 15, a hemicycle, has Attic vases, among them a *Cup* (16545) with Athena, Jason and the Dragon, an episode from the myth of the Argonauts, signed by Duris 86 the famous painter of the 5th century B.C., and an important black-figured *Amphora* (16757) signed by Exekias which can be dated about 540–530 B.C. It portrays on one side Achilles in a Corinthian helmet and Ajax with a long beard playing dice or, more probably, *morra.* The mantles of the warriors are exquisitely patterned. On the other side Castor and Pollux are being welcomed home by their parents Tyndareus and Leda.

In the last decade of the 6th century B.C. Attic ceramic technique was revolutionized by the introduction of red figures, painted on the natural surface of the vases. In Room 16 upstairs a good example of this technique is a *Hydria* with Apollo (16568). The god has a bow and quiver behind him and a plectrum in his right hand with which to sound his lyre as he passes over the ocean on a great winged tripod. This work is attributed to the Berlin painter *c.* 490 B.C. The fine *Amphora of Achilles* (16571) has given its name to the author, the Painter of Achilles, a disciple of the Painter of Berlin, who was a contemporary of Phidias. The hero stands firmly, resting on his lance, and turns his head towards Briseis who is depicted on the other side. At the centre of his corselet is the tiny head of a gorgon. Datable *c.* 440 B.C. On a pillar is a polychrome *Krater* from Vulci (16586) which shows, against a white-cream background, Hermes consigning the orphan Dionysus to an aged Silenus.

We descend the Staircase of the Assyrian Reliefs and proceed to the Atrium of the Quattro Cancelli.

III The Vatican Library and Annexes

The Vatican Library was founded by Nicholas V with a nucleus of about 340 books which he increased to some 1200. Sixtus IV brought the total to 3650. During the sack of Rome in 1527 about 400 volumes were lost, but thereafter the contents of the library steadily increased until today there are over 60,000 manuscripts, 7000 incunabula and well over 1,000,000 other printed books. The Library proper may only be visited by scholars with recommendations.

A Museum of Pagan Antiquities

This is approached from the Quattro Cancelli and was designed to house medals and coins. It was begun in 1767 and completed in the time of Pius VI when it was decorated and furnished by Valadier. In the niche to the right in the entrance wall is a bronze *Head of Augustus* (14), *c.* 31 B.C. In the cases are bronzes, ivories, statues and mosaics. We pass into the Clementine Gallery which was added to the Library by Clement XII in 1732. In the various sections of the Gallery are gifts from Heads of States to the popes. The Alexandrine Room, the Pauline Rooms and the Library of Sixtus V have paintings, bronzes and plans of Rome. The last contains the largest and smallest manuscripts in the Library: the *Hebrew Bible of Urbino* dated 1295 and the *Masses of St Francis and St Anne* decorated with 16th century miniatures. On the left is:

B The Sistine Hall

This is named after its founder Sixtus V and was built by Domenico Fontana 1587–1589. It is richly decorated with compositions glorifying literature and eulogizing the pontificate of Sixtus V. The most precious possessions of the Library are exhibited in glass cases. In Case 1, containing Greek manuscripts, are the Codex Vaticanus B, an uncial text of the Bible, 4th century, and a Fragment of the Gospel of St Matthew written in gold and silver on faded purple parchment, 6th century. In Case 2, containing Latin manuscripts, are four Virgils: the Vatican Virgil, 4th century, the Roman Virgil, 4th century, with miniatures, the Augustan Virgil, ? 3rd to 4th century, and the Palatine Virgil, 5th century. There is also a Palimpsest of Cicero's *De Republica*, 4th century. Cases 3, 4 and 5 contain examples from the Library's famous collection of illuminated manuscripts. These are changed from time to time. Case 6 has 15th century illuminated books and manuscripts including a Ferrarese Dante and a magnificent *Crucifixion* (38) by Pinturicchio from a missal. Case 7 contains drawings and designs by

Giuliano da Sangallo, Botticelli, Raphael and Michelangelo. Case 8 contains miniatures and paintings of famous persons, including Federico da Montefeltro and Benedict XIV, and caricatures by Pietro Ghezzi and Bernini. Case 9 has autograph letters from St Thomas Aquinas, Michelangelo, Raphael, Martin Luther, Savonarola, and a little bound volume of love-letters in French from Henry VIII to Anne Boleyn. Case 10 has maps, designs and illustrated books of the 15th and 16th centuries. Case 11 contains early bibles, including the earliest, the Gutenberg Bible of 1455–1456. Case 12 has illuminated books and missals, including a Florentine Homer of B. Merli 1488, and beautifully-bound books of the 15th and 16th centuries. Case 13 has books and manuscripts of the 6th to 16th centuries from the Middle East. Remarkable is a Syriac text of the 6th century. Case 14 has letters, manuscripts and maps from the Far East, including a letter in Japanese presented to Paul V in 1612. Passing through the two Sistine Rooms and the Gallery of Urban VIII where there are astronomical instruments, globes and sailing charts, we enter:

C Museum of Christian Art
Known as the Museo Sacro, which was founded by Benedict XIV in 1756 and enlarged by successive popes. Room I contains Palaeochristian art from the Catacombs of which the most important are a Cameo with a Winged Victory, a disc believed to portray the earliest representations of St Peter and St Paul and a Byzantine mosaic of St Theodore, 12th century. Room II contains an important collection of gold glass from Catacombs of the 3rd to 5th centuries. Room III contains ceramics, enamels, ivories and church furnishings in silver and gold. The ceramics are mainly from the Renaissance, the enamels from the 2nd to the 17th century. The twelfth case on the left contains ivory diptychs and triptychs of which the most important is the Ramboyna Diptych, *c.* 900. Retracing our steps and passing through a door on the left we enter the Room of the Aldobrandini Marriage which is named after one of the most famous of Roman paintings, a fresco discovered in 1605 on the Esquiline, preserved in the Villa Aldobrandini, restored in 1817 on the orders of Pius VII and placed in this room in 1818. It is probably a copy made in the reign of Augustus of a Greek original of the 4th or 3rd century, possibly the picture by Aëtion of the Marriage of Alexander the Great and Roxana, *c.* 328 B.C. There are many copies, one by Poussin is in the Doria Gallery. The ceiling frescoes are by Guido Reni and on the upper part of the walls are four frescoes of the 1st century B.C. representing episodes from the

Odyssey. Lower down are paintings of famous women from Greek tragedy, five of them from Tor Marancia, 3rd century A.D. and paintings of children from Ostia 1st century A.D.

At the end is the Chapel of St Pius V. In the glass case is a large enamelled Cross presented by St Paschal I, 817–824, which was used as a reliquary for fragments of the True Cross. A large Greek Cross of 9th century gold filigree work also contained a fragment of the True Cross. A cushion in the shape of a Greek Cross, stitched in gold thread, is Byzantine work of the 8th century. In a case in the next room are woven vestments of the 16th century presented to Clement VIII by the Grand Duke Ferdinand I of Tuscany.

D The Borgia Rooms

These are entered through a door on the left and a small anteroom. The Borgia Apartment is named after Alexander II the Borgia (Spanish, Borja) pope, who had it decorated by Pinturicchio and assistants, and lived and died there. Room I, Of the Sibyls, takes its name from the twelve half-figure sibyls, each accompanied by a prophet, which peer out of the lunettes. This juxtaposition of Christian and pagan symbols comes from a medieval tradition which linked Israel and the world of the Gentiles in the expectation of the coming of the Messiah. The whole decoration is probably by Antonio da Viterbo. Room II, Of the Creed, is named after the fluttering scrolls on which are written the articles of the Creed, and which are held by the twelve Apostles. Each is accompanied in the lunette by a prophet who holds a scroll on which a passage from his prophecies is quoted referring to the article of the Creed displayed by his companion Apostle. The frescoes are by a secondary painter, possibly Tiberio d'Assisi or Pier Matteo d'Amelia. Room III, Of the Liberal Arts, takes its name from the seven liberal arts of the medieval Trivium and Quadrivium, which are personified in the lunettes. In this room the influence of Pinturicchio is felt, but the work was probably done by Antonio da Viterbo. The Arch of Justice in the middle was decorated about 1520. The marble bust of Pius II is attributed to Paolo Taccone. The great chimney-piece is perhaps by Simone Mosca from designs by Sansovino.

Room IV, Of the Staints, has frescoes planned and probably largely carried out by Pinturicchio himself. The room is divided by an arch into two cross-vaulted areas forming six lunettes. In the lunette in the wall opposite the window is the *Disputation of St Catherine*, one of 87 Pinturicchio's masterpieces. The action takes place in the open air and

87. Pinturicchio (*c.*1454–1513)
*Disputation of St Catherine, c.*1495
oil on panel

the Arch of Constantine rises in the centre. On the left the Emperor
Maximian sits on a throne, surrounded by his court. The identification
of the Emperor as Cesare Borgia and the saint as his sister Lucrezia is
mistaken. However, the man with the drooping moustache on the left
of the throne is Andrew Palaeologus, despot of Morea. Behind him
are Antonio da Sangallo the Elder holding a square rule and Pinturicchio himself with his thin face and black hair. Prince Djem, a friend of
Cesare Borgia, is said to be the oriental on the right of the emperor. In
the smaller lunette on the right is *St Anthony Abbot's Visit to St Paul
the Hermit* in the desert. The *Visitation* in the next lunette may be by
the hand of the master. The *Martyrdom of St Sebastian* occupies the
space above the window. The fancifully-dressed bowmen are the
most interesting part of the picture, particularly a janissary in the right-
hand corner. The Colosseum is seen on the horizon. *Susanna and the
Elders,* over the small door, has a charming garden. *The Legend of St
Barbara* is very decorative. It is rather curious to find, on the ceiling,
mixed up with these religious scenes, episodes from the Egyptian
myth of Isis, Osiris and the bull Apis, but the last is inserted here in
order that a reference may be made to the Borgia's heraldic animal. In
a round frame over the door is a *Madonna and Child* by Pinturicchio.
The inlaid benches around the wall by Giovannino de'Dolci date from
the time of Sixtus IV and come from the Vatican Library.

Room V, Of the Mysteries of the Faith, contains frescoes of the *Annunciation*, the *Nativity*, the *Adoration of the Magi* and the *Resurrection* by Pinturicchio and assistants. The *Resurrection* is not entirely painted by Pinturicchio, but it contains his masterpiece of portraiture, the superb figure of Alexander VI, in a magnificent gold cape glittering with jewels, kneeling with folded hands in adoration. The series concludes with the *Ascension, Pentecost* and the *Assumption*. This last contains a portrait of the donor, praying on the right, who may be Francesco Borgia. In the eight groins of the double cross-vaulted ceiling are frescoed medallions with half-figures of the prophets. Room VI, Of the Popes, was originally covered by a heavy beamed ceiling which collapsed in 1500 and nearly killed Alexander VI. The present false vault was decorated at the time of Leo X with stuccoes by Giovanni da Udine and grotesques by Perin del Vaga. The ten lunettes commemorate various popes. Tapestries were to be hung illustrating the inscriptions on the wall but they were never woven and in their place are seven 16th century carpets depicting the myth of Cephalus and Procris. The room contains some interesting bronzes and Bernini's model of the figure of Charity for the monument to Alexander VII in St Peter's.

We retrace our steps to the entrance to the Borgia Rooms, go through the door on the left and take the stairs to:

E The Sistine Chapel
The Chapel was built for Sixtus IV by Giovannino de' Dolci in 1473–1481. It is a rectangle 133 feet long and 43 feet wide, with six windows rather high up on either side and a barrel-vaulted ceiling. An elegant marble screen by Mino da Fiesole, perhaps assisted by Giovanni Dalmata and Andrea Bregno, divides the chapel into a large choir and a smaller nave. The same artists were responsible for the cantoria, or choir-gallery, which is decorated with delicate reliefs taken from classical models. The 15th century mosaic pavement is a fine example of *opus alexandrinum*.

The first two series of frescoes (Life of Moses left, Life of Christ right) began with the *Finding of Moses* and the *Nativity* by Perugino, but these were sacrificed to give place to Michelangelo's *Last Judgment*. Today the series, 1481–1483, begins with the *Journey of Moses into Egypt* on the left and the *Baptism of Jesus* on the right, both by Perugino with the assistance of Pinturicchio. The second fresco on the left, *The Burning Bush*, with Moses slaying the Egyptian, 88 meeting the daughters of Jethro, and driving the Midianites from the well, is a masterpiece by Botticelli. The daughter of Jethro carrying a distaff, the bride-to-be, is a miracle of lyrical tenderness. The *Crossing of the Red Sea* is of dubious authorship but may be by Cosimo Rosselli, with portraits and landscapes by Piero di Cosimo. The *Giving of the Tables of the Law* is probably by Cosimo Rosselli without assistants. In the following fresco Botticelli deals with the *Punishment of Korah, Dathan and Abiram*. This is an incident unusual in art, but it must be remembered that the subjects were chosen by Sixtus IV and this one was used to allude to a revolt by certain bishops. This magnificent fresco is full of movement, it swirls like a refining fire. In the background are the Arch of Constantine and the Septizonium, at that time still adorned with columns. *Testament of Moses* by Luca Signorelli is a great contrast to the activity of the former fresco. The weary Moses and the superb figure of the naked youth of the tribe of Levi are solemn and monumental. The *Dispute and Mourning Over the Body of Moses* by Signorelli was destroyed and replaced during the period of Gregory XIII by a poor mannerist composition.

On the right, after the *Baptism,* is the *Cleansing of the Leper* and the *Temptation in the Wilderness* by Botticelli, two subjects which do not make a whole. In the background is the hospital of Santo Spirito. Domenico Ghirlandaio's *Calling of Peter and Andrew* has a fine background of the Sea of Galilee, with a large crowd on the other side including many portraits. *Sermon on the Mount* and *Healing of the Leper* by Cosimo Rosselli and Piero di Cosimo is an unsuccessful
89 combination of subjects. The *Delivery of the Keys,* a beautifully balanced composition with a magnificent Temple of Jerusalem, is Perugino's masterpiece. Repeated symmetrically on either side is the Arch of Constantine. The series ends with the *Last Supper* by Cosimo Rosselli. The final episode, the *Resurrection* by Ghirlandaio, his masterpiece, was destroyed (with Signorelli's *Death of Moses*) when the architrave over the door leading into the Sala Regia collapsed. In the niches between the windows are 28 portraits of the early popes.

The ceiling frescoes were forced upon Michelangelo, much against his will, by Julius II in 1508, but he was given permission to do what he wished. The original design had been twelve Apostles in the spandrels and the central field decorated with geometric ornament, but once Michelangelo got started he saw that he had to treat

88. (opposite above) Botticelli (*c.*1445–1510) *The Burning Bush, c.*1482 fresco height 137 in. (348·5 cm.)
89. (opposite below) Perugino (*c.*1445/50–1523) *The Delivery of the Keys, c.*1482 fresco height 110¼ in. (335 cm.)

the vault as a unity, with a formal interdependence of the mass of figures with the mass of the architecture. The result is one of the greatest works of art ever created. The Sistine ceiling is a torture to the spectator, who has to bend back, twist and turn and strain to get the full effect. The great Swiss art historian Heinrich Wölfflin recommends that the visitor should ignore the *Last Judgment*, that is go up and turn his back on it, as the colossal proportions of this picture dwarf the figures on the ceiling. The general design is architectural, though the main divisions take little account of the actual ceiling formation, and represents the creation of the world and Old Testament episodes from Genesis up to Noah. The frescoes, however, were executed in reverse order to the chronological sequence and the *Flood* was the first episode painted. Along the sides and at the end are colossal figures of Prophets and Sibyls and on the frame sit *ignudi* (slaves or athletes). Essentially it is a composition of nude figures.

In the first series painted, the *Flood*, the *Sacrifice of Noah* and the *Drunkenness of Noah*, Michelangelo had not solved the problems of fresco painting. The *Flood* is too crowded, but he achieved in the *Drunkenness of Noah* a concentrated composition. From this point he cut down everything to the barest essentials, linear rhythm is combined with spatial depth to increase the impressiveness of the theme. In the *Fall and Expulsion* the Garden of Eden consists only of a few leaves, yet an effect of richness is obtained by the sweeping lines of the figures. God the Father first appears in the *Creation of Eve* and His majestic bulk is offset by Eve's beautiful gesture as she rises. The figure of Adam in the *Creation of Man* is a marvellous invention, com- IX bining latent strength and present helplessness. *God Hovering Over the Waters* is a splendid rendering of all-pervading benediction. Most remarkable of all is the *Creation of Sun and Moon* where God appears twice. With a thrusting movement of both arms, He creates the sun with His foreshortened right arm, while His left arm is thrown back towards the moon. In His second appearance God rushes 'into the depth of the picture like a cyclone' to create Vegetable Life. In the *Separation of Light from Darkness* God is borne along on sweeping clouds in a Blake-like vision.

The Prophets and Sibyls, seated alternately in square niches be-

IX. (opposite above) Michelangelo (1475–1564) *The Creation of Man, c.* 1510 fresco width 224⅜ in. (570 cm.)
X. (opposite below) Fra Angelico (*c.* 1387 or perhaps *c.* 1400–1455)
St Peter Ordaining St Stephen as Deacon (right), *St Stephen Distributes Alms* (left), 1447–49 fresco

90. Michelangelo (1475–1564)
*The Prophet Jonah, c.*1511

neath the nude youths, are the largest figures of all, each representing a different spiritual experience. On the Left Wall are: Jeremiah, a simple but touching figure; the Persian Sibyl holding a book; an agitated Ezekiel with a scroll; the monumental Erythraean Sibyl; Joel, sharply outlined. On the Right Wall: the Cumean Sibyl, an aged giantess; Daniel writing; the grandly conceived Delphic Sibyl; Isaiah in deep meditation. At the east end is Zachariah consulting a book and
90 at the altar end the most remarkable figure of all, Jonah issuing from the great fish.
91   The twenty *ignudi* sit above the thrones of the Prophets and are their *animae rationali.* Michelangelo probably intended them to be mediators between the physical and spiritual worlds. With their powerful muscular development, their athletic postures and their vigorous movements, they are unequalled in the painting of the nude.

In the lunettes over the windows are figures of the forerunners of Christ and in the spaces on either side of the prophet-sibyl sequence the Saviours of Israel, of which the most remarkable is *Judith and Holofernes,* where a wonderful emotional tension is created by Judith glancing back at the bed on which Holofernes lies.

More than twenty years later, in 1536–1541, Michelangelo painted his immense fresco of the *Last Judgment,* which is 66 feet by 33 feet. Unfortunately the surface has deteriorated, owing to the smoke of incense, damp stains, repaintings and restoration. Michelangelo was a profoundly religious man and he was tremendously affected by the

91. Michelangelo (1475–1564) *A Slave* (ignudo), *c.*1511 fresco

Sack of Rome in 1527 which seemed to him, as to many of his contemporaries, as a kind of visitation of God's judgment. Hence the Dantesque quality of the composition. Christ appears as an avenging Apollo, an inexorable judge, with right arm raised in condemnation. The figure is colossal, square, over-muscled, with thickened limbs, and makes a complete break with the classical tradition. The Virgin in a strange sinuous pose shelters under Christ's uplifted arm. Above are two groups of angels bearing the instruments of the Passion, beneath on the left the saved are ascending to heaven and on the right the damned are being dragged into hell. In the centre the Judgment Angels blow their trumpets. Below the surging mass of the condemned, an unparalleled assemblage of bodies in violent movement, are Charon in his bark and Minos, the guide to the infernal regions. Minos, unconventionally, has ass's ears and a serpent coiled round his loins. His face is a portrait of Biagio da Cesena, who was Master of Ceremonies to Paul III and who had objected to the nudity of the figures. Later, Pius IV ordered Daniele da Volterra to paint loin-cloths over some of the figures, which earned for the painter his nickname of Il Braghettone, the breeches-maker.

The *terribilità* of the *Last Judgment*, the abandonment of classical figures in harmony and proportion, broke up the tradition which Michelangelo had established in his earlier work and his *Conversion of St Paul* and *Crucifixion of St Peter* in the Pauline Chapel herald a new phase in Italian painting.

92. Michelangelo (1475–1564) *The Last Judgment* (detail), *c.* 1540
fresco

IV Gallery of Tapestries, Stanze and Loggia of Raphael

We return to the Quattro Cancelli, enter the Hall of the Greek Cross, go upstairs past the Room of the Chariot, through the Gallery of the Candelabra and enter the Gallery of Tapestries. Ten of these, later woven in Brussels by Pieter van Aelst, were executed after Raphael's death from cartoons by his assistants. They are: (1) *Adoration of the Shepherds;* (2) *Adoration of the Magi;* (3) *Presentation in the Temple;* (4), (5), (6) are scenes from the *Massacre of the Innocents;* (7) *Resurrection;* (8) *Christ Appearing to Mary Magdalene;* (9) *Supper at Emmaus;* (10) *Ascension.* The *Descent of the Holy Spirit* does not belong to the series.

The Gallery of Maps was decorated by Antonio Danti 1580–1583 with maps and plans, under the direction of his brother Ignazio, the famous Dominican cosmographer, mathematician and architect. They represent ancient and modern Italy and the papal territory of Avignon. Of the town plans and views of seaports the best is that of Venice. We proceed into the Gallery of Pius V in which are two fine Tournai tapestries of the *Passion* and the *Creed,* 15th century, and on to the Ladies' Audience Room added by Paul V. The frescoes by Guido Reni represent the *Transfiguration, Ascension* and *Pentecost.* In the centre is a cabinet presented by the French catholics which contains translations into many languages of the bull proclaiming the dogma of the Immaculate Conception. Passing through the Sobieski Room and the Hall of the Immaculate Conception we reach the:

Stanze and Loggia of Raphael

This series of rooms was built by Nicolas V and they were decorated by Andrea del Castagno, Piero della Francesca, Luca Signorelli and Benedetto Bonfigli. Later Julius II employed a number of artists to continue the decoration, including Perugino, Sodoma, Bramantino, Baldassare Peruzzi and Lorenzo Lotto. On the suggestion of the architect Bramante, an Umbrian, Raphael was called to Rome in 1509 and asked to undertake a piece of trial work. The result was so successful that Julius dismissed all the other painters, ordered their works to be destroyed, according to Vasari, and commissioned Raphael to decorate the whole of this part of the Vatican.

In order to follow the development of the work of Raphael and his assistants it is necessary to begin with the Room of the Segnatura although it comes second after the entrance. In the room the pope signed bulls and briefs, hence its name. It was painted in 1509–1511 entirely by Raphael, who had conceived a plan to represent the highest attainments of the human spirit, Religion, Poetry and Philosophy and Justice. The earliest of the frescoes, on the right as we enter, is the *Disputa* (or Disputation on the Holy Sacrament) wrongly so-called owing to the misunderstanding of a passage by Vasari. It really represents 'The Triumph of Religion'. In the centre is the symbol of the Eucharist and above it Christ seated in majesty between the Madonna and the Baptist. Over his head God the Father appears accompanied by angels and beneath his feet the Holy Spirit, flanked by four cherubs carrying the gospel, links heaven and earth. On either side of the central group apostles, saints and patriarchs sit in a hemicycle on the clouds. Beneath, on either side of the altar, stand or sit the four Doctors of the Church, Jerome, Gregory, Ambrose and Augustine, and behind them stand popes, monastic founders and a throng of believers. The man pointing upwards with his right hand is said to be Pietro Lombardo. The composition is remarkable for admirable distribution of masses, variety of poses, symmetrical design and the balance of upright figures contrasted with others in vigorous movement.

On the opposite wall is the *School of Athens* symbolizing Truth in the form of Philosophy and Justice. At the sides of a portico are statues of Apollo and Minerva; steps ascend to a lofty vault in the style of Bramante where, framed by an arch, are the two supreme masters, Plato with his *Timaeus* and Aristotle with his *Ethics*. Plato points upward to the realm of ideas while Aristotle, with his palm turned earthwards, indicates the vast realm of nature as his province. To the left of Plato, Socrates expounds a syllogism to a group of young men, among whom are Alcibiades, Xenophon and Aeschines. Alexander the Great, in shining armour, looks on. At the extreme left is Zeno, in bearded profile, with a child propping up a book which Epicurus, crowned with vine-leaves, is reading. In the foreground Pythagoras, seated a little to the right, points out a passage in his book to Empedocles, who is taking notes. A youth beside him holds a tablet showing the harmonic tables. Leaning over Pythagoras is Averroes, the Moslem commentator on Aristotle, in a white turban. The handsome young man in white with the aloof smile may be Francesco Maria della Rovere. Standing with his foot on a marble block is Anaxagoras and sitting alone, resting his head on his arm, is Heraclitus, with the face of Michelangelo. Sprawled across the steps like a church beggar is Diogenes, who links the groups. On the extreme right, in the corner, Ptolemy, wearing a crown, holds a terrestial globe while Zoroaster beside him displays a celestial one. Stooping to the ground, Euclid is measuring a geometrical figure.

On the other wall is the third fresco *Parnassus*. The window gave Raphael the idea of building over it a hill where Apollo is playing a lyre surrounded by the Muses. Sappho, a rich classical figure, is there and the blind Homer, dictating a poem to Ennius, Virgil and Dante. The rest of the poets flock around the slopes of the hill. There is a feeling of overcrowding here, but the whole design is a marvel of grace and freshness.

On the ceiling above the *Disputa* is Theology, above the *Parnassus* Poetry, above the *School of Athens* Philosophy and above the window wall Justice.

We proceed to the Room of Heliodorus where the frescoes are historical and, because the subjects were chosen by Julius II, political. These masterpieces were painted by Raphael in 1512–1514 in the Grand Manner of the High Renaissance. On the left wall is the *Expulsion of Heliodorus from the Temple in Jerusalem*, alluding to Julius II's policy of ridding the States of the Church from foreign usurpers. In the centre of the fresco at the back, beneath a series of golden domes, the High Priest Onias is praying before the Ark of the Covenant. On the left is Julius II surrounded by his suite, a witness of the judgment of God. On the right are Heliodorus and his men struggling with the three avenging angels, two with whips and one armed in gold riding a rearing white horse, a tremendously dramatic scene.

To the right is the *Mass of Bolsena*, a representation of the miracle of 1263, which alludes to God's miraculous intervention in defence of the integrity of the faith and to the vow made by Julius when, on his first expedition against Bologna in 1506, he stopped at Orvieto to pay homage to the sacred relic. Here again use is made of a window. Above it the priest celebrating is stunned by the miracle of the bleeding Host. Opposite him kneels Julius, represented as assisting at the mass. On the right are cardinals and Swiss guards and on the left the excited crowd. There is great play with light, from the altar and from the flickering flames of the candles held by the boys, which adds to the dynamic perspective of the architecture. The Swiss Guards are coloured in red, bluish-black, green and yellow, which makes this the most splendidly chromatic of the frescoes.

On the next wall is *Leo I Repulsing Attila*. Again there is an equal distribution of figure masses on each side but there is no clear central scene. The intention of Julius in selecting this episode was to show how the See of St Peter is guarded by Providence. On the left the papal procession advances with Leo I on a white mule, while Attila on his rearing horse is struck with terror at seeing St Peter and St Paul appear in the sky armed with swords, visible to him alone. Behind lies Rome with the Colosseum, an aqueduct and Monte Mario ablaze.

On the fourth wall is the *Deliverance of St Peter*. Raphael is again restricted by a window, above which are the bars of the prison. Behind them the saint, with hands and feet chained, is asleep, while two guards in armour are leaning against the wall. The angel in a phosphorescent circle of light bends to strike the saint on the shoulder and points to the open door. On the right the apostle, with the transfigured face of Julius, appears at the head of the stairs, led by the hand of the angel. Beneath them two soldiers lie in heavy sleep and, on the other side, the guards are waking in the dim light of a torch and a crescent moon. This is the first great nocturnal scene in Renaissance art and is unique inasmuch as the light comes from five different sources.

The Hall of the Fire, the first room, has on the ceiling four roundels of the *Glorification of the Holy Trinity* by Perugino. The walls were painted in 1517 by Raphael's assistants, Giulio Romano and Giovan Francesco Penni in continuation of the style of the Room of Heliodorus. Facing the window is the *Fire in the Borgo* which was developed from sketches of Raphael by Giulio Romano, with possible assistance from Penni in the central group. It refers to an incident in 847 when Leo IV, by making the sign of the cross, extinguished a great fire which endangered the whole quarter. It is, however, Troy that is in flames, not Rome, as is seen from the figure of Aeneas carrying his father Anchises on his back, followed by his wife Creusa and their son Ascanius. The most famous figure is that of a woman seen from the back bearing a jar on her head who has a truly Raphaelesque poise. On the right wall is the *Coronation of Charlemagne* by Leo III in 800, an obvious reference to the meeting of Leo X and Francis I at Bologna in 1513. It is a mediocre work probably by Penni with assistance from Raffaelino del Colle. On the left wall is the *Victory of Leo IV Over the Saracens at Ostia* in 849, which alludes to the crusade against the Turks proclaimed by Leo X. Here, as in the *Fire in the Borgo*, Leo IV has the features of the Medici pope. It is a good composition, well carried out by Giulio Romano. Raphael may have had a hand in it, but it is much damaged and repainted. On the window wall is the *Oath of Leo III* with which the pope publicly cleared himself of charges brought against him in 800. The allusion is to the Lateran Council of 1516 which established that the pope need only answer for his acts before God.

The Hall of Constantine, the last room, was painted between 1517 and 1524, almost entirely after the death of Raphael in 1520, by

Giulio Romano with the assistance of G. F. Penni and Raffaelino del Colle. On the wall facing the window is the *Victory of Constantine Over Maxentius* near the Milvian Bridge in 312. The composition, based on sketches by Raphael which still exist, is mainly by Giulio Romano and is lively and spirited, if full of ostentatious antiquarian detail. In the middle of the fight Constantine is mounted on a white horse, on the right Maxentius is being carried away by the current of the river. On the wall opposite the entrance is *The Appearance of the Cross to Constantine* in the same style and again chiefly by Giulio Romano. The emperor is addressing his soldiers gathered in the field to do battle against Maxentius when a golden cross shines. On the entrance wall is the *Baptism of Constantine* by St Sylvester, a portrait of Clement VII, as yet without a beard. This fresco, by Penni, is in a very different manner and is as flat and apathetic as the first two pictures are fiery and spirited. On the window wall is *Constantine's Donation*, where the emperor is seen in the act of presenting the pope with temporal authority. Most of the picture is by Raffaelino del Colle, but the better figures are probably by Giulio Romano.

We proceed next to the Room of the Chiaroscuri, or Of the Palafrenieri (Grooms), which has a magnificent carved and gilded ceiling with Medici arms. It was decorated in 1517 by Raphael, whose work was modified by Pius IV and finally destroyed. The existing frescoes were added by order of Gregory XIII in 1582. The adjoining Chapel of Nicholas V has a fine series of frescoes by Fra Angelico painted 1447–1449, damaged by rain and frequently repainted. The four Doctors of the Church in the corners have suffered most. The Stories of St Stephen, the upper series, start on the right with *St Peter Ordaining St Stephen as a Deacon.* The noble figure of St Peter sits on a throne with two rows of apostles assisting at the ceremony. In the second half of the lunette *St Stephen Distributes Alms* to a group of needy brethren. In the background are some white houses against a cobalt sky. The *Preaching of St Stephen* takes place out of doors in some Tuscan city with high fortress-like buildings. The men in 15th century costume are painted in great detail. The *Appeal of St Stephen* follows the bible, and his adversaries, dressed in fanciful clothes, gnash their teeth as the saint points to heaven. *St Stephen Being Led to Martyrdom* outside the Aurelian walls is accompanied by very mild-looking executioners. The *Stoning of St Stephen* takes place at the foot of the walls in a Tuscan landscape. The Stories of St Laurence, the lower series, start with *St Laurence Ordained as a Deacon by St Sixtus.* The ceremony takes place in a basilica, with beautifully-dressed priests in blue and pink. *St Laurence Receiving the Goods of the Church from St Sixtus* is upset by two armed soldiers who are trying to take the saint prisoner. The elegant façade of the building has the strange, spiritual character common in this painter's work. *St Laurence Distributing Alms* takes place on the threshold of a severe 15th century church and has fine figures of the poor. The most monumental is *St Laurence Before the Tribunal* of the emperor, which has a splendid imperial castle in pink marble. The greater part of the *Martyrdom of St Laurence* fell away in the time of Gregory XIII but we can still see the niches containing the Cardinal Virtues and a few people around the emperor on the roof terrace.

The Loggia of Raphael is a long gallery of 13 arches overlooking the Courtyard of St Damascus. It was begun by Bramante in 1512 and completed by Raphael in 1519. The vault of each arch has four small paintings and the whole is enlivened by gaily-coloured grotesques. In spite of the damage wrought by time and the hand of man, the decoration of the Loggia with its stucco facings still remains the finest example of the Renaissance conception of the ancient classical style. The paintings of the vaults, the so-called Bible of Raphael, have nothing like the same perfection as the Roman stuccoes. The supervision of the work was assigned to Giulio Romano, who had the assistance of G. F. Penni, Perin del Vaga and Polidoro da Caravaggio. It is difficult to assign each piece of work but the first to the ninth vaults were probably sketched by Penni and completed by Giulio Romano, while the hand of Giovanni da Udine can be clearly seen in the stuccoes and the grotesques. A number of the later vaults are probably by Perin del Vaga.

We now return to the Hall of the Fire, where a door on the left leads to the Chapel of Urban VIII, richly decorated with frescoes by Pietro da Cortona. From the chapel a staircase leads down to the Borgia Rooms and the Library, but as this is usually closed it will normally be necessary for us to retrace our steps to the Quattro Cancelli and to the exit.

The Director-General is Count Paolo della Torre. The Curator is Dr Deoclecio Redig de Campos.

The Vatican museums and galleries are open on weekdays from 9 a.m. to 2 p.m., closed on Sundays and on all the principal festivals of the church.

Out of doors and incidentals

Rome was built on Seven Hills and this gives the city an advantage over most of the other great cities of the world by providing numerous vantage points from which its marvellous harmony of colour and line can be studied. These vantage points are frequently sites of great monuments and architectural masterpieces. In Rome it is best to walk and most of the important free-standing monuments can be seen in four walking tours.

Itinerary 1. A splendid viewpoint, famous for centuries, is that from the Arch of Titus, which stands on a spur of the Palatine. It takes in 93 the Arch of Constantine and the Colosseum, whose correct name is 94 the Flavian amphitheatre. Begun by Vespasian in 72 A.D. this stupendous building was finished eight years later by Titus. In spite of pillage and destruction it remains the grandest and most awe-inspiring of the Roman monuments. It was built at a time when the city had a population of 1½ millions, rather more than at the beginning of the present century, and could hold about 80,000 spectators. The triumphal

93. *The Arch of Titus*

94. *The Arch of Constantine with the Colosseum*

Arches of Titus and Constantine, like the Columns of Trajan and Marcus Aurelius, served two purposes. The first was to glorify the emperor and the second was to provide a documentary account of great military exploits which the common people could understand, as the illiterate in the Middle Ages learned the Bible stories from stained-glass windows and the sculptured figures on the façades of churches. In addition the arches had the function of purifying the victorious generals who marched under them. The Arch of Titus has fine scenes, particularly the relief showing the emperor's triumph after the conquest of Judea in 71 A.D. Here the sculptor has made an attempt at perspective and gets the procession nearly right. The imperial chariot and horses on the other side are impressive, but rather awkward. The Arch of Constantine, erected in 315 A.D. in honour of the emperor's victory over Maxentius at Saxa Rubra near the Milvian Bridge, shows considerable deterioration in style and execution, apart from the borrowings from earlier buildings, but it has its own nobility. The statues above the main cornice were taken from a monument of Trajan, as were the great reliefs of the battle scenes. The eight medallions with scenes of hunting and sacrifice date from Hadrian's reign and the eight reliefs above the longer sides of the cornice represent scenes from the life of Marcus Aurelius.

Passing along the Via dei Fori Imperiali we see the Markets of Trajan with the 13th century Torre delle Milizie rising behind them and reach the Forum of Trajan, designed by the imperial architect Apollodorus of Damascus and perhaps the greatest architectural

95. *Trajan's Column,* A.D.113 and
SS Nome di Maria marble
height about 137 ft (41 metres)

achievement of the ancient world. Against the background of Santa 95
Maria di Loreto and SS Nome di Maria stands Trajan's Column, whose
hand-carved shaft is the best example of sculptural documentation in
Rome. It is, incidentally, the prototype of many columns, including the
Vendôme Column in Paris. Constructed of eighteen drums of marble
the column is 100 Roman feet (97 ft) high and the spiral frieze, 650 ft
long and 3 ft high, has some 2500 figures, vigorously carved, illustrating the Dacian campaigns. How magnificent it must have looked,
brilliantly coloured from top to bottom, with the sunlight falling on
the gilded armour of the soldiers.

Passing the egregious Monument of Victor Emmanuel II, called the
'Wedding Cake' by French soldiers during World War I and by a
later generation the 'Pre-war typewriter', we approach the Capitoline
Hill, the smallest and lowest but the most famous of the seven and the
political and religious centre of ancient Rome. The Temple of Jupiter
Optimus Maximus, the most venerated in the city, stood there until
the 6th century. In the 8th century it came into the possession of the
monastery of S. Maria in Capitolio. In 1143 the Romans revolted
against the domination of the papacy and resuscitated the Senate,
which gave the hill fresh importance. On the left is the flight of 124
steps, built in 1348 by the survivors from the plague, which leads to
the blank façade of Santa Maria in Aracoeli, where Gibbon, meditating
on the ruins of the Capitol on October 15, 1764, got the idea of writing
the decline and fall of the city. The magnificent square, planned by
Michelangelo in 1536 and completed in the 17th century, is bounded

96. (left) *Statue of Marcus Aurelius with the Palazzo Senatorio*
97. (right) *S. Maria in Cosmedin and Bizzaccheri's Fountain*

by three buildings, the Palazzo Senatorio (centre), the Palazzo del Museo Capitolino (left) and the Palazzo dei Conservatori (right). The square remains much as it was envisaged by Michelangelo when he designed it for the reception of the emperor Charles V. It is approached by a flight of shallow steps leading to a balustrade ornamented with two colossal statues of the Dioscuri and in the centre stands the statue

96 of the emperor Marcus Aurelius, the only equestrian bronze preserved from antiquity, which owes its existence to a mistaken belief that it represented the first Christian emperor, Constantine the Great. Traces of the original gilding are still visible. The roads to the right and left of the Palazzo Senatorio provide magnificent views of the Roman Forum.

Turning sharp left after leaving the Capitol we arrive at the majestic remains of the Theatre of Marcellus, begun by Julius Caesar and completed in 13 B.C. by Augustus. In 1712 the Orsini family built a palace in the ruins. Further down on the right are the elegant fluted columns of the Temple of Fortuna Virilis and the erroneously-named

97 circular Temple of Vesta. On the left is the church of Santa Maria in Cosmedin, one of the most beautiful of the medieval Roman churches, with its Romanesque tower of seven stories. Beneath the portico is the Bocca della Verità, a large marble disc of a face which was originally a drain cover. In medieval times it was used as an ordeal to convict perjurers. If anyone told a lie while holding his right hand in the stone

98. The Farnese Palace

mouth his fingers were snapped off. Opposite the church is a fountain, 1717, by Carlo Bizzaccheri.

We proceed along the Tiber to the Ponte Sisto and take the Via Giulia on the right until we reach the back of the Farnese Palace. The 98 Via dei Farnesi leads to the Piazza Farnese. The Farnese Palace is a magnificent structure begun in 1514 by Antonio da Sangallo the Younger for Cardinal Alessandro Farnese, afterwards Paul III, and completed by Michelangelo and Giacomo della Porta. It is now the French Embassy. The gallery contains splendid frescoes by Annibale and Agostino Carracci and still has claims to be considered one of the half dozen most beautiful rooms in the world. It is open on Sundays from 11 a.m.–12 p.m. On the right is the elegant 18th century Palazzo Roccagiovine and on the left the church of the Swedish St Bridget, built on the site where she died on July 23, 1373. The twin fountains are probably by Girolamo Rainaldi, 1626. The water spurts from a Farnese lily and falls into small marble cups and thence into two colossal bathtubs of grey Egyptian granite, which were found in the Baths of Caracalla.

Itinerary 2. We begin at the Piazza San Bernardo in the Via Venti Settembre. On the N.W. side is Santa Susanna dating from the 3rd century. Remodelled in 1475, it was provided with a dynamic façade by Carlo Maderno in 1603. Opposite is the round church of San

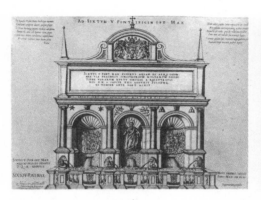 

99. (left) *Contemporary engraving of the Moses Fountain,* 1589
100. (right) *Lion* (detail of the Moses Fountain), 19th century

Bernardo alle Terme and to the left of it is the Fontana dell'Acqua
99 Felice, known as the Moses Fountain, the first of the great fountains
of Rome to be built, 1585–1587, in modern times. The main design is
by Domenico Fontana and the statue of Moses by Prospero da
Brescia. This squat figure in a toga received such severe criticism that
100 the sculptor died of a broken heart. The four lions are copies of antique
Egyptian originals. On the other side of the street is the church of
Santa Maria della Vittoria built by Maderno 1608–1620, with a
façade of 1626 by G. B. Soria resembling that of Santa Susanna. Inside
101 is Bernini's marvellous Cornaro Chapel with the *Ecstasy of St Teresa,*
which Bernini thought was the most beautiful thing he had ever done.
We go down the Via Barberini to the Piazza Barberini, where, in the
102 centre, is Bernini's famous Triton Fountain, *c.* 1642–1643. Four dolphins rear up from the pool, a huge shell opens and the sea-god
emerges. The tremendous figure of the Triton combines with the other
figures to make an organic whole which is the most attractive and
imaginative fountain in Rome. We walk up the Via della Quattro
Fontane past the Barberini Palace and at the junction with the Via
Venti Settembre see the four little wall fountains built in 1588–1589
for Sixtus V. Turning to the right we walk the length of the Quirinal
Palace, passing on the left Bernini's elegant church of S. Andrea al
Quirinale, until we reach the Piazza del Quirinale, known as Monte
Cavallo. In the centre of the square are two colossal groups of the
103 Dioscuri (Castor and Pollux) over 18 ft high. Marble statues of two
men attending two horses had been on the Quirinal Hill, the highest
point of old Rome, since classical days and were known as the 'Horse-

101. (above left) Gian Lorenzo Bernini (1598–1690) *Ecstasy of St Teresa,* Cornaro Chapel, S. Maria della Vittoria life size
102. (above) *Dolphins on the Triton Fountain,* Palazzo Barberini
103. (below) *The Dioscuri, Obelisk and Fountain,* Piazza del Quirinale

104. *The Trevi Fountain*

tamers'. Sixtus V ordered Domenico Fontana to turn them so that they faced the Via del Quirinale and to erect a fountain in front of them. This fountain was demolished in 1782 by Pius V and an obelisk placed between the two groups. In 1818 Pius VII made a new fountain out of a huge granite basin found in the Forum. The Dioscuri and their horses are copies of Greek originals of the 5th century and have an air of Phidias about them. On the side of the square opposite the Quirinal Palace, the official residence of the President of the Republic, is the Palazzo della Consulta, 1739, a refined and virtuoso work by Ferdinando Fuga which now houses the Constitutional Court. Lower down on the left is the Rospigliosi Palace built 1611–1616 by Vasanzio (Jan van Santen) and Maderno. It contains the important Pallavicini collection of pictures, to see which special permission must be obtained. In the Casino is Guido Reni's celebrated *Fresco of Aurora*, 1614, which can be viewed on the 1st of each month from 10 a.m.–12 p.m. and 3 p.m.–5 p.m. Opposite the Palace is a magnificent double staircase, 1618, with a fine balustrade, leading into the Villa Colonna.

We go down the steps on the right of the Quirinal Palace, turn right

105. *The Pantheon with Obelisk and Fountain*

into the Via di San Vicenzo and reach the Trevi Fountain, which occupies the south front of the Palazzo Poli. In the 15th century it was a simple basin by Leon Battista Alberti, used by washerwomen. Urban VIII had it restored and Bernini made a sketch for the present structure, which Niccolò Salvi was commissioned to carry out in 1732. It was completed after Salvi's death in 1751 by Giuseppe Pannini in 1762. Salvi had the courage to take up an idea of Pietro da Cortona and build the fountain into the palace front on a base resembling natural rock formation. The rococo elements in the design are strictly subordinated to the baroque figure of Neptune in the central niche of the triumphal arch. The whole is one of the gayest spectacles in Rome. The prudent traveller who wishes to return to Rome will throw a coin over his left shoulder into the waters.

Itinerary 3. One of the principal centres of Rome is the Piazza Colonna, in the middle of which stands the Column of Marcus Aurelius, behind a graceful fountain by Giacomo della Porta, 1575. Like Trajan's Column it originally towered over a group of monuments and similarly it owes its survival to ecclesiastical ownership and protection. The reliefs spiralling up the shaft celebrate the emperor's vic-

106. *Elephant and Obelisk,* Piazza della Minerva

tory over the Marcomanni, Quadi and Sarmathians. Originally the column had on it a statue of Marcus Aurelius, but this was replaced in 1589 by a statue of St Paul. The shaft, like that of Trajan's Column, measures 100 Roman feet (97 ft). On the right is the Chigi Palace, a late mannerist work by Giacomo della Porta which contrasts interestingly with Bernini's baroque Palazzo di Montecitorio up on the right, the seat of the Lower House. In the middle of the square is an obelisk from Heliopolis, originally erected by Psamettichus II *c.* 590 B.C., which was brought to Rome by Augustus who erected it in the Campus Martius. In 1792 it was placed on its present site.

We go down the Via della Guglia, turn right into the Via dei Pastini and reach the Piazza della Rotonda where stands the grand pile of the Pantheon, an engineering feat of the first order. In the centre of the square is a charming fountain of 1578, originally designed by Giacomo della Porta, surmounted by an obelisk of Rameses the Great. Proceeding along the Via della Minerva we arrive at the Piazza della Minerva. In the middle of the square stands a delightful marble elephant supporting a small obelisk from the Temple of Isis, which stood near by. Alexander VII was particularly interested in the hieroglyphic inscriptions on this obelisk and owing to the mention therein of the elephant as a bringer of the rays of the sun he got Bernini to plan this group, which was executed in 1666–1667 by Ercole Ferrara. On the left side of the square is S. Maria sopra Minerva, the only Gothic church in Rome.

107. *The Piazza Navona*

Leaving the square by the Via di Santa Chiara on the right we reach the Piazza di Sant'Eustachio and proceed along the Via dei Staderari to the junction with the Corso del Rinascimento. Turning right we pass the Palazzo Madama, the seat of the Senate, and turn left into the Piazza Navona, the most beautiful in Rome, which still preserves the 107 outline of the Stadium of Domitian. The narrow oval was used during the Renaissance, and long after, for jousts and, when flooded with water, for mock naval battles. In the centre is the huge Fountain of the Four Rivers by Bernini, who envisaged a great rock with the Four Rivers of the World, Nile, Danube, Rio de la Plata and Ganges, springing from it. The fountain, made of travertine, was built by many hands, from Bernini's careful designs, 1648–1651. Bernini is traditionally supposed to have finished the rock, palm tree, lion and horse. Bernini only refurbished the Fountain of the Moor at the southern end of the 109 square, which was originally built by Giacomo della Porta c. 1575, but he did provide the designs for the Moor with a spouting fish standing on a great conch. On the west side of the square is the church of Sant'Agnese in Agone begun by Carlo Rainaldi, carried on by Bernini's great rival Francesco Borromini, who was responsible for the magnificent façade, and finished by Rainaldi. The interior is of remarkable richness.

Itinerary 4. We start at another centre of Rome, the Piazza di Spagna. Above the charming Barcaccia c. 1627–1629, a fountain in

108. Engraving of the *Spanish Steps* showing the *Fountain of the Barcaccia* in the foreground

108 the form of a boat by Gian Lorenzo Bernini, the splendid Spanish Steps weave up and up to the church of the Trinità dei Monti. The double flight of 137 steps was built in 1721–1725 by Francesco de Sanctis as the result of a bequest by the French ambassador Etienne Gueffier. No one has left a finer memorial to himself in Rome in modern times. On the right of the Steps (No. 26) is the house in which Keats died on February 23, 1821. It now houses the Keats-Shelley Memorial.

Proceeding along the Via del Babuino we reach the Piazza del Popolo, a superb ensemble which grew up over a period of three hundred years. As we see it today this spacious oval owes its existence to Giuseppe Valadier, who planned and designed it after the return of Pius VII from France in 1814. Three streets meet here, the Via di Ripetta, the Via del Corso in the middle and the Via del Babuino. They are separated by a pair of Baroque churches, S. Maria di Montesante, 1662–1675, and S. Maria dei Miracoli, 1675–1679, begun by Carlo Rainaldi and completed by Bernini with the assistance of Carlo Fontana. At the end of the oval is the great church of S. Maria del Popolo, with its host of treasures. Beside the church stands the

109. (left) Detail from the *Fountain of the Moor*
110. (right) *The Obelisk of Flaminius,* Piazza del Popolo

historic Porta del Popolo. The inner face of the gate was executed by
Bernini in 1655 on the occasion of the entry into Rome of Queen
Christina of Sweden. In the middle is the Obelisk of Flaminius which 110
celebrates the glories of the pharaohs Rameses II and Merenptah. It is
accompanied by four Egyptian lions, reminiscent of the lost fountain
of 1572, who spout Acqua Vergine.

    From the Piazza del Popolo we proceed on foot or by bus to the
Ponte S. Angelo, originally built by the Emperor Hadrian in 136 A.D.
Clement IX soon after his accession commissioned Bernini to modern-
ize the bridge and decorate it with ten marble angels; these were
finished in 1669. Bernini's personal contribution was the *Angel with
the Crown of Thorns* and the *Angel Carrying the Superscription
I.N.R.I.* These were placed in S. Andrea della Frate to protect them
from the weather. We cross the bridge and proceed along the Via della
Conciliazione which was opened up in 1937, a blunder of monumental proportions. The Piazza San Pietro is Bernini's large-scale 111
masterpiece, 1656–1667. The conception is extremely simple – an
enormous oval surrounded by colonnades of free-standing columns –

111. *The Piazza San Pietro*

but the effect is tremendous, giving as it does greater height to St Peter's. Bernini himself compared his colonnades to the motherly arms of the church 'which embrace Catholics to reinforce their belief'. The piazza was to have been enclosed by a third arm to give an effect of surprise as one passed through the opening and saw the great church. The Borgo Nuovo and the Borgo Vecchio used to provide, before their destruction, this moment of delighted surprise. Matters were made worse by the tasteless buildings constructed at the end of the Via della Conciliazione in 1950. In the middle of the piazza is an obelisk $82\frac{1}{2}$ feet high. It was brought from Heliopolis in 37 A.D. by Caligula and was placed on its present site by Sixtus V in 1586. It took 900 men, 140 horses and 47 windlasses to get it into place. On each side of the obelisk is a magnificent fountain. The one on the right by Carlo Maderno dates from the time of Paul V while the one on the left designed by Bernini was erected in 1677.

In some ways the greatest monuments of Rome, certainly the most conspicuous, are the walls that encircle it, the Republican Wall inside and the Aurelian Wall outside. The latter has set the bounds of the city until the present day, so that St Peter's and the Vatican are 'outside the walls'.

Art for sale

Rome is no longer a centre for great auctions and although there are sales rooms what is sold in them is of little importance. The difficulties of exporting works of art are considerable, owing to the restrictions imposed by the Directorate-General of Fine Arts in the Ministry of Public Instruction, and these difficulties are enormously increased if the objects come from well-known sources. Even within Italy taxation and restrictions make the purchase and re-sale of valuable works of art far from easy. Rome is full of antique shops *(antichità),* but few of them have much of importance to offer, authentication is dubious and prices are likely to be high. It will, therefore, be advisable only to mention three long-established and reliable dealers. The firm of Sestieri, Piazza di Spagna 81, run by the brothers Marcello and Carlo, is the outstanding one in Rome. It has its own clientèle and deals in pictures, porcelain and silver up to the beginning of the 19th century. It specializes in Old Masters, particularly Italian painters and those connected with Italy. Alberto di Castro e Figlio, Via del Babuino 102, was established over a hundred years ago and deals in all kinds of antiques – pictures, furniture, porcelain, silver, tapestries – from the 16th century until 1870. Sangiorgi, Via di Ripetta 117, is housed in the great Borghese palace, the 'Roman harpsichord'. The present head of the firm, which was founded at the beginning of this century, Sergio Sangiorgi, recalls the early days of the gallery when his predecessors dealt with the great Russian museums and the Russian aristocracy. The firm maintains a huge stock of antiques dating from 1200 to 1900.

Rome has sixty or so galleries dealing in contemporary art and art of this century, but only ten or a dozen of them deserve mention. The most important international gallery is the Marlborough, Via Gregoriana 5. This is the third Marlborough Gallery and it was opened in June 1962 with a splendid exhibition of Masters of the 19th and 20th centuries which shook Rome. The artists ranged from Armitage and Balla to Turnbull and Vlaminck. The director, Bruno Herlitzka, has a wide knowledge of his subject and for part of the year he has the benefit of the expertise of the ubiquitous Frank Lloyd. The gallery

112

exhibits both figurative and non-figurative art and also deals in Old Masters. The aims of the gallery are to make contemporary Italian painters and sculptors better known abroad and to stimulate interest in Italy in internationally-known foreign artists. Among those associated with this gallery are Lucio Fontana, Gastone Novelli, Beverly Pepper, Arnaldo Pomodoro, Toti Scialoja, Emilio Vedova and the heirs of the late Luigi Spazzapan.

113   Also at Via Gregoriana 5 are two other galleries, Il Levante and La Salita. Il Levante is a branch of the Milan gallery, founded in 1961, which is directed by Emilio Bertonati and there is another branch in Munich. The Rome branch is run by Laura Drudi Gambillo. Exhibitions travel between Milan, Munich and Rome and feature foreign, particularly German, artists. Gustav Klimt in 1962, Félix Vallaton in 1964,

112. (above left) Arnaldo Pomodoro (b.1926) *Sphere No. 6,* 1963–65 bronze diameter 45¼ in. (120 cm.) Marlborough Galleria d'Arte
113. (above right) Frank Kupka (1871–1957) *Rhythms in Black and White,* 1921 gouache 12½ × 7⅞ in. (32 × 20 cm.) Il Levante
114. (above) Giacomo Balla (1874–1958) *Decor for Stravinsky's 'Feux d'Artifice',* 1917 L'Obelisco

115. (left) Tano Festa (b.1938) *Da Michelangelo N. 2,* 1966
enamel on canvas 51⅛×38⅛ in. (130×97 cm.) La Salita
116. (right) Max Ernst (b.1891) *Aeolian Harp,* 1963
oil and collage on panel 44⅞×34⅝ in. (114×88 cm.) Iolas Galatea

Frank Kupka in 1965 and Maurice Denis in 1966 are the most important of the one-man shows, but the gallery also claims to have
introduced to Italy Kirchner, Dix, Feiniger, Grosz and others. La Salita 115
was founded in 1957 by Gian Tomaso Liverani and deals mainly in
non-figurative art. Alberto Burri and Emilio Vedova were shown in the
earlier days, but preference is now given to promising younger artists
such as Accardi, Battaglia and Tano Festa. The gallery has arranged
exhibitions as far afield as Tokyo.

At Via Sistina 146 is L'Obelisco, founded in 1946 by two lively and 114
intelligent people, Gaspero del Corso and Irene Brin. They were the
first to introduce to Italy scores of outstanding foreign artists and they
arranged the world première of Rauschenberg. The gallery is now con-
cerned with themes such as Perpetuum Mobile 1965, Sound, Movement and Colour 1966 and White + White 1966, when all the guests
were in white and artificial snow fell gently on them. At present a
series of exhibitions demonstrating the growth of Giacomo Balla's art
is being arranged. At Via Capo le Case 4 Angelica Savinio, daughter of

117. (left) Pini Pascali (b.1935) *Decapitated Rhinoceros and Giraffe,* 1966 cloth stretched on wooden frames L'Attico
118. (right) Claudio Bruni with Luigi Russolo's (1885–1947) *I Capelli di Tina,* 1911 oil on canvas 28⅛×19¼ in. (71·5×49 cm.) La Medusa

Alberto Savinio and niece of Giorgio De Chirico, specializes in graphic art, of which she has a widely representative collection.

116   The Iolas-Galatea Gallery at Piazza di Spagna 9 opened in April 1967. It is associated with the Iolas galleries in Paris, Geneva and New York and with the Galatea Gallery of Turin. So far exhibitions of Max Ernst, Jean Tinguely and Paul Klee have taken place. Mara Chiaretti Buffa di Perrero is in charge. The permanent collection includes works by Picasso, Braque, Leger, Magritte, Bacon and other

117 distinguished artists. At No. 20 is L'Attico, opened in 1957. Fabio Sargentini does not see his gallery as a commercial proposition, he is only interested in new talent. He does not recognize as valid the distinction between figurative and non-figurative art. Between November 1966 and June 1967 he held exhibitions devoted to Vasarely, Pino Pascali, Valerio Adami, Jannis Kounellis and Ridolfo Aricò.

118   La Medusa, Via del Babuino 124, has been run since 1953 by Claudio Bruni, the most enterprising and purposeful of the younger gallery directors. He has no group of artists associated with his gallery because he wishes at all times to have good paintings by the best people. He tries to bring as many important artists as possible to the notice of the Roman public. In short, he sees his function as that of an educator. He has a large permanent stock of painters of the older

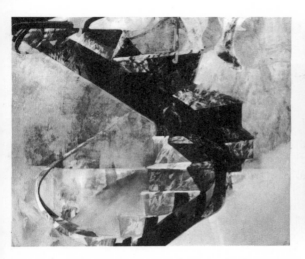

119. (left) Renzo Vespignani (b.1924) *Steps to the Swimming-pool,* 1967
oil on canvas 51⅛ × 38⅜ in. (130 × 100 cm.) Il Fante di Spada
120. (right) Carlo Lorenzetti (b.1934) *Structure in Steel and Yellow Enamel,* 1966
80¾ × 20½ × 16½ in. (205 × 52 × 42 cm.) Galleria Arco D'Alibert

generation such as De Chirico, De Pisis, Morandi and Campigli. In
1967 he staged a very good exhibition of European Masters from
Boldini to Sutherland. At Via Alibert 25 (a small street off the Via del
Babuino) is Il Torcoliere, founded in 1956 and run by Virginia Gag-
liani, which has a workshop, produces prints by a large number of
foreign and Italian artists and issues books illustrating the work of
some of them such as Guttuso and Vespignani.

Il Fante di Spada, Via di Ripetta 254/5, was founded in 1962 by the 119
Group 'Il Pro e il Contro' but it is now directed by Camilla Roncaglia.
The gallery specializes in the work of Vespignani and has associated
with it a number of important younger painters and sculptors. In 1965
the gallery arranged an exhibition by Francis Bacon. At Via Ferdinando
di Savoia 2 is L'Arco d'Alibert, founded in 1963 and directed by Mara 120
Coccia, who has got together a group of younger Italian artists. She
has also arranged exhibitions of Gino Severini and Alexander Calder.

Plinio de Martis, who directed until recently La Tartaruga in the
Piazza del Popolo, has the last word. His gallery was the most avant-
garde in Rome and had op-art, pop-art and the latest of everything. He
said: 'I have closed down the gallery temporarily and opened a bar.
The Romans are not interested in the things of the spirit, so I am selling
them spirits instead.'

Galleries, museums and salerooms

It should be noted that while the important art dealers have regular hours of opening and closing, the commercial galleries exhibiting contemporary art keep no fixed hours. It can be assumed that they will be open from about 10.30 a.m. to 1.30 p.m. and from 5 p.m. to 8 p.m. They are mostly closed on Monday mornings. These galleries generally close from August 1 to September 20. The exhibition season is from November to July.

Commercial galleries

1 **Marlborough**
Via Gregoriana 5
684678

2 **Il Levante**
Via Gregoriana 5
681415

3 **La Salita**
Via Gregoriana 5
672841

4 **L'Obelisco**
Via Sistina 146
465917

5 **Il Segno**
Via Capo le Case 4
671387

6 **Iolas-Galatea**
Piazza di Spagna 9
686293

7 **L'Attico**
Piazza di Spagna 20
671036

8 **La Medusa**
Via del Babuino 124
686546

9 **Il Torcoliere**
Via Alibert 25
687317

10 **Il Fante di Spada**
Via Ripetta 254/5
684409

11 **L'Arco d'Alibert**
Via Ferdinando di Savoia 2
687448

Art dealers

12 **Sestieri**
Piazza di Spagna 81
689798

13 **Alberto di Castro e Figlio**
Via del Babuino 102
672269

14 **Sangiorgi**
Via di Ripetta 117
670861

Galleries and museums

15 **National Gallery of Rome,
Palazzo Barberini**
Via delle Quattro Fontane 13
474591

16 **National Gallery of Rome,
Palazzo Corsini**
Via della Lungara 10
652323

17 **Villa Farnesina**
Via della Lungara 230
651858

18 **Capitoline Museums and
Gallery**
Piazza del Campidoglio
661 extension 3071

19 **Museum of the Palazzo Venezia**
Via del Plebiscito
688865

20 **Doria Pamphilj Gallery**
Piazza del Collegio Romano 2
674365

21 **Colonna Gallery**
Via della Pilotta 17

22 **Gallery of the Academy of
St Luke**
Piazza dell'Accademia di San
Luca 77
689243

23 **Spada Gallery**
Piazza Capo di Ferro 3
561158

24 **Barracco Museum**
Corso Vittorio Emanuele 168
650848

25 **Museum of Rome**
Piazza di San Pantaleo 10
655880

26 **Roman National Museum
(Museo delle Terme)**
Via delle Terme
489319

27 **Borghese Museum and Gallery**
Villa Umberto I
858577

28 **National Etruscan Museum of
the Villa Giulia**
Piazzale di Villa Giulia
350719

29 **National Gallery of Modern Art**
Viale delle Belle Arti 135
802751

30 **National Military and Art
Museum, Castel Sant'Angelo**
Lungotevere Castello 1
655036

31 **Vatican Galleries and Museums**
Viale del Vaticano
698

Author's Acknowledgements

The author wishes to express his great gratitude to Professor Italo Faldi for giving up to him so much of his valuable time. He also wishes to thank the following for assistance and advice: Professor Maria Vittoria Pace Brugnoli, Dr Palma Bucarelli, Sir Kenneth Clark, Professor S. J. Freedberg, Dr Peter Murray and Dr Deoclecio Redig de Campos.

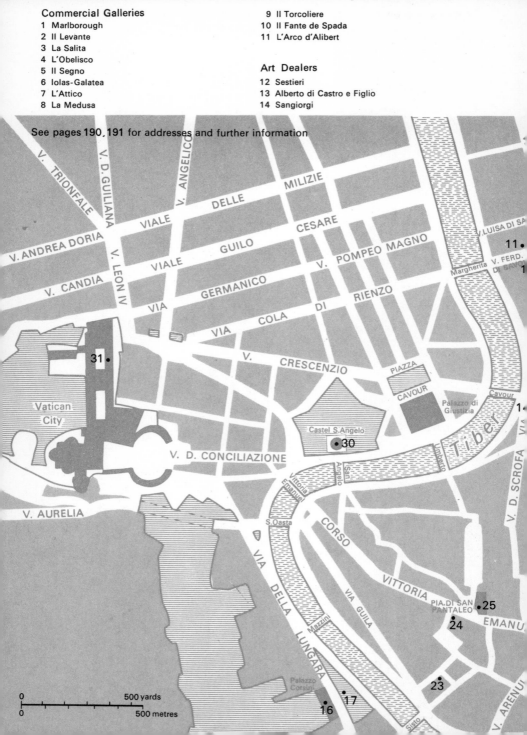

Commercial Galleries

1 Marlborough
2 Il Levante
3 La Salita
4 L'Obelisco
5 Il Segno
6 Iolas-Galatea
7 L'Attico
8 La Medusa
9 Il Torcoliere
10 Il Fante de Spada
11 L'Arco d'Alibert

Art Dealers

12 Sestieri
13 Alberto di Castro e Figlio
14 Sangiorgi

See pages 190, 191 for addresses and further information